B 20

D0218460

Humanists and Holy Writ

HUMANISTS
AND HOLY WRIT

New Testament Scholarship
in the Renaissance

Jerry H. Bentley

PRINCETON UNIVERSITY PRESS

PRINCETON, NEW JERSEY

Copyright © 1983 by Princeton University Press

Published by Princeton University Press, 41 William Street,
Princeton, New Jersey 08540
In the United Kingdom: Princeton University Press,
Guildford, Surrey

All Rights Reserved

Library of Congress Cataloging in Publication Data will be
found on the last printed page of this book

ISBN: 978-0-691-15560-9

Publication of this book was made possible (in part)
by a grant from the Publications Program of the National
Endowment for the Humanities, an independent
Federal agency.

This book has been composed in Linotron Galliard type

Clothbound editions of Princeton University Press books are
printed on acid-free paper, and binding materials are chosen
for strength and durability

Printed in the United States of America by Princeton
University Press, Princeton, New Jersey

For my parents,

BILLIE AND CAREY
BENTLEY

Contents

Preface

GIVEN the profound influence of the New Testament in western civilization, it is hardly surprising that over the past two millennia, countless scholars have devoted their best efforts to its study. The following account examines a short period in the tradition of New Testament scholarship: all the major works analyzed here were produced within the century 1440 to 1540. However short, this was a period of significance, for it witnessed a wrenching reorientation in the western tradition of New Testament study. The agents of this development were the Renaissance humanists, who devoted much attention to Christian as well as classical antiquity. A cultural and educational movement of the years ca. 1300 to 1600, humanism exercised great influence on the methods and assumptions governing scholarship on the New Testament. Hence the title of this study. I do not examine the work of every humanist who dealt with New Testament problems, but by subjecting the work of several particularly influential humanists to deep analysis, I seek to shed light on the meaning of humanism for New Testament scholarship. To be a bit more precise, my study argues that the Renaissance humanists laid the foundations for characteristically modern scholarship on the New Testament.

The study could never have emerged without the generous support of many people. Four colleagues read the book in manuscript: thanks to the efforts of Robert Kolb, Helen Nader, James D. Tracy, and Charles Trinkaus, many errors have exited the pages that follow. Several other friends and colleagues—including Reuel Denney, Robert Littman, Donald Raleigh, and Richard Vuylsteke—read all or part of the manuscript and offered advice from the viewpoint of a more general readership. While expressing my appreciation for the efforts of all these readers, I wish to absolve them from responsibility for any remaining errors. Besides the above-named, many others have aided and abetted my work in myriad ways—mental, moral, and otherwise—and I wish to express my appreciation here also for the advice and counsel of Bernard S. Bachrach, Father Henri Gibaud, Jozef IJsewijn, Walter Johnson, H. J. de Jonge, Daniel W. Y. Kwok, Stanford E. Lehmberg, Richard Marius, John Olin, John B. Payne, and Lewis W. Spitz. I am indebted to the National Endowment for the Humanities and the American Council of Learned Societies for travel grants that underwrote large portions of my research. Finally, with good humor and consistent support, my wife Jeani has provided the encouragement and exhibited the tolerance that all works such as this one require.

Honolulu
12 August 1982

A Note on Editions, Translations, and Citations

UNLESS otherwise stated, all citations to the Greek New Testament refer to K. Aland et al., eds., *The Greek New Testament*, 2nd ed. (New York, 1968). Unless otherwise stated, all citations to the Vulgate New Testament refer to J. Wordsworth and H. J. White, eds., *Novum Testamentum latine. Editio minor* (Oxford, 1911), which is based on the same editors' *Novum Testamentum latine domini nostri Jesu Christi*, 3 vols. (Oxford, 1889-1954). I have also consulted the Greek and Latin texts printed in E. Nestle, ed., *Novum Testamentum graece et latine*, 25th ed. (Stuttgart, 1969).

Unless otherwise stated, all translations into English are my own.

In references to New Testament manuscripts by letter (for uncials) or number (for minuscules), I employ the standard listing system of C. R. Gregory, *Textkritik des Neuen Testaments*, 3 vols. (Leipzig, 1900-1909).

I see little virtue in superfluous citation. Most of the works discussed in the following study—manuscripts, editions, translations, and annotations to the New Testament—follow the traditional order of the New Testament canon. I cite them all at least once in the notes for bibliographical purposes, but most later citations refer only to the New Testament passage where the works' texts, translations, or discussions are relevant to my argument. I cite specific pages or folios only when the evidence I refer to may be difficult to locate because it does not follow the traditional order of the New Testament canon.

Abbreviations

AHR	*American Historical Review*
ARG	*Archiv für Reformationsgeschichte*
CHB	*Cambridge History of the Bible*, 3 vols. (Cambridge, 1963-1970)
EE	*Opus epistolarum Des. Erasmi Roterodami*, ed. P. S. Allen et al., 12 vols. (Oxford, 1906-1958)
Ferguson	*Erasmi opuscula*, ed. W. K. Ferguson (The Hague, 1933)
Histoire de l'exégèse	O. Fatio and P. Fraenkel, eds., *Histoire de l'exégèse au XVIe siècle* (Geneva, 1978)
Holborn	*Desiderius Erasmus Roterodamus. Ausgewählte Werke*, ed. H. and A. Holborn (Munich, 1933)
JWCI	*Journal of the Warburg and Courtauld Institutes*
LB	*Opera omnia Des. Erasmi Roterodami*, ed. J. LeClerc, 10 vols. (Lugdunum Batavorum, 1703-1706)
PL	*Patrologiae cursus completus. Series latina*, ed. J.-P. Migne, 221 vols. (Paris, 1844-1890)
RABM	*Revista de archivos, bibliotecas y museos*
RQ	*Renaissance Quarterly*
SCJ	*Sixteenth Century Journal*

Humanists and Holy Writ

ONE

The Renaissance and the History of Scholarship

THIS BOOK seeks to contribute to our understanding of the history of scholarship, more specifically to account for a turning point in the development of New Testament studies. Humanist scholars of the Renaissance, so my argument runs, explored and charted virgin territory in New Testament scholarship: they studied the original Greek text of the New Testament instead of the Latin translations used by western scholars during the Middle Ages; they based their analyses on philological and historical criteria instead of the theological considerations that governed medieval study of the New Testament; they opened the door on a new era of scholarship by developing the methods, principles, and insights employed by students of the New Testament all the way up to the present day; they prepared and published editions of the New Testament that scholars relied upon until the late nineteenth century. These humanists may therefore be recognized as the founders of modern philological scholarship on the New Testament.

Implications of Humanism for New Testament Studies

Straightforward as it may seem, this thesis opens a Pandora's box of problems. Almost every element calls for some clarification or justification, beginning with the notion of scholarship itself and the question whether it may be said to have a history. Scholarship in general is simply the preservation, clarification, and extension of human learning. The present study concentrates on only a small segment of this vast enterprise, New Testament scholarship, and the limitation will make it possible to base generalizations on reliable detail. Still, New Testament scholars in the Renaissance took on a broad range of assignments and carried them out in various ways. Throughout this study I shall distinguish three general areas of New Testament scholarship: the editing of texts, production of translations, and explanation of works edited or translated.

From one age to another, New Testament scholars in performing these tasks have depended upon entirely different methods. As one of the ways by which a civilization transmits and interprets its cultural legacy, scholarship reflects the values and views of the civilization from which it arises. As these things change, so does scholarship, though not necessarily by mechanical, one-to-one correspondence. If one can trace and account for change, development, and growth in scholarly aims and methods, then one is entitled to speak of the history of scholarship. Until quite recently, strange to say, historians evinced little interest in this sort of history, properly speaking, of scholarship. J. E. Sandys's massive, encyclopedic volumes dominated the topic for so long that they perhaps obscured the need for studies concentrating on the development of

4

scholarship.[1] Though immensely valuable as a source of reference, Sandys's work—chiefly a chronological review of names, dates, titles, and anecdotes about classical scholars and their writings—provides no adequate substitute for properly historical studies of scholarship, its character, and especially its development. While it has recently become possible to consult such works, no study yet accounts for the entire tradition of classical or New Testament scholarship, though several volumes present intelligent interpretations of long periods of those traditions.[2] And one might see in a number of recent articles and monographic studies the groundwork for more reliable treatments of scholarship and its development.[3]

[1] J. E. Sandys, *A History of Classical Scholarship*, 3 vols. (Cambridge, 1903-1920).

[2] Easily the most impressive of these studies is Rudolf Pfeiffer's *History of Classical Scholarship from the Beginnings to the End of the Hellenistic Age* (Oxford, 1968). Though helpful, the sequel lacks the originality and power of the earlier volume: *History of Classical Scholarship from 1300 to 1850* (Oxford, 1976). One thinks also of the following works: Sebastiano Timpanaro, *La genesi del metodo del Lachmann* (Florence, 1963); E. J. Kenney, *The Classical Text* (Berkeley, 1974); L. D. Reynolds and N. G. Wilson, *Scribes and Scholars*, 2nd ed. (Oxford, 1974); and R. R. Bolgar, *The Classical Heritage and Its Beneficiaries* (Cambridge, 1954). For New Testament scholarship one may consult Bruce M. Metzger, *The Text of the New Testament*, 2nd ed. (New York, 1968), esp. pp. 95-185; and Werner G. Kümmel, *The New Testament: The History of the Investigation of Its Problems*, trans. S. M. Gilmour and H. C. Kee (Nashville, 1972).

[3] To limit citations to studies of Renaissance scholars, four especially important works come quickly to mind: G. Billanovich, "Petrarch and the Textual Tradition of Livy," *JWCI* 14 (1951):137-208; Winfried Trillitzsch, "Erasmus und Seneca," *Philologus* 109 (1965):270-93; Anthony Grafton, "On the Scholarship of Politian and Its Context," *JWCI* 40 (1977):150-88; and Silvia Rizzo, *Il lessico filologico degli umanisti* (Rome, 1973). Other interesting literature includes the following works: Remigio Sabbadini, *Il metodo degli umanisti* (Florence, 1920); Sesto Prete, "Leistungen der Humanisten auf dem Gebiete der lateinischen Philologie," *Philologus* 109 (1965):259-69; the same author's pamphlet, *Observations on the History of Textual Criticism in the Medieval and Renaissance Periods* (Collegeville, Minn., 1970); Vittore Branca, "Ermolao Barbaro and Late Quattrocento Venetian Humanism," in *Renaissance Venice*, ed. J. R. Hale (Totowa, N.J., 1973), pp. 218-43; and Charles

In a similar vein, I propose here not so much to add to our knowledge of the details concerning New Testament scholars and their work, but rather to contribute to our understanding of the character and quality of their work, and further to show how the Renaissance humanists expanded the boundaries of New Testament scholarship as a discipline. The developments examined here in some ways resemble a scientific revolution, as some analysts have recently come to understand that process.[4] The various disciplines of natural science are branches of scholarship, after all, which undergo change, development, and growth. Like the makers of scientific revolutions, Renaissance humanists changed the questions asked in New Testament scholarship, the methods used to answer them, and the rules governing the interpretation of data—as later chapters will show in detail. I do not mean to suggest an exact parallel between the development of natural science and that of New Testament scholarship. There is no precise equivalent in New Testament studies to Thomas Kuhn's periods of "normal science," for example, when scholars identify anomalies unexplained by the prevailing scientific explanations of the world. Nor have New Testament scholars ever worked with such strict reference to an all-embracing synthesis as, say, physicists, who in order to contribute usefully to their discipline have had to take into account an Aristotelian, Newtonian, or Einsteinian paradigm of the physical world. A loose analogy between natural science and New Testament studies, however, may help to illustrate the character of the develop-

G. Nauert, "Humanists, Scientists, and Pliny: Changing Approaches to a Classical Author," *AHR* 84 (1979):72-85. These lists make no pretense to completeness, but only cite some of the more important contributions to the history of scholarship known to me.

4 The following discussion takes its inspiration from Thomas S. Kuhn, *The Structure of Scientific Revolutions*, 2nd ed. (Chicago, 1970); also from David A. Hollinger, "T. S. Kuhn's Theory of Science and Its Implications for History," *AHR* 78 (1973):370-93.

mental process that transformed New Testament scholarship during the Renaissance.

Finally, I should like to argue that the history of scholarship, though not well understood, is significant. Scholarship profoundly influences society and civilization because of its importance in education. Scholars teach students what they themselves discover about their disciplines, but what they discover depends upon their methods, principles, and approach to their work. These things must be analyzed if we are to understand how past generations viewed the world. Furthermore, the analysis of scholarship can help to account for important developments in cultural history on a broader scale. Thus later chapters show that with humanist scholars of the Renaissance, the New Testament emerged as an object of philological and historical study—a development that eventually would diminish the importance of the Christian scriptures as a guide to living in the modern world. The time seems to me long overdue that historians began to pay attention to the history and development of scholarship in general and New Testament studies in particular, given their roles in molding the minds of society's leaders and elites.

A SECOND cluster of problems emerges from the summary thesis presented above, this one concerning the notions of humanism, Renaissance, and modernity. It has become almost obligatory for historians to refer with appreciation to the authority of Paul O. Kristeller when speaking of Renaissance humanism, and I have no wish to break precedent. Kristeller's work rescued the notion of humanism from the swamps of ideological debate and rendered it a useful concept for students of Renaissance culture.[5] By his account, humanism was a broad cultural, educational, and literary movement of the

---

[5] See especially his *Renaissance Thought: The Classic, Scholastic, and Humanist Strains* (New York, 1961).

period ca. 1300 to 1600. The movement took no particular stand on philosophical or ideological issues, though almost to a man the humanists were Christians, of one stripe or another. In general, the humanists were bound by a common appreciation of classical literature, and they usually encouraged cultivation of an eloquent, or at least a pure writing style.

Most historians find little to object to in this formulation, but some recent students have added to it in a way important for the following study.[6] If humanists in general adhered to no peculiar ideology, their special interests—language and history—led them to understand the world in terms different from those of their chief intellectual rivals, the scholastic philosophers and theologians. The humanists found meaning in neither the abstract syntheses nor the petty logical quarrels of the scholastics, but rather in practical matters of politics and morality and—especially important for us—in the unique and particular elements of literature and history. The humanists therefore approached the New Testament, among other things, with different purposes in mind than the scholastics. The humanists' interests lay not in the construction of a comprehensive theological system that answered all possible questions bearing on salvation, and that did so with logical rigor worthy of an Aristotle. They valued the New Testament instead as the source of pure moral and religious doctrine and as the record of early Christian experience. They consequently lavished their attention on details of the text itself, declining the opportunity, often taken by scholastics, to derive heady theological doctrine from the intellectually modest writings of the New

[6] What follows reflects the influence of two papers which add texture and a sense of dynamism to Kristeller's neutral and static definition of humanism: Charles G. Nauert, "The Clash of Humanists and Scholastics: An Approach to Pre-Reformation Controversies," *SCJ* 4 (1973):1-18; George M. Logan, "Substance and Form in Renaissance Humanism," *Journal of Medieval and Renaissance Studies* 7 (1977):1-34.

Testament. This study will assess the scholarly implications of humanism by examining three of the humanists' more important scholarly projects on the New Testament—those of Lorenzo Valla (1407-1457), who annotated the Vulgate in the light of the Greek New Testament; a group of scholars gathered at the University of Alcalá (near Madrid) by Cardinal Francisco Ximénez de Cisneros of Spain, scholars who prepared the first edition of the Greek New Testament ever set in print; and Erasmus of Rotterdam (1466-1536), who produced the first edition of the Greek New Testament ever published and distributed, and accompanied it with a fresh Latin translation and copious annotations.

Humanism was no high road to modern philological scholarship, however, and it may serve the interests of balanced history to recall at least briefly some of the other scholarly trails explored by humanist (or humanist-influenced) students of the New Testament. Marsiglio Ficino produced a long commentary on the Epistle to the Romans, but he rarely addressed problems of text and translation in the work, even though he was a competent student of Greek and the translator of Plato's works into Latin. Philological clarifications occur only as incidental digressions from Ficino's chief purpose, the bolstering of his elaborate Neoplatonic theology.[7] Similarly, the work of John Colet informs us less about philology than theology on the eve of the Reformation. Colet lacked Greek and based his exegesis of the Pauline epistles on the Vulgate New Testament; his work reveals the influence not of humanist philologists, but of Neoplatonic theologians, especially Ficino and the Pseudo-Dionysius. Though routinely hailed

[7] Ficino's commentary on Romans and a few other minor writings on the New Testament are found in his *Opera omnia*, 4 vols. (Basle, 1576), 1:425-91. The best study is that of Charles Trinkaus, *In Our Image and Likeness*, 2 vols. (Chicago, 1970), 2:613, 734-53, esp. 744-53. See also Walter Dress, *Die Mystik des Marsilio Ficino* (Berlin, 1929), pp. 151-216.

as a harbinger of Reformation exegesis, Colet's real achievement was simply to provide a running literal commentary in the patristic fashion, abandoning the late medieval style of exegesis, which often subordinated the scriptures to the needs of scholastic theology.[8]

Other Renaissance humanists approached more closely the philological scholarship of the subjects studied here, but without illuminating very clearly the development of that scholarship. Giannozzo Manetti, for example, translated afresh the Greek New Testament, but left no notes or other explanation of his work, so that it is impossible to evaluate accurately the quality of his scholarship. Furthermore, his translation apparently influenced no other scholar of his own or later times: it remains even today in manuscript.[9] Even less material survives to illuminate the New Testament scholarship of Guillaume Budé. A preeminent and somewhat imposing philologist, Budé devoted himself to the classical tradition and left only a few sketchy observations on the New Testament. Historians therefore lack the information necessary to evaluate Budé as a New Testament philologist.[10]

---

[8] The most accessible edition of Colet's works remains that of J. H. Lupton. See especially the *Enarratio in epistolam S. Pauli ad Romanos* (London, 1873); the *Enarratio in primam epistolam S. Pauli ad Corinthios* (London, 1874); and the exposition of Rom. 1-5 in the *Opuscula quaedam theologica* (London, 1876). Professor C.A.L. Jarrott will soon publish a new edition of Colet's exegesis of 1 Cor. The more accurate literature includes the following works: Eugene F. Rice, "John Colet and the Annihilation of the Natural," *Harvard Theological Review* 45 (1952):141-63; C.A.L. Jarrott, "John Colet on Justification," *SCJ* 7 (1976):59-72; P. Albert Duhamel, "The Oxford Lectures of John Colet," *Journal of the History of Ideas* 14 (1953):493-510; and Sears Jayne, *John Colet and Marsilio Ficino* (Oxford, 1963).

[9] See Trinkaus, *In Our Image*, 2:571-78; and Salvatore Garofalo, "Gli umanisti italiani del secolo XV e la Bibbia," *Biblica* 27 (1946):354-65.

[10] Budé's New Testament scholarship is limited to a few points on translation raised in correspondence with Erasmus (*EE*, no. 403, 2:228-33); a few reflections on Lorenzo Valla's work and problems in the gospel of Luke raised in the course of Budé's monumental *Annotationes in Pandectas* (in his *Opera*

More problematical is the case of Budé's countryman and contemporary, Jacques Lefèvre d'Étaples. Lefèvre produced a series of widely celebrated scholarly works on the New Testament: a fresh Latin translation and exegesis of the Pauline epistles (1512); brief commentaries on the gospels (1522) and catholic epistles (1527); a French translation of the whole New Testament (1523); and several polemical works attacking various interpretations of Erasmus, John Fisher, and others. He based his work on the Greek text of the New Testament, and he exhibited a sometimes impressive independence of thought. Yet he influenced the development of philological scholarship only marginally, for lack of an adequate critical faculty. His credulity extended so far that in his edition of the Pauline epistles he presented as genuine writings of St. Paul the apocryphal Epistle to the Laodiceans and spurious correspondence between Seneca and Paul.[11] Indeed, recent studies have made it abundantly clear that Lefèvre was only superficially interested in philological matters. In one issue, one controversy, one problem after another, he allowed his deep piety, his commitment to tradition, or his mystical theology to override philological considerations.[12]

Later chapters will make some reference to these figures of

---

omnia, 4 vols., Basle, 1557, 3:56 D-57 A); and a few marginal additions and corrections that Budé himself entered into five manuscripts of the Greek New Testament copied by George Hermonymus (Bibliothèque Nationale, MSS. grecques 59, 108-111).

[11] See his *Pauli epistolae* (Paris, 1512), fol. 188rv, 226r-229v.

[12] Jean-Pierre Massaut, *Critique et tradition à la veille de la Réforme en France* (Paris, 1974); Guy Bedouelle, *Lefèvre d'Étaples et l'intelligence des écritures* (Geneva, 1976); John B. Payne, "Erasmus and Lefèvre d'Étaples as Interpreters of Paul," *ARG* 65 (1974):54-83; Helmut Feld, "Der Humanisten-Streit um Hebräer 2, 7 (Psalm 8, 6)," *ARG* 61 (1970):5-35. See also two articles in the *Histoire de l'exégèse*: Jean-Pierre Massaut, "Histoire et allégorie dans les Evangiles d'après Lefèvre d'Étaples et Clichtove," pp. 186-201; and Guy Bedouelle, "La lecture christologique du psautier dans le *Quincuplex Psalterium* de Lefèvre d'Étaples," pp. 133-43.

lesser importance—particularly Manetti, Colet, and Lefèvre—
but will concentrate on the three projects mentioned above.
Selection of this group is not entirely arbitrary, but may be
justified on the grounds that Valla, the Complutensian circle,
and Erasmus most clearly illustrate the gradual, sometimes
painful process by which philological methods came to dominate study of the New Testament. Moreover, these scholars
offer several other advantages to the historian of scholarship.
In the first place, it is possible to trace the influence of the
scholars on each other. Valla's notes on the New Testament
were well known to Erasmus, who first published them, and
to the scholars of Alcalá; Erasmus and the scholars of Alcalá
were themselves comtemporaries, and they kept close watch
on each others' works, though they did not always enjoy cor-
dial relations. Thus it is possible to determine how these scholars
received, accepted, rejected, or modified each others' methods
and principles of scholarship. This information offers to the
historian the opportunity to compare, contrast, and evaluate
their work with no small accuracy, and thus to form reliable
judgments about the development of early philological scholarship.

In the second place, limiting this study to the work of Valla,
the circle at Alcalá, and Erasmus makes it possible to take
advantage of a peculiar but important unity of time. Many,
perhaps most historians today think of the Renaissance simply
as the period ca. 1300 to 1600. For the purposes of intellectual and religious history, however, the onset of the Reformation and the sundering of Christendom form a great wa-
tershed dividing the period as a whole. Our subjects all
undertook their labors before the Reformation. Erasmus and
some of the Spanish scholars continued their work during the
early years of the Reformation, but the great religious and
theological controversies did not deeply influence the charac-

ter of their work. They continued in the 1520s and 1530s to employ, and even to develop further the same methods they used in their earliest works, begun long before anybody outside Germany recognized the name of Martin Luther. This is important because, as the last chapter will show, the Reformation created a new and not always a healthy environment for philological studies on the New Testament. Theology came often to dominate philology in the later sixteenth century. Too much doctrine was invested in certain passages of scripture to allow full rein to critical philologists, who might undermine cherished interpretations. Limiting this study to pre-Reformation scholarship will enable us to avoid many problems introduced into New Testament study by scholars' prior theological commitments, and to concentrate attention instead on a purer philological tradition in New Testament scholarship.

Finally, the subjects chosen for study here offer the advantage of geographical diversity. The group includes a preeminent Italian humanist, a peripatetic, cosmopolitan Dutchman, and a circle of Spaniards whose work was probably coordinated by a Greek emigré. Historians usually confine their basic research to a single country or a small group of like-minded figures, and not without good reason. All over western Europe, however, humanist scholars were influenced by many of the same intellectual currents. Only by analyzing their various reactions to these currents may one draw valid general conclusions about the nature, development, and significance of Renaissance scholarship.

The most important of these general conclusions is that the philological strain of Renaissance scholarship deeply influenced the development of modern New Testament studies. The question of the Renaissance and its relationship to the modern world has been endlessly debated.[13] Few if any his-

---

[13] For a thoughtful and provocative discussion of the Renaissance and its

torians today accept in unmitigated form Jakob Burckhardt's thesis, that the Renaissance drove daemonically toward secular, individualist modernity. The Renaissance failed to anticipate the modern world in every particular. Yet it seems to me well established that one may trace to the Renaissance certain fundamental departures from previous practice, and further that these developments significantly shaped modern ways of doing things. Scholars have demonstrated, for example, that the resident ambassador and modern diplomatic protocol have their origin in the Renaissance; that Renaissance artists developed new techniques and new ways of thinking about antiquity that brought to an end the long medieval tradition of representational art; that Renaissance historians began the early experimentation with modern historical methods, and even anticipated historicist ideas and techniques.[14] Modern diplomats, artists, and historians of course do not slavishly imitate their Renaissance counterparts, but modern practice in diplomacy, art, and historiography owes no small debt to Renaissance developments.

And so it is also with New Testament scholarship. In a way, the following study parallels those alluded to above. I do not pretend that Renaissance philologists would feel at home in modern universities, but in several important respects, the humanists helped lay the foundations for modern New Testament scholarship.

---

relation to modernity see William J. Bouwsma, "The Renaissance and the Drama of Western History," *AHR* 84 (1979):1-15. The following pages will show that I cannot agree with Bouwsma in every respect, though in general I think his essay offers a wise alternative to previous characterizations of the Renaissance.

[14] Garrett Mattingly, *Renaissance Diplomacy* (Baltimore, 1964); Erwin Panofsky, *Renaissance and Renascences in Western Art* (New York, 1969); Donald R. Kelley, *Foundations of Modern Historical Scholarship* (New York, 1970); Nancy S. Struever, *The Language of History in the Renaissance* (Princeton, 1970).

LIKE ALL men, the humanists were deeply influenced by the events of their own times, and their scholarly achievements reflect broader cultural patterns of the Renaissance. It seems to me that three developments in particular help to explain the humanists' foundation of a new brand of scholarship: the revival of Greek learning, the emergence of philological criticism, and the invention of printing.

From the earliest days of Christianity through St. Jerome, and even until the time of Bede (d. 735), scholars often based their New Testament commentaries on the Greek scriptures. The Church Fathers recorded variant readings in both Latin and Greek texts of the New Testament; they evaluated the Latin as a translation of the Greek; and they intelligently debated the accurate interpretation of the original Greek New Testament. From the eighth until the end of the fourteenth century, however, knowledge of Greek language and literature all but vanished in western Europe. Theological, political, and economic differences separated Byzantines and western Europeans. Latin Christians regarded Greeks as schismatics and heretics, and Greek letters fell under suspicion by association. Only toward the end of the Middle Ages did some westerners begin to recognize the importance of education in Greek. Roger Bacon (1220-1292) insisted that Bible students learn Hebrew and Greek, produce accurate texts of scripture, and base their expositions on study of the Hebrew and Greek texts. In 1312 Ramon Lull persuaded the Council of Vienne to decree that chairs of Greek, Hebrew, Chaldean (i.e., biblical Aramaic), and Arabic be established at the universities of Paris, Bologna, Salamanca, and Oxford. Pierre d'Ailly (1350-1421) echoed Bacon, though cautiously, after a century's time. Yet none of these calls was heeded. The Council of Vienne notwithstanding, the first regular teaching of Greek began only in 1397, when Manuel Chrysoloras was called to Florence. Elsewhere Greek did not make its way into school and university curricula until the mid-fifteenth century.[15] In the meantime, New Testament scholarship had been severely hampered by western scholars' ignorance of the Greek text. Beginning in the twelfth century a peculiar misunderstanding of St. Jerome's prologue to the Pentateuch even prompted many medieval scholars to assert that the Latin scriptures were more reliable than the Greek, and the Greek more reliable than the Hebrew![16] Only with the Renaissance and the revival of interest in Greek did western scholars begin again to study the original text of the New Testament. The significance of Greek scholarship in the humanists' works will be evident on almost every page of the following study.

Knowledge of Greek by itself, however, would not necessarily have led to a new brand of New Testament scholarship. Byzantine scholars had used the Greek scriptures for a millennium without anticipating modern scholarship. The Byzantines devoted their philological talents to the classical tradition; they seemed to recognize only doctrinal and theological problems in the Christian scriptures. The most likely expla-

[15] On the knowledge of Greek in the Middle Ages see Bernhard Bischoff, "Das griechische Element in der abendländischen Bildung des Mittelalters," in his *Mittelalterliche Studien*, 2 vols. (Stuttgart, 1967), 2:246-75; and the same author's "The Study of Foreign Languages in the Middle Ages," in ibid., 2:227-45. On calls for language study in the late Middle Ages see Francis A. Cardinal Gasquet, "Roger Bacon and the Latin Vulgate," in *Roger Bacon Essays*, ed. A. G. Little (Oxford, 1914), pp. 89-99; and Louis Salembier's very interesting but little known work on d'Ailly, "Une page inédite de l'histoire de la Vulgate," published in eight installments in the *Revue des sciences ecclésiastiques* 56-62 (1887-1890). On the revival of Greek instruction see Sabbadini, *Il metodo degli umanisti*, pp. 17-27.

[16] A. Landgraf, "Zur Methode der biblischen Textkritik im 12. Jahrhundert," *Biblica* 10 (1929), esp. pp. 445-56. Landgraf does not discuss Jerome's text, which occurs in *PL*, 28:184 A. Jerome said Latin manuscripts would be better than Greek and Greek better than Hebrew only as the result of a false condition. The medieval scholars failed to recognize that the condition was contrary to fact. Erasmus exposed the error in his preface to Lorenzo Valla's *Adnotationes* to the New Testament: *EE*, no. 182, 1:411.

nation for this puzzling state of affairs is that the Church of Constantinople had long since adopted as a standard text of the New Testament the edition prepared by the martyr Lucian of Antioch (d. 312). About the turn of the fourth century Lucian examined Greek texts of the New Testament from all parts of the Mediterranean. He of course noticed variant readings, literary rough spots, and significantly different texts in his manuscripts. He prepared his own edition on what might be called a catholic editorial principle: he harmonized his wildly varying manuscripts by conflation and assimilation, and he smoothed over the literary indelicacies found in many or most of his texts. His edition soon found its way to Constantinople, whence it spread throughout the Byzantine Empire. Later Byzantine scholars therefore were largely spared the necessity of producing improved editions of the scriptures. Rarely would they be likely to encounter a copy of the New Testament that differed significantly from Lucian's, which was profusely multiplied by Byzantine scribes. If errors crept into new copies of the New Testament, they need only be removed by collation with the standard reference copies of the scriptures preserved in the important churches of the Empire.[17]

Thus Byzantine scholars had little need to develop the faculty of philological criticism that plays so large a role in modern New Testament studies. A critical philologist pays close

---

[17] On Lucian of Antioch and the Byzantine text of the New Testament see B. H. Streeter, *The Four Gospels* (New York, 1925), pp. 1-148, esp. pp. 109-27 and 144-48 on the origin and character of the text and pp. 39-45, 61-64, 102-106 on its diffusion. See also Metzger, *The Text of the New Testament*, pp. 131-32, 169-73. I know of no study on Byzantine New Testament scholarship, but the main outlines of Byzantine scholarship in general may be gathered from the following works: Hans-Georg Beck, *Kirche und theologische Literatur im byzantinischen Reich* (Munich, 1959); Sandys, *History of Classical Scholarship*, 1:347-439; Karl Krumbacher, *Geschichte der byzantinischen Literatur*, 2nd ed. (Munich, 1897); J. M. Hussey, *Church and Learning in the Byzantine Empire, 867-1185* (New York, 1963); Reynolds and Wilson, *Scribes and Scholars*, pp. 37-68; and Bolgar, *The Classical Heritage*, pp. 59-90.

attention to words and the problems entailed in their transmission, translation, and explanation. Unless scholars notice these problems they can hardly become philologists. Byzantine scholars of the New Testament could regard editorial problems as largely solved; they could ignore problems of translation, since they used the New Testament in its original language; and the problem of explaining the Greek language was obviously less difficult for them than for westerners. Thus when they studied the New Testament, they concentrated their efforts on homiletics and theology. The Renaissance humanists, however, noticed problems overlooked by the Byzantines with respect to the transmission of the New Testament, and they addressed further problems raised by its translation and explanation in Latin. Since they interested themselves so deeply in language, grammar, and words, it is not surprising to find them developing and employing novel and sophisticated insights regarding these problems and their solution. Again, almost every page of this study will testify to the significance and the extent of the humanists' use of philological criteria to resolve the thorny problems they encountered in their study of the New Testament.

The combination of Greek studies and philological criticism thus enabled the humanists to develop a new brand of scholarship; the invention of printing enabled the new scholarship to flourish.[18] The press provided scholars with an excellent means of communication, by which they could take advantage of each others' works. Through the new medium knowledge was rapidly reported, accumulated, assimilated—or rejected— improved, expanded, and advanced. In fact, in a peculiar way printing aided scholarship so much that it obscured the rep-

[18] By far the most interesting recent work on early printing is Elizabeth L. Eisenstein, *The Printing Press as an Agent of Change*, 2 vols. (Cambridge, 1979). For the impact of printing on New Testament scholarship, see especially 1:329-67.

utation of the Renaissance humanists in their capacity as scholars: scholarship progressed so fast as to make it unnecessary very soon to consult the humanists' works. If one enjoys access to the works of Scaliger in the seventeenth century, Bentley in the eighteenth, or Lachmann in the nineteenth, there will be little point in returning to the less rigorous investigations of Valla, Politian, or Erasmus. Printing therefore ensured that humanist scholarship would soon suffer eclipse; but at least it guaranteed the survival of the humanists' works, which were so widely scattered as to enable at least a few copies to endure the ravages of time, men, and worms.

This survival of the humanists' works makes it possible at long last to locate the humanists themselves in the history of scholarship. Renaissance humanists invested a prodigious amount of time and energy in ferreting out manuscripts; editing, publishing, and translating them; analyzing, explaining, and popularizing their contents. Many of the humanists owed their reputations among contemporaries chiefly to their scholarly activities. Yet few aspects of Renaissance culture are less understood today than the humanists' classical and biblical scholarship. This study of the humanists as New Testament scholars seeks to set right this state of affairs, to rescue the humanists from the oblivion assigned them by the invention of printing, and to clarify their role in the history of New Testament scholarship.

The study proceeds by analysis of the humanists' manuscripts, editions, translations, and annotations on the Greek and Latin New Testament. These sources best display the humanists' efforts to produce accurate texts of the Greek and Latin New Testament, an accurate Latin translation of the Greek New Testament, and an accurate historical explanation of what New Testament writings meant to their earliest audiences. Analysis of these sources will show that in several general ways the humanists penetrated the boundaries that confined their medieval predecessors and began to mark the paths that modern New Testament scholars would follow. The humanists, for example, began to assemble the basic data—manuscripts and variant readings—that had to be controlled before editors could produce accurate texts of the New Testament. They published the first standard editions of the New Testament, editions that all scholars could use and against which new textual discoveries could be evaluated. They formulated a number of specific principles and methods of textual analysis which modern scholars still invoke when confronted with knotty textual problems. Finally, they developed a detached, historical attitude toward biblical antiquity that made possible a more accurate understanding of the original meaning of New Testament writings. In short, this study deals with a topic that ought to interest all modern scholars—the dawn of modern scholarly attitudes and methods.

New Testament Scholarship in the Late Middle Ages

Before delving into the humanists' works, it will be useful to discuss the state of the art in New Testament scholarship during the later Middle Ages. There can be no question here of providing a complete review of medieval scholarship on the Bible or New Testament: that must be sought elsewhere.[19] It will be easier to appreciate the character and quality of the humanists' achievement, however, if it is viewed in the context of the methods and principles used by their immediate predecessors in New Testament scholarship.

---

[19] Still the most judicious survey is Beryl Smalley, *The Study of the Bible in the Middle Ages*, 2nd ed. (Oxford, 1952). See also Henri de Lubac, *Exégèse médiévale*, 4 vols. (Paris, 1959-1964); C. Spicq, *Ésquisse d'une histoire de l'exégèse latine au Moyen Age* (Paris, 1944); and pertinent articles in the *CHB*.

In fact this is a particularly important setting of the stage, because historians of exegesis have largely ignored the tradition of biblical scholarship in the late Middle Ages. They have called the later medieval period a time of "stunted growth," or even "decadence" in the field of biblical studies in general.[20] They have neglected to examine the New Testament scholarship of even the greatest of the later medieval exegetes, Nicholas of Lyra (1270-1349), author of the enormous *Postilla litteralis*, a literal commentary on the whole Bible which required nearly a decade to prepare (1322-1331), and a shorter *Postilla moralis* (1339) which summarized allegorical and spiritual exegesis on all the Bible except the apostolic epistles. On the strength of these works Lyra acquired a reputation as a reliable, up-to-date commentator, especially with respect to the literal sense of scripture. His familiarity with the Hebrew language and Jewish scholarship lent further prestige to his exposition of the Old Testament. His works were accepted as authority in the later Middle Ages; indeed, they were reprinted and used as standard reference works for centuries after his death. Yet there exists no study of Lyra's New Testament scholarship! Historians have discussed Lyra's life, hermeneutics, and Old Testament exegesis; but beyond a short account of his commentary on the Epistle to the Hebrews, almost nothing is known of the methods and principles he employed in his New Testament studies.[21] Lyra's work set the

[20] Beryl Smalley, "The Bible in the Medieval Schools," *CHB*, 2:216-19; and Lubac, *Exégèse médiévale*, 4:369-91.

[21] On Lyra's life and influence see Charles-Victor Langlois, "Nicolas de Lyre, frère mineur," *Histoire littéraire de France* 36 (1927):355-400. On his hermeneutics and Old Testament exegesis see James Samuel Preus, *From Shadow to Promise* (Cambridge, Mass., 1969), pp. 61-71; Herman Hailperin, *Rashi and the Christian Scholars* (Pittsburgh, 1963), pp. 137-246; and Lubac, *Exégèse médiévale*, 4:344-67. Kenneth Hagen discusses Lyra's treatment of Hebrews as part of the background to Martin Luther's lectures on that epistle: *A Theology of Testament in the Young Luther* (Leiden, 1974), pp. 1-70 *passim*.

pace for biblical scholarship in the later Middle Ages; by investigating it one may gain the clearest possible view of the immediate background of humanist scholarship on the New Testament.

Lyra tacitly assumed the accuracy and reliability of the Vulgate New Testament. In the Old Testament portion of his *Postilla litteralis* he compared the Vulgate's translation with the original Hebrew text, and he criticized and corrected many passages where the Vulgate inadequately represented the Hebrew.[22] But this critical interest did not carry over into Lyra's scholarship on the New Testament. He knew no Greek and so was unable to consult the original text or to evaluate the Vulgate as a translation of the New Testament. He occasionally noted readings found in many common Vulgate manuscripts, but not *in libris correctis*, volumes that had been checked for errors. Even more rarely he undertook to explain the origin of incorrect readings: at Acts 23:24 and 1 Tim. 3:14, for example, he pointed out that a whole sentence and a phrase, respectively, had found their way from a gloss into the Vulgate's text. Lacking Greek, however, Lyra could not comment with much authority on the accuracy of the Vulgate's text and translation. Thus criticism played a negligible role in his exposition of the New Testament, and straightforward exegesis predominated even more than in his scholarship on the Old Testament.

Since his own day Lyra has been noted primarily as an ex-

---

[22] There is no standard or critical edition of Lyra's works, but the *Postilla litteralis* may be consulted in scores of editions published between the fifteenth and eighteenth centuries. I have used the text printed in a magnificent *Biblia sacra cum glossa interlineari, ordinaria, et Nicolai Lyrani postilla, eiusdemque moralitatibus, Burgensis additionibus, & Thoringi replicis*, 6 vols. (Venice, 1588). The last two volumes cover the New Testament. For Lyra's Old Testament criticism see the general prologue to the *Postilla litteralis* (vol. I, fol. 3r-4r in the edition just cited) and Langlois, "Nicolas de Lyre," pp. 385-97.

ponent of the literal sense of scripture—and not without reason. In the general prologue to his *Postilla litteralis* Lyra lamented the degree to which recent commentators had indulged themselves in speculative allegorical and spiritual exegesis. The literal sense provides necessary support for all successful exegesis, he insisted: allegorical and spiritual explanations not firmly grounded on the literal sense will collapse like a house without a foundation. Lyra therefore took as his main object the clarification of the literal sense of the scriptures.[23] And he provided a treatment of the literal sense that was indeed elaborate. He commented on every verse of the New Testament, every phrase, and sometimes every word in the verse. Usually he explained his text by means of a pious paraphrase that expanded on the text and pointed to its moral implications. The result was a reverent, uncontroversial comment such as that to 2 Tim. 2:22, where the author of the epistle advised Timothy to "flee from adolescent desires; seek instead justice, faith, charity, and peace with those who call on the Lord with pure intentions." Lyra explained "adolescent desires" as those activities that delight the flesh; only by avoiding them altogether might one conquer them. Timothy must therefore flee them and pursue justice toward his neighbor, faith toward God, charity toward both, and peace with all, especially with the faithful. So Lyra expounded this text.

Lyra's high regard for literal exegesis, however, must not be allowed to obscure the fact that he maintained a healthy respect for allegorical and spiritual as well as literal exegesis.[24] He prepared also a *Postilla moralis* (sometimes entitled simply *Moralia*) to complement his literal commentary. It is a much shorter work than the *Postilla litteralis*: Lyra thought its brev-

[23] See again the general prologue to the *Postilla litteralis*.
[24] Lubac argues (correctly, I think) that Lyra's exegesis was not so one-sidedly literal as most interpretations suggest. See his *Exégèse médiévale*, 4:344-67.

ity excusable on the ground that exegetes had long since devoted considerable attention to the spiritual sense of scripture.[25] The fact remains, however, that Lyra considered allegorical and spiritual explanations an important part of a complete exegesis of the scriptures. For the most part, Lyra kept his spiritual exegesis within reasonable boundaries, even though he passed beyond the meaning intended by the authors of scripture. He explained Zechariah (Luke 1:5), for example, as a model illustrating the qualities of the good prelate, who keeps the memory of God in his heart and seeks salvation for himself and his flock. The woman taken in adultery (John 7:53-8:11) represented those cut off from faith in Christ, entangled in mortal sin because of their intercourse with the devil. The scribes and pharisees who try to bring her to judgment signified demons, who similarly try to drag the faithless into hell, while Jesus' intervention illustrated the saving power of Christ. The mention of St. Paul's occupation (Acts 18:3) prompted Lyra to compare tents with Pauline doctrine. Tents protect their inhabitants from heat, rain, and wind; so Paul's teaching shelters Christians from the heat of cupidity, the rains of carnality, and the winds of pride and vanity.

Lyra generally limited himself to this sort of tame allegory, but he was capable at times of advancing truly arcane explanations in his *Postilla moralis*. Jesus' genealogy (Matt. 1:1-18)—by any odds one of the driest passages of the entire New Testament—was fraught with mysterious significance for Lyra. The line of descent breaks down into three parts, each of fourteen generations. The three sections, Lyra said, represent the Trinity; the fourteen generations signify the combination of the Ten Commandments and the four gospels. In similar vein, Lyra said Jesus did not accidentally appoint twelve disciples

---

[25] See the prologue to the *Postilla moralis* in the *Biblia sacra* cited above, I, 4ʳ.

at Mark 3:14: he meant the number twelve to signify the proclamation of the Trinity to the four corners of the world. The star seen by the wise men (Matt. 2:2) he explained by reference to the Virgin Mary, the star who guides those navigating their way through the world to a safe port, i.e., to Christ.

It is not surprising to find this sort of explanation in the *Postilla moralis*. That Lyra set great store by spiritual exegesis is more evident from its presence also in the *Postilla litteralis*. He presented an allegorical exposition, for example, for the entire twenty-fifth chapter of Matthew. The parable of the ten virgins (Matt. 25:1-13), he explained, refers to contemplatives, that of the talents (Matt. 25:14-30) to prelates, and that of the sheep and goats (Matt. 25:31-46) to laymen. In each case he developed detailed schemes by which the parables foreshadow the fortunes these classes of men may expect. Other allegorical explanations occur elsewhere in the *Postilla litteralis*—in Lyra's comments, for example, to Matt. 7:17 and 1 Pet. 3:19-20.

Without question, Lyra placed high value on exegesis of the literal sense of scripture, but overemphasis of this point has obscured his attachment to allegorical and spiritual explanations, and indeed to the medieval exegetical tradition in general. Like other branches of scholarship, scriptural exegesis reflects the broader culture from which it emerges. By Lyra's time allegorical and spiritual exegesis had long been regarded as an important, even necessary ingredient in any complete exposition of the New Testament. Since Lyra was thoroughly committed to the medieval Catholic tradition, it should cause no surprise to find him employing the characteristic medieval methods of allegorical and spiritual exegesis.

Lyra's New Testament scholarship reflects medieval culture also in another way which few historians have recognized: he resorted frequently to Aristotelian philosophy and scholastic theology to solve scriptural problems and to support interpretations relevant to his own times. In fact this dependence upon Aristotelian and scholastic authorities strikes me as the most distinctive feature of Lyra's New Testament scholarship. It is not unique to Lyra's work: other late medieval postillators commonly relied on these same authorities.[26] Nor is it difficult to see why the authors of *postillae* found such authorities useful. The postillators in general took it as their mission to bring biblical commentary up to date, to explain the scriptures in the most advanced terms available. They naturally began to consult the works of Aristotle—available in Latin dress only since the thirteenth century—and Aristotle's medieval disciples, chief among them St. Thomas Aquinas. The result was a sort of scientific exegesis best illustrated in Lyra's *Postilla litteralis*.

Lyra betrayed Aristotle's influence even before beginning his commentary proper. In prefaces to both the gospels and the Pauline epistles he outlines the four (Aristotelian) causes of evangelical and Pauline doctrine. In the case of the gospels Lyra identified Christ as the efficient cause (since he actually provided the doctrine required by his ministers), the material cause (since he served as subject of the gospels), and the final cause (since the gospels proposed to lead believers to him). The formal cause varied with the individual gospel, Lyra said, since it depended on each author's peculiar emphasis and manner of argument: thus in general, Matthew emphasized Jesus' humanity, John his divinity, Luke his ministry, and Mark his kingdom.[27] In the case of the Pauline epistles and their

---

[26] See Smalley's superb discussion of the late medieval postillators and their work in her *Study of the Bible in the Middle Ages*, pp. 264-355. Unfortunately, she does not extend her survey into the fourteenth century, and thus she excludes Lyra from her study.

[27] *Postilla litteralis*, prologue to the gospels, in the *Biblia sacra* cited above, V, fol. 2ʳ.

doctrine, Lyra found the four causes to be a bit more complicated. The efficient cause he identified with the author of the
epistles, i.e., Paul himself as a sort of agent, but Christ ultimately. The material cause was God's love and the redemption
it brings. The formal cause varied with the individual epistle:
it depended upon the addressee (whether Roman, Greek, or
Hebrew) and the manner of expression (whether explanatory,
analytical, or laudatory). The final cause of Pauline doctrine
Lyra defined as the profit (*utilitas*) of the Church.[28]

The tone of Lyra's New Testament commentary was thereby
firmly established, for Aristotle's influence does not end with
the prefaces, but spices the whole *Postilla litteralis*. The disciple Thomas wanted to experience the risen Christ by both
touch and sight, so Lyra explained at John 20:25, because
these are the two most reliable human senses—witness the
Metaphysics (I, 1). Jesus' counsel to "enter by the narrow gate"
(Matt. 7:13) reminded Lyra of the *Ethics* (II, 6-9): the gate is
called narrow, he said, because of the difficulty of holding to
the mean, the narrow path of virtue threading its tenuous way
through Aristotle's opposing vices. Lyra invoked Aristotle's
teachings on the powers of the mind (*De anima*, III, 4) in
refuting astrological explanations of John 2:4: the mind does
not depend upon bodily organs, so that the stars cannot explain Jesus' reluctance to perform a miracle. Lyra even imported Aristotelian natural science into his commentary: at
Acts 9:6 he cited the *Physics* (I, 1) to illustrate how cognitive
powers develop over time, enabling individuals to distinguish
the perfect from the imperfect.

Where Aristotle held his silence, medieval scholastic theologians came to Lyra's aid, especially St. Thomas Aquinas,
chief of the Christian Aristotelians. Lyra consistently introduced the terms and categories of the scholastics into his ex-

---

[28] *Postilla litteralis*, prologue to the Pauline epistles, in the *Biblia sacra* cited
above, VI, fol. 2ᵛ-3ʳ.

egesis. He often followed very closely the explanations advanced by St. Thomas in his own commentaries on the New Testament, and occasionally he even copied passages verbatim from Thomas's work.

A diligent researcher, in fact, could extract most of the essential features of scholastic theology from Lyra's *Postilla litteralis* on the New Testament. Perhaps the most important categories of the medieval theologians were those of *gratia* and *fides*, grace and faith, both of which were divided into many subcategories. The scholastics distinguished, for example, between *gratia gratis data* (grace freely given by God), which did not sanctify but only prepared an individual for salvation, and *gratia gratum faciens* (justifying grace), which rendered the individual acceptable to God. Now, at 1 Cor. 12:4 St. Paul spoke of "varieties of graces." Following St. Thomas, Lyra explained that Paul intended to discuss *gratia gratis data* in 1 Cor. 12, then turn to *gratia gratum faciens* in the following chapter.[29] Medieval theologians distinguished in similar fashion between *fides informis* (incomplete faith), which might be found apart from the state of grace, and *fides charitate formata* (faith perfected by love), which could exist only in conjunction with the state of justifying grace. Lyra found this distinction relevant at Rom. 1:17, the passage that Martin Luther later considered so important in his own spiritual development: "For the justice of God is revealed in [the gospel] from faith into deeper faith" (*ex fide in fidem*). According to Lyra, God's justice is revealed in the gospel proceeding from *fides informis* toward *fides charitate formata*. At Apoc. 3:18 Lyra entered into a complicated discussion of meritorious works involving three important scholastic concepts: *facere quod in se est* (doing one's level best), *meritum de*

---

[29] For St. Thomas's exegesis I use the texts published in his *Opera omnia*, 25 vols. (Parma, 1852-1873). His most important New Testament commentary, that on the Pauline epistles, appears in vol. 13 of the Parma edition.

congruo (an act that God out of sheer generosity recognizes as partially worthy), and *meritum de condigno* (a truly meritorious deed worthy of salvation). If an individual strives to fulfill the obligation of the principle *facere quod in se est*, so Lyra explained, God recognizes his effort as a *meritum de congruo* and bestows *gratia gratis data* upon him; the individual then becomes capable of performing *merita de condigno*, enabling him to grow in grace and eventually win salvation.

Scholastic theology therefore suggested novel interpretations of individual passages, but Lyra carried his scholastic commentary much further than this. In his exegeses of many texts he presented detailed summaries of scholastic thought on specific doctrines or theological problems. At Rom. 5:21, for example, he offered a compendium of scholastic thought on original sin, its definition, the manner by which it passes from one generation to another, its effect on the individual, and the countereffect of baptism. His long discussion reflects the influence of St. Thomas's comment to Rom. 5:12, considered by Latin theologians since Augustine the best scriptural proof-text for the doctrine of original sin. At 2 Cor. 3:5 Lyra again followed St. Thomas in summarizing orthodox thought on the freedom of the will, its powers and limitations. Like many other medieval exegetes, Lyra considered Heb. 11:1 a carefully constructed definition of faith: "Faith is the substance of things hoped for, the proof of things unseen." It was therefore natural for him to expound this passage at length and to follow St. Thomas in showing how the biblical "definition of faith" harmonized with scholastic teachings.

A further set of comments in Lyra's *Postilla litteralis* summarizes scholastic theology on the sacraments. Thus one finds a compendium of eucharistic theology at Matt. 26:26. In comments to other passages Lyra addressed some of the finer points of scholastic thought on the eucharist: at John 6:53, for example, he defended the practice of withholding the cup

29

and offering only the bread to laymen; at 1 Cor. 11:24 he employed the characteristic Aristotelian and scholastic categories of substance and accident in order to explain scientifically the conversion of the hosts. At 2 Cor. 7:10 Lyra closely followed St. Thomas's exegesis in discussing the sacrament of penance. At 1 Cor. 1:13 he copied St. Thomas's work almost verbatim—we would call it plagiarism—in explaining scholastic thought on baptism.

Thus for Lyra the New Testament confirmed medieval doctrines and was in turn illuminated by medieval theology, philosophy, and science. His *Postilla litteralis* grandly succeeded in its primary purpose—to explain the New Testament in the most advanced terms available and to place it in the context of sophisticated medieval theology. Yet by reason of this very accomplishment, Lyra's work throws more light on medieval thought and values than on those of the early Christian world. The authors of the New Testament wrote their works unburdened by scholastic categories of grace and faith, medieval theology of the sacraments, or the fine points of Aristotle's teachings. To explain the New Testament with reference to these things is necessarily to distort the original meaning of the Christian scriptures.

This point must not be understood as a condemnation of Lyra's work, still less of medieval scholarship on the New Testament in general.[30] Recent studies have proven that medieval biblical scholarship does not deserve the tarnished reputation it bore for so long.[31] They have disproved the old canard that medieval exegesis was vitiated by a mechanical application of

[30] For that one may consult F. W. Farrar, who found in the Middle Ages "very little except the 'glimmerings and decays' of patristic exposition" in his review of exegesis from the seventh to the sixteenth century. "Not one writer in hundreds," he continued, "showed any true conception of what exegesis really implies." See his *History of Interpretation* (London, 1886), pp. 245-46.

[31] See especially the works cited above, n. 19.

the *quadriga*—the fourfold method of exegesis, by which each text could be explored for literal, allegorical, tropological, and anagogical meanings. They have shown instead that, especially in Old Testament studies, there was a long and lively tradition of advanced scholarship during the Middle Ages. The medieval schools encouraged studies based on the original Hebrew text of the Old Testament, enabling scholars to evaluate the Vulgate's text and translation against a reliable standard, and to explain with some accuracy the original meaning of the Hebrew scriptures.

Thus medieval scholarship on the Bible appears today as a much more interesting and impressive enterprise than used to be thought. Still, medieval scholarship—especially that on the New Testament—faithfully reflected medieval assumptions, values, and doctrines. The Renaissance humanists were determined to set aside the medieval tradition of New Testament study and replace it with a brand of scholarship that aimed to recover or reconstruct the assumptions, values, and doctrines not of the Middle Ages, but of the earliest Christians. The following examination of the humanists' annotations to the New Testament, along with their Greek and Latin manuscripts, their editions and translations of the New Testament, will show how they came to understand these earliest Christian writings much more accurately than their predecessors.

TWO

Lorenzo Valla: Biblical
Philologist

LORENZO Valla introduces a new world of thought. Most brash and least compromising of the Italian humanists, Valla had no patience with medieval scholars nor any use for their methods. He exhibited an independence of thought that often refreshed, but not infrequently agitated his contemporaries. He had the provocative habit of formulating old problems in new terms, then establishing new rules and employing new methods in order to solve them. Thus he attempted in his *Dialectical Disputations* to renovate all philosophy by subjecting it to the authority and demands of rhetoric. The dialogue *On the True and False Good* challenged traditional, ascetic moral thought with its frank espousal of Epicurean values, however Christianly Valla understood them. Another dialogue, that *On Monastic Vows*, relied heavily on philological as well as theological considerations in arguing that laymen equaled or even excelled monks in their piety. Like these and other works, Valla's notes to the New Testament take a creative, fresh approach to an old problem—in this case the problem of accurately understanding and explaining the New Testament.

Valla was the first westerner since the patristic age to enjoy

32

a thorough knowledge of Greek and to apply it extensively in his study of the New Testament. This alone would have rendered his work one of capital importance for the history of biblical studies, though it need not have inaugurated a new brand of scholarship. Valla might have followed the example of the Byzantine scholars, who had always studied the original Greek text of the New Testament, but had placed their work in the service of speculative theology or homiletic exegesis. Instead, he enriched his command of Greek with an awareness of the demands of philology. Above all else, Valla was a connoisseur of words. Doubters may consult his *Elegantiae linguae latinae*, an enormous and erudite study of Latin words, their meanings, nuances, problems, and proper usage. It is not surprising, then, that Valla trained his study not on the doctrine, moral teaching, or theology of the New Testament, but rather on its words.

To be sure, Valla's studies harbored weighty implications for traditional doctrine, moral teaching, and theology. Indeed, several recent commentators have called attention to these implications in their analyses of Valla's New Testament scholarship. Mario Fois portrays Valla as a fundamentally orthodox Roman Catholic; Salvatore Camporeale suggests that he was an ardent proponent of a revived Pauline theology; and Charles Trinkaus shows that Valla's philological approach had the potential to undermine traditional doctrine.[1] I have no wish to dispute these interpretations—recent scholarship on Valla has been conducted on an impressively high plane—for each contributes to our understanding of Valla's complexity. I wish instead to emphasize here a different aspect of Valla's work, his contribution to the discipline of New Testament scholar-

---

[1] Mario Fois, *Il pensiero cristiano di Lorenzo Valla* (Rome, 1969), pp. 397-440; Salvatore Camporeale, *Lorenzo Valla. Umanesimo e teologia* (Florence, 1972), esp. pp. 3-4, 288, 300-302; and Charles Trinkaus, *In Our Image and Likeness*, 2 vols. (Chicago, 1970), 2:571-78.

ship.[2] Granted that Valla occasionally took the opportunity to develop the religious or theological significance of his philological analysis, he set as his main task the evaluation of the Vulgate as a translation of the Greek New Testament. If his notes occasionally challenged traditional doctrine, they invariably taught by example how to employ philological criteria in the study of scripture. The following chapter will show that Valla did not always apply his methods in thoroughgoing or systematic fashion. Nevertheless, his efforts to solve problems of New Testament text, translation, and explanation inaugurated the modern tradition of critical, philological scholarship on the New Testament.

Development and Sources of Valla's Work

Valla's notes to the New Testament survive in two redactions. The earlier of the two, entitled *Collatio novi testamenti*, was a product of Valla's Neapolitan period (1435-1448), along with the *Dialectical Disputations*, the *Elegantiae*, the treatise on the Donation of Constantine, and other works. Valla began the *Collatio* probably in 1442; by the end of 1443 he was circulating a draft of the work. It remained virtually unknown and unpublished until recently. The second redaction stems from the period 1453 to 1457, after Valla had returned to

---

[2] See two short studies conducted along somewhat similar lines: Salvatore Garofalo, "Gli umanisti italiani del secolo XV e la Bibbia," *Biblica* 27 (1946):343-53; and Anna Morisi, "La filologia neotestamentaria di Lorenzo Valla," *Nuova rivista storica* 48 (1964):35-49. See also two studies comparing Valla's New Testament scholarship with that of Erasmus: Jerry H. Bentley, "Biblical Philology and Christian Humanism: Lorenzo Valla and Erasmus as Scholars of the Gospels," *SCJ* 8, no. 2 (1977), pp. 9-28; and Jacques Chomarat, "Les *Annotations* de Valla, celles d'Érasme et la grammaire," in *Histoire de l'exégèse*, pp. 202-28.

Rome and become acquainted with the Greek refugees there, of whom the most notable and most important for Valla's career was Cardinal Bessarion. In 1504 Erasmus stumbled across a manuscript of this second redaction at the abbey of Parc, near Louvain. In 1505 he published the work under a new title, the *Adnotationes* to the New Testament. For the sake of convenience I shall refer here to the two redactions as the *Collatio* and the *Adnotationes*, though Valla always called his work a "collatio." The *Adnotationes* reveal a more mature scholar than the *Collatio*, as much evidence in this chapter will show, but it seems that Valla never considered even the *Adnotationes* a finished product. He allowed the works to circulate only in a small, select group of scholars, and they remained largely unknown from Valla's death (1457) until Erasmus' publication of the *Adnotationes* (1505).[3]

There can be little question why Valla prepared his notes to the New Testament, for he gave his reasons in at least four places. He pointed out that already in the fourth century, St. Jerome had complained that he found as many texts (*exemplaria*) as manuscripts of the New Testament. "Now if after 400 years so muddy a stream flowed from the fount," so Valla reasoned, "what marvel if after 1,000 years—for so many there are between Jerome and the present age—this stream, no part of which has been cleaned or tidied up, has become scummy and squalid?" If the temple of scripture leaks when it rains, it must be patched up; and Valla offered himself as one of the few craftsmen with the necessary tools—Latin, Greek, and a thorough knowledge of the Bible—to undertake this project. More specifically, Valla attempted to patch up the Latin scriptures and render them a more faithful reflection of the Greek.

---

[3] For the texts see the *Collatio novi testamenti*, ed. A. Perosa (Florence, 1970); and Valla's *Opera omnia*, 2 vols., ed. E. Garin (Turin, 1962), 1:801-95. On the tangled history of the two redactions see Perosa's introduction to the *Collatio*, pp. xxiii-l; and Camporeale, *Lorenzo Valla*, pp. 350-74.

Thus he presented in his work for the most part a "collatio," a comparison of the Latin Vulgate with the Greek New Testament. He set for himself a straightforward scholarly task: the evaluation of the Vulgate as a translation of the Greek New Testament. In carrying out this task he found many passages, he said, vitiated by unlearned or negligent copyists; others he found corrupted by conscious alteration on the part of audacious scribes; still others he found inaccurately translated from the Greek. In his "collatio," then, Valla annotated these passages in order to offer Latin Christians the clearest possible understanding of the New Testament.[4]

Textual Criticism

Lorenzo Valla was rarely given to false modesty, but his remark about "patching up" the temple of scripture perhaps obscures the fact that he also took care to inspect the building's foundations. That is to say, he devoted some attention to the "lower criticism," the establishment of the text of the New Testament. He of course consulted manuscripts of the Greek New Testament in preparing the *Collatio*, but in this first redaction of his notes he neither mentioned his Greek manuscripts nor cited variant readings in the Greek text. In the *Adnotationes*, however, he saw fit to provide more complete information about his manuscripts and readings they

[4] See especially Preface II to the *Collatio*, pp. 6-9. (Despite its order, this was the earlier of the two prefaces that introduce the *Collatio*, and we may take it as providing the best description of Valla's original intentions with respect to his New Testament scholarship. Preface II has been dated to the Spring of 1443; Preface I, to mid-1453. See Camporeale, *Lorenzo Valla*, pp. 350-74, and Perosa's introduction to the *Collatio*, pp. xxiii-l.) Valla justified his work in similar terms also in Preface I to the *Collatio*, p. 6, and in two polemical works directed against his bitter enemy, Poggio Bracciolini, for which see his *Opera*, 1:270, 339.

preserve for both Greek and Latin texts of the New Testament. He mentioned four Latin and four Greek manuscripts at Matt. 28:8, three Latin and three Greek at Matt. 27:22, and seven Greek at John 7:29-30. At John 18:28 there occurs what is unfortunately the most specific description of Valla's Greek manuscripts. There he mentioned five codices discovered in and around Milan by that indefatigable world traveler, Cyriaco d'Ancona, and two others written "in a marvelous, old script" found at Rome by Giovanni da Tivoli.

I know of only a single attempt to identify Valla's manuscripts of the Greek New Testament, and even it is not very persuasive. Arthur T. Russell argued unsystematically and unconvincingly that Valla used primarily MS. S of the gospels and MS. L[ap] (Codex Angelicus, which Russell cited as MS. G) for the remainder of the New Testament.[5] Possibly Valla did indeed consult these manuscripts (housed respectively at the Vatican Library and the Biblioteca Angelica in Rome) while working on his *Adnotationes* at Rome. The *Collatio*, however, more likely depended on manuscripts available in Naples, where Valla began his New Testament scholarship. Furthermore, at many passages where Russell found Valla agreeing with MSS. S and L[ap], Valla made the same point in both the *Collatio* and the *Adnotationes*. These Roman manuscripts therefore could have determined Valla's position only on a few texts, if any. Thus Valla's chief manuscripts of the Greek New Testament remain unidentified. Only extensive collations between Valla's readings and Greek manuscripts available in his day might reveal which ones he used, and one doubts the effort would be justified by the knowledge gained.

At any rate, Valla invested the time and effort required to

---

[5] *Life of Bishop Andrewes* (London, 1863), pp. 282-310. As always, I cite manuscripts of the Greek New Testament according to the system of C. R. Gregory. See the "Note on Editions, Translations, and Citations," above, p. xi.

collate at least seven Greek and four Latin manuscripts of the New Testament. Valla the philologist could hardly have avoided noticing and addressing problems of textual criticism. Usually he reported readings in the Greek New Testament simply in order to support his criticism or clarification of the Vulgate. Not infrequently, however, he encountered variant readings in Greek or Latin texts or both, and so found it necessary to render judgment as to which was better. Unfortunately, he usually delivered merely the judgment, without discussing the evidence and explaining the reasoning standing behind it. At 1 Cor. 6:20 he said that "the best Greek manuscripts" read "you were purchased at a price," and thus implied tacitly having seen other codices that agreed with the Vulgate's "you were purchased at a great price." At Rom. 16:25 he reported that only "the rarest Greek manuscripts" include the so-called Wandering Doxology (Rom. 16:25-27, sometimes found following 14:23 or 15:33). Valla's comments on these passages help incidentally to illustrate the growth of his textual scholarship. In both cases he addressed the problem of the Greek text only in the *Adnotationes*; in the *Collatio* he commented on the passages in order to make different points.

Only rarely in his notes to the New Testament did Valla comment fully enough to allow some insight into his thinking on Greek textual problems. His remarks at 2 Cor. 12:1, however, reveal his attention to the philological aspects of textual problems—again in such fashion as to underline the development of his textual scholarship. In the *Collatio* he presented a minor criticism of the Vulgate's translation: "Si gloriari oportet, non expedit mihi," in Valla's manuscripts—"Even if I am obliged to boast, it is not useful for me." In the first redaction of his notes Valla suggested only a slight alteration in the translation of the main clause: "Si gloriari oportet, gloriari non expedit mihi"—"Even if I am obliged to boast, boasting is not useful for me." By the time he prepared the *Adnota-*

tiones, however, Valla had noticed a more fundamental problem in the Greek text. The Greek word δεῖ ("oportet"—"it is necessary") is identical in sound to the particle δὴ ("now"), so that a scribe copying from dictation could easily confuse the two words. Valla found δὴ in most of his Greek manuscripts and considered δεῖ and its Latin counterpart, "oportet," the inferior readings. Thus he proposed to alter the passage entirely: "Gloriari non expedit mihi"—"Boasting does not profit me." In the *Adnotationes* he pointed out other homonyms (or near-homonyms) causing corruption or confusion in the Greek text at Acts 5:3 and Apoc. 15:6. Modern editors enjoy more and better textual data than Valla, and they reject his readings at 2 Cor. 12:1 and Acts 5:3. The fact remains, however, that Valla grappled intelligently with the problem: homonyms often lead to textual corruption, but with proper philological awareness, scholars can restore purity to the text.

Observations of this sort show plainly the philological—as opposed, say, to theological—character of Valla's New Testament scholarship. Yet he contributed but little to the development of the discipline of textual criticism and emendation, at least as it applies to the Greek New Testament. He made no attempt to edit the entire Greek New Testament, nor to form a complete collection of variant readings. He did not even employ some of the methods he used in his textual scholarship on classical works. There Valla resorted often, for example, to conjectural emendation—a risky, but often successful method of restoring correct readings not preserved in manuscripts, by means of intelligent inference based on the context of the corrupted passage, the author's style, or other such considerations. In his translations of Herodotus and Thucydides, Valla conjectured many Greek readings and rendered them accordingly into Latin. Modern scholars still profess admiration for the ingenuity and exceptional quality of his emendations to the text of Livy. In fact, conjectural emendation may almost be considered the hallmark of Valla's textual scholarship on classical literature.[6] Yet this method plays a negligible role in Valla's criticism of the Greek New Testament. I find not a single instance of true conjectural emendation in his notes to the New Testament. At most Valla infers variant readings in the Greek text by means of peculiar or inaccurate translations in the Vulgate. Thus, in the *Adnotationes* only, at Philem., v. 6, he accepted ἐνεργὴς ("effective" or "active") as the correct reading, but inferred the variant ἐναργὴς ("visible" or "distinct") on the basis of the Vulgate's "evidens" ("evident" or "manifest"). Perhaps Valla did not consider scripture open to the more speculative methods of textual scholarship, however appropriate they might be for classical studies.

Nor, despite a recent suggestion to the contrary, did Valla often have recourse to the Church Fathers as textual witnesses.[7] He often cited their works in proposing an improved Latin translation of the New Testament, but the evaluation of a translation is a business quite separable from the establishment of the text of the New Testament. St. Jerome and the Greek Fathers especially recorded many variant readings for the Greek text in their commentaries on the New Testament. A later chapter will show that Erasmus extensively mined the Fathers' works and vastly enlarged the body of textual data available for the Greek New Testament. But only rarely did Valla depend on the Fathers to supply him with textual information, as at 1 Cor. 15:51, a passage to be examined later in detail, where in the *Adnotationes* he cited Jerome as a witness

---

[6] See G. B. Alberti, "Erodoto nella traduzione latina di Lorenzo Valla," *Studi italiani di filologia classica* (1957), esp. pp. 240-49; also G. Billanovich, "Petrarch and the Textual Tradition of Livy," *JWCI* 14 (1951):137-208.

[7] Camporeale, *Lorenzo Valla*, p. 289, says Valla looked to the Fathers in order to "recover traces of a more primitive Latin translation or a more accurate text."

for his Greek text. Valla evidently did not consider this sort of research particularly relevant to his main enterprise—the evaluation of the Vulgate as a translation of the Greek New Testament.

Thus in the final analysis, criticism of the Greek text played but a small role in Valla's notes to the New Testament. He set out, after all, to evaluate the Vulgate, not to edit the Greek New Testament. Thus we find Valla addressing problems in the Latin text more frequently—and more successfully—than the Greek. Again, he noticed that confusion of homonyms (or near-homonyms) caused textual impurities. He showed at Luke 15:8 that "evertit" ("she overturns") stood incorrectly in place of "everrit" ("she sweeps"), so that the woman of the parable was said to overturn, not to sweep out her house while searching for a lost coin. He showed at John 18:28 that "ad" ("to") had replaced the correct preposition, "a" ("from"), so that Jesus was said to have been taken *to* Caiapha, where he already was, instead of *from* Caiapha. He showed at John 21:22 that the confusion of "si" ("if") and "sic" ("thus") led to a puzzling variant of the proper text: "*If* I wish him to remain until I shall come, what is that to you?" In all three cases, recourse to the Greek text shows clearly that the variant readings originated in the Latin tradition: Greek manuscripts present straightforward texts with no difficulties for these passages. Thus Valla's comparison of Vulgate and Greek New Testaments proved quite successful in suggesting solutions to hitherto baffling problems. Nor did Valla shrink from drawing attention to the value of his methods. In his comments to both of the Johannine passages cited above, he curtly corrected St. Augustine, who had labored mightily to make sense of the corrupted Latin translations, but had not inspected the Greek text. Valla therefore took the opportunity to reiterate one of his favorite points: New Testament scholarship not based on the Greek text is ipso facto vitiated.

Since Valla concentrated his analysis on the Vulgate, it is not surprising that he exhibited a more sophisticated awareness of textual problems in the Latin than in the Greek New Testament. He passed beyond the problem of homonyms and pointed out, for example, that corruption in the Vulgate often sprang from the problem of assimilation—the tendency of scribes consciously or accidentally to add to one passage a word or phrase that correctly belongs to a different, though similar passage. Already in the *Collatio* Valla pointed to a case of assimilation at Luke 6:26. The Greek text reports Jesus' warning to his congregation: "Woe to you when men speak well of you, for so their fathers behaved toward the false prophets." Valla found many Vulgate manuscripts, however, which read not "false prophets" ("pseudoprophetis"), but "prophets" ("prophetis")—a reading hard to reconcile with the spirit of the Sermon on the Mount. Valla easily explained the difficulty: a copyist corrupted the true text by assimilating it to Luke 6:22-23, which presents a different teaching, but in similar language: "Blessed are you when men despise you . . . for so their fathers behaved toward the prophets." Valla employed the same reasoning at other points in the *Collatio*, e.g., at Matt. 4:19 and Matt. 17:2. In the *Adnotationes* he added yet other passages to the list of texts corrupted by assimilation, e.g., Matt. 24:36, Matt. 27:39-40, and John 7:29-30; in the last cited passage Valla found an entire sentence assimilated from John 8:55. These passages noted only in the *Adnotationes* illustrate once again how, over time, Valla conducted further research on the Vulgate's text, how he applied more extensively the analytical techniques first developed in the *Collatio*, long after compiling his notes on the New Testament in the first redaction.

Modern editors of the Vulgate do not always agree with Valla where he diagnosed assimilation: at Matt. 4:19, 17:2, and 24:36, for example, they present readings that Valla thought corrupted. Their decisions are grounded, however, on a thorough knowledge of Vulgate manuscripts, which Valla was not privileged to share. In every case, Valla's charge of assimilation is both reasonable and plausible. One might argue that even his mistakes pointed the way to an improved philological understanding of the New Testament, since he identified a common cause of New Testament textual corruption and by his own example showed others how to recognize the problem.

Assimilation can result from the innocent carelessness of sleepy scribes—though Valla thought differently at Luke 6:26, where he charged copyists with deliberate alteration of the text—but textual corruption in the New Testament occurs often by design as well as accident. Valla stood alert to such intentional changes, at least in the text of the Vulgate. At Matt. 4:6 and Matt. 21:26 he noticed copyists altering verb tenses so as to make prophecy or conversation fit better into its context. "In many manuscripts I have found corruption in place of correction," he averred at Philem., v. 12, where copyists smoothed out a correct, though coarse reading. In the Vulgate, St. Paul asks Philemon to receive Onesimus, "that is, my very flesh"—"tu autem illum, id est viscera mea suscipe." Many manuscripts present not "id est," but "ut" or "sicut," however, so that Paul asks Philemon to receive Onesimus "as though he were my very flesh." The variant "ut" or "sicut" renders the passage less peculiar, or even offensive, but does so at double cost. In the first place, it corrupts the text, for the original Vulgate beyond doubt presented "id est." Furthermore, the smoother variant may very well obscure the intensity St. Paul felt as he addressed Philemon. Thus, Valla's criticism of the Vulgate's text amounted to more than refined pedantry: it helped positively to promote an accurate understanding of what the New Testament meant to its authors and earliest readers.

There remains one especially puzzling omission in Valla's criticism of the Vulgate text—his neglect to comment on the discrepancy between Greek and Vulgate texts at 1 John 5:7-8. Most Vulgate manuscripts present here a so-called *comma Johanneum* mentioning the "three heavenly witnesses" to Christ's truth: "Et tres sunt qui testimonium dant in caelo, pater, verbum, et spiritus, et hi tres unum sunt"—"And there are three who give testimony in heaven, the Father, the Word, and the Spirit, and these three are one." Latin theologians from the early Middle Ages forward had taken this text as providing the clearest scriptural support for the doctrine of the Trinity. In all the world, however, only four Greek manuscripts mention the heavenly witnesses. Two of them were copied very late in the Middle Ages; in the other two the passage occurs as a marginal addition by modern hands.[8] It is entirely possible that when Valla wrote, not a single Greek manuscript included the *comma*. Yet Valla did not take the opportunity to correct or even to comment on the Vulgate's text at this significant passage. Whatever the explanation for this lapse, it was not that Valla failed to notice the difference between the Greek and Vulgate texts: in the *Adnotationes* he slightly corrected the Vulgate's translation at 1 John 5:8, and the glaring discrepancy between the two texts could not have escaped his notice. Nor does it seem likely that theological scruples by themselves induced him to hold his peace: in other works Valla expressed such critical and unorthodox views concerning the Trinity that some scholars have seen fit to suggest affinities between Valla and the anti-Trinitarian heretics of the sixteenth century.[9] Why then did he not expose and emend the

[8] Bruce M. Metzger, *A Textual Commentary on the Greek New Testament*, 3rd ed. (New York, 1971), pp. 716-18.

[9] Delio Cantimori, *Eretici italiani del Cinquecento* (Florence, 1939), pp. 1-3, 42-44, 239-41, 366-68, 413; and G. Zippel, "La 'Defensio quaestionum in philosophia' di Lorenzo Valla, e un noto processo dell'inquisizione napo-

Vulgate's corrupted text at 1 John 5:7-8? We can hardly do more than speculate: perhaps Valla considered it too impolitic to meddle with the proof-text for a doctrine so important to the Roman Church as that of the Trinity. It bears pointing out that Valla was not the only Renaissance scholar to deal gingerly with this text. His contemporary, Giannozzo Manetti, included the *comma* in his fresh translation of the Greek New Testament into Latin.[10] And a later chapter will show that, under pressure of conservative critics, even Erasmus had to proceed cautiously when treating this sensitive passage.

In at least one place, then, Valla allowed the Vulgate to go uncorrected by better Greek texts. In general, however, if there was a weak side to Valla's textual criticism, it was his too facile reliance on the integrity of the Greek text of the New Testament. He reported a few variant readings in the Greek text, but he failed to realize how confused, tangled, and corrupted the Greek New Testament had become over the preceding fourteen centuries. Thus he assumed too quickly that Greek manuscripts always present better texts than Latin. Usually they do, but in some places the Vulgate preserves readings that reflect the original Greek text better than Greek manuscripts produced in the later Middle Ages and afflicted by later corruptions. In notes to several passages—to Matt. 6:25 and 2 Pet. 2:18 in both the *Collatio* and the *Adnotationes*, for example, and to Mark 6:11 in the *Adnotationes* only—Valla emended the Vulgate's translation on the basis of an inferior Greek text. But his comment at Matt. 6:13 (in both the *Collatio* and the *Adnotationes*) best illustrates how his assumption

letana," *Bollettino dell'istituto storico italiano per il Medio Evo e archivio muratoriano* 69 (1957):319-47.

[10] Manetti's translation is preserved in two Vatican manuscripts, Pal. lat. 45 and Urb. lat. 6. I rely on the better of the two, the latter, but in checking I have found that the two manuscripts agree on all readings cited in this chapter.

led to inadequate criticism. Almost all Greek manuscripts add a clause to the end of the Lord's Prayer (Matt. 6:13): "for thine is the kingdom and the power and the glory forever. Amen." But no Vulgate manuscript includes the clause, for the good reason that the ascription crept into the Greek New Testament quite late, by way of Greek liturgical works.[11] When Valla noticed the discrepancy between Greek and Vulgate texts, he complained loudly that the Latin scriptures omitted "a good chunk of the Lord's Prayer." In fact, the Vulgate here reflects the original prayer better than most Greek manuscripts. Valla's mistake at this point was perhaps inevitable at a time when Greek manuscripts of the New Testament were poorly known. The Complutensian scholars and Erasmus later came to an improved understanding of the textual problem at Matt. 6:13, thanks to their deeper knowledge of Greek manuscripts and liturgy. But like Valla, Giannozzo Manetti fell victim to inadequate manuscript resources: he included the apocryphal clause in his translation of the Lord's Prayer. Valla's error thus illuminates the chief limitation of his New Testament scholarship—his neglect of textual problems in the Greek New Testament. Valla happily applied his critical talents to the text of the Vulgate New Testament; had he done the same to the Greek text, he would have increased vastly the importance of his work and the understanding of the Greek New Testament itself.

As in the lower, so also in the "higher criticism"—critical analysis of the authorship, authenticity, and composition of texts—Valla failed to advance New Testament scholarship as much as one might have expected. This is particularly surprising, since in general Valla's efforts at the higher criticism stand out even today as his most strikingly original contributions to the development of philological scholarship. Best known, of

[11] Metzger, *Textual Commentary*, pp. 16-17.

course, was his exposé of the Donation of Constantine, a work brilliant for its interweaving of humanist polemic and philological criticism. Valla exercised his critical talents also on other problems than that of the Donation's authorship. He argued, for example, that the Apostles' Creed was not the work of Jesus' twelve disciples—legend taught that each disciple contributed one of the creed's twelve articles—but was composed rather by the Councils of Nicaea (A.D. 325) and Constantinople (A.D. 381).[12] In a lost work he also disputed the authenticity of the apocryphal correspondence between Seneca and St. Paul.[13]

In his notes to the New Testament, strange to say, Valla's attempts at the higher criticism lack the rigor and insightfulness of his efforts elsewhere. In notes to Mark 1:4 and 1:6 in the *Adnotationes*, he held correctly that Mark composed his gospel in Greek, not in Latin, as hoary legend maintained. But he advanced contradictory and ill-considered judgments on other books of scripture. He said twice, for example, that Matthew composed his gospel in Greek, and twice that he composed it in Hebrew.[14] He wavered similarly on the question of the authorship of the Epistle to the Hebrews, traditionally but incorrectly ascribed to St. Paul. At the end of his notes to Hebrews in the *Collatio*, Valla cited St. Jerome, who had testified that many people doubted the traditional attribution on stylistic grounds. In the *Adnotationes*, however, he took a firm stand in favor of Pauline authorship in his note to Heb. 10:34. Valla's Greek text there read: "For you have suffered in my chains. . . ." Valla took this passage as proof of

---

[12] See Valla's *Opera*, 1:357-62, 800-800a.

[13] See Valla's *Opera*, 1:428, where he mentioned the work.

[14] He argued for Greek twice in the *Collatio*, in Preface I (p. 8) and the note to Rom. 11:25. He argued for Hebrew once in the *Collatio*, commenting on Matt. 13:55-56, and once in the *Adnotationes*, commenting on Matt. 1:16.

Pauline authorship. He did not discuss his reasoning, which seems tenuous; evidently he considered the mention of "my chains" an authentic reference to Paul's imprisonment reported in the Book of Acts. Finally, Valla wavered also on the authorship of the catholic epistles. In the *Collatio* he again cited Jerome, who had reported the doubts of many contemporaries on the authorship of the Epistles of James, 2 Peter, 2 and 3 John, and Jude. The citations of Jerome suggest that as he prepared the *Collatio*, Valla at least entertained the possibility that Jesus' disciples did not write these letters. In the *Adnotationes*, however, he mentioned Jerome's testimony only with respect to 2 John.[15] The suppression of the other citations perhaps came as a result of Valla's bitter controversy (1451-1453) with Poggio Bracciolini, who among other things attacked the *Collatio*, charging Valla with scorning the scriptures and slinging darts at Christ.[16] Poggio's vicious assaults in several ways induced Valla to speak more cautiously in the *Adnotationes* than in the *Collatio*, as will be seen.[17] It seems a reasonable conjecture that in the *Adnotationes* Valla withheld critical comment on the authorship of the catholic epistles in order to forestall further attacks on his New Testament scholarship. At any rate, Valla clearly did not devote his best efforts to the higher criticism of the New Testament.

But let us not deprive Valla of his due. Armed with a thorough knowledge of Latin and Greek, equipped with a finely honed critical faculty, Valla attacked some of the important textual problems that confront the New Testament scholar. These problems call less for theological than philological anal-

[15] See the notes to James 5:16; 2 Pet. 2:20 (also 2 Cor. 10:4); 3 John, v. 10; Jude, v. 22—all in the *Collatio*—and 2 John, v. 1 in the *Adnotationes*.

[16] See Poggio's *Opera omnia*, ed. R. Fubini, 4 vols. (Turin, 1963-1969), 1:199-200, 210, 231-34, 248.

[17] For the influence of the controversy on Valla's notes to the New Testament, see also Camporeale, *Lorenzo Valla*, pp. 350-74.

ysis; they arise less from doctrinal considerations than from the difficulties of transmitting texts in the pre-Gutenberg era. Ancient and medieval scribes, like other men, sometimes proved to be lazy, ignorant, or otherwise incompetent. They produced corrupt texts of scripture in abundance because they misunderstood the form, sound, or meaning of the words they copied. Textual corruption may be recognized, explained, and removed only if scholars study their manuscripts while bearing in mind the problems that complicate the scribe's task. Valla's achievement was to show by example how to do this. He unfortunately never wrote a manual or textbook setting out systematically the scholarly methods and principles he employed, but his notes to the New Testament marked some of the paths that later philologists could travel. It would be too much to label him a modern critical scholar: he neither developed his philological techniques so thoroughly nor applied them so widely as Erasmus, for example, as a later chapter will show. Nonetheless, we catch in Valla the first glimmer of the critical attitudes and methods that characterize modern New Testament scholarship.

Translation

Valla's scholarly works on the New Testament thus show that his critical powers and knowledge of languages led him to a sophisticated understanding of textual problems in the Latin and, to a lesser extent, the Greek New Testament. Had he chosen to concentrate his efforts on the text, he would surely have thrown new light on many dark passages of the New Testament. But in his notes to the New Testament Valla did not accept the establishment of the text as his primary responsibility. In fact, both the lower and the higher criticism appeared only as a sideline to Valla's main effort in his notes—

the evaluation of the Vulgate as a translation of the Greek New Testament. Valla kept his eyes open for cracks in the foundation of the temple of scripture, but he took as his main task the mending of the building itself, so that the temple might prove worthy of the divine affairs carried on within it. The following analysis of Valla's comments on the Latin scriptures will reveal that he found three main problems with the Vulgate New Testament: it presented scripture in an inferior or inappropriate literary style; it inaccurately translated many passages of the Greek text; and it in general obscured the meaning of the original Greek New Testament.

Valla enjoyed the luxury of taking such a critical stand partly because he denied the traditional belief that St. Jerome translated the Vulgate New Testament. The Vulgate went out from the beginning under Jerome's name, and his prominence naturally strengthened the Vulgate's authority during the Middle Ages. So far as I know, Valla was the first scholar to challenge this ascription, though he unfortunately never developed a detailed argument on the question. In several passages, however—e.g., at Luke 16:2 and 1 Cor. 2:9 in the *Adnotationes*—he pointed out significant discrepancies between the Vulgate and translations of New Testament passages found in Jerome's commentaries and other works. Valla concluded that either Jerome had not translated the New Testament, or his work had been transmogrified by impudent scribes. Valla developed this line of thought at least partly as a result of his controversy with Poggio, who accused Valla of deprecating the authority of the eminent doctor by attacking his translation of the scriptures.[18] Whatever his motive, Valla's position is important for the history of scholarship for two reasons: first, because it

[18] See the Prefaces to the *Collatio*, pp. 6, 10; and the comment in the *Adnotationes* to 2 Cor. 2:9. On the connection between the quarrel with Poggio and Valla's thought on the translator of the Vulgate, see Camporeale, *Lorenzo Valla*, pp. 350-53.

illustrates again Valla's fresh, critical, philological approach to long unchallenged traditions; and second, because it is right. Most students of Jerome today believe that he translated afresh no part of the New Testament, that he revised earlier versions of the gospels, and that he only slightly amended earlier translations of the Acts, Epistles, and Apocalypse.[19]

Like most of the Renaissance humanists, Valla placed high value on proper Latin style and usage. He saw no reason to exempt the scriptures from stylistic criticism, and he complained frequently that the Vulgate presented the New Testament in shabby literary dress. At Acts 9:27 he scored the translator for using an archaic and awkward word (*fiduciali-ter*—"faithfully") when more standard and pure alternatives were available (e.g., *fidenter*—"resolutely"—or *constanter*—"steadily"). At Mark 4:41 he commented on an almost opposite problem: in good Latin the word *alteruter* properly means "one or the other," but the Vulgate uses it to mean "each other"—a usage Valla could find witnessed no earlier than Boethius, who did not qualify in Valla's judgment as a reliable arbiter of Latin style. At Luke 1:79 and 1 Tim. 6:17-18 he found the translator violating parallel structure by mixing gerunds with infinitives. All these comments appear in the *Collatio*; only that to Mark 4:41 recurs in the *Adnotationes*. Valla did not altogether ignore stylistic matters in preparing the second redaction of his notes: at Matt. 13:9, for example, he discussed in the *Adnotationes* a new problem, not treated in the *Collatio*, involving the correct usage of gerunds. In general, however, purely stylistic criticism played a larger role in

[19] See F. Cavallera's conclusive demonstration: "St. Jérôme et la Vulgate des Actes, des Épitres et de l'Apocalypse," *Bulletin de littérature ecclésiastique* 21 (1920):269-92. Cavallera's argument remains widely accepted: J.N.D. Kelly, *Jerome* (New York, 1975), pp. 88-89; H.F.D. Sparks, "Jerome as Biblical Scholar," *CHB* 1:517-22; and Bruce M. Metzger, *The Early Versions of the New Testament* (Oxford, 1977), pp. 356-59.

the first redaction of Valla's notes. In keeping with their more serious and scholarly character, the *Adnotationes* usually addressed problems not of style, but of the accuracy and sense of the Vulgate's translation of the New Testament.

Yet one stylistic criticism in particular appears regularly in both the *Collatio* and the *Adnotationes*—Valla's charge that the translator abused his office by introducing into the Vulgate a rhetorical variety absent in the Greek New Testament. The translator of the Vulgate often represented a single Greek word by several Latin words, apparently in the interest of more varied speech. Valla saw no need to enliven Latin scripture in this artificial way. At 2 Cor. 6:8 he alluded approvingly in both redactions of his notes to the opinion of certain learned men that "there is more majesty in the simplicity of Homer than grace in the fashioned festivity of Vergil." Similarly, Valla himself preferred St. Paul's honest simplicity to the Vulgate's rhetorical variety. Thus he became annoyed when the Vulgate translated πρεσβύτερος ("elder") as both *senior* ("elder") and *presbyter* ("priest");[20] φρόνιμος ("prudent") as both *prudens* ("prudent") and *sapiens* ("wise")[21] and νοῦς ("mind") as both *mens* ("mind") and *sensus* ("understanding").[22] He became incensed at Rom. 4:3-8, where λογίζομαι ("to calculate" or "to credit") occurs five times in the Greek, but appears under three different Latin guises. "Who would suspect," Valla inquired, "that in the Greek, that is in the source, a single word stands behind all these: *reputare*, *imputare*, and *accepto ferre?*"

Thus Valla desired a Latin New Testament that presented the scriptures in good Latin style, but did so without artifi-

[20] See, for example, his comments in both the *Collatio* and the *Adnotationes* to Matt. 2:3-4, Acts 15:2, and 1 Pet. 5:1.

[21] See, for example, his comments in both redactions to Rom. 8:6 and Rom. 11:25.

[22] See, for example, his comments in both redactions to Rom. 12:2 and 1 Cor. 14:14-15.

cially complicating the plain style of the original Greek. Valla considered the Greek New Testament elegant in its simplicity, if not formally eloquent; to deck scripture out in fancy Latin dress was to misrepresent the character of the original Greek. And so in his comments to the passages cited above (and to others) he recommended translating a given Greek word consistently with a single Latin word. In most cases such a principle of translation would do little positive harm, and might lead at many points to a clearer version, if the translator shared Valla's sensitivity to words, their meanings, nuances, and proper usage. If applied too mechanically, however, the rule could lead to obscurity, since it would reduce a translator's flexibility and make it harder to produce a sensitive and accurate version. Valla never attempted a complete translation of the New Testament and perhaps did not appreciate a translator's need for maximum flexibility in his choice of words. Erasmus did, however, and a later chapter will show that while agreeing with Valla in general, Erasmus often found it necessary to violate Valla's principle in his own translation.

Beyond matters of style, Valla found hundreds of points where he could offer a translation more accurate than that of the Vulgate. Sometimes his corrections seem minor, as at Rom. 1:17, where the Vulgate reads: "Iustus autem ex fide vivit"— "The just man lives by faith." The Greek text, Valla noted, presents the verb ζήσεται (future tense), which calls for *vivet* in Latin: "Iustus autem ex fide vivet"—"The just man will live by faith." In other places his comments and revised translations made possible a more precise understanding of the sense of the Greek New Testament. According to the Vulgate, St. Paul taught at 1 Tim. 6:10 as follows: "Radix enim omnium malorum est cupiditas"—"For the root of all evils is desire." Desire, Valla pointed out, can refer to many things. There is desire for glory, for example, or for power. The Greek word φιλαργυρία ("love of money") makes it plain that St. Paul had in mind desire for wealth at this point, and Valla suggested *avaricia* ("greed"), *amor pecuniae* ("money lust"), or *amor argenti* ("love of silver") as more accurate translations of the Greek term. The larger part of Valla's notes in both redactions is given over to clarifications of this sort. There would be little point in multiplying examples here, since the discussion will soon turn to several particularly significant corrections offered in Valla's notes. Suffice it to say that Valla's attempt to capture precisely the right shade of meaning beyond doubt rendered his translations more faithful reflections of the Greek New Testament than the Vulgate.

It was Valla the lexicographer who spoke in such notes as those just cited, the author of the *Elegantiae linguae latinae*, the literary scholar sensitive to the meanings, connotations, and nuances of Greek and Latin words. Valla did not stop with words, however, but engaged himself further to see that Latin scriptures properly expressed the whole sense of the Greek. Many times he censured the Vulgate because, although it presented a basically accurate translation, for one reason or another it obscured the sense or meaning of the Greek New Testament. At Rom. 2:11 in the *Collatio* Valla set aside the Vulgate's excessively literal translation and advanced a new one designed, he said, to express the sense rather than the words of the Greek. At 2 Cor. 1:11, again in the *Collatio*, Valla called the Vulgate's translation "without doubt an obscure and confused passage." He went on to say that "the blame belongs not to Paul, but to the translator. The fault, I repeat, lies with the translator, who was determined to translate literally [*ad verbum*], opposing the nature of the Latin tongue." Valla repeated both these comments in the *Adnotationes*, though in less explicit language.

In some places Valla discovered the Vulgate's translator indiscriminately translating not only word for word, but also case for case. This practice can lead to deep confusion, since the uses and functions of cases vary between the Greek and Latin languages. Latin, for example, uses the ablative case to express comparisons between persons or things; lacking an ablative, Greek uses the genitive. The Vulgate followed the Greek cases as well as words at Heb. 3:3 and presented a Latin text marred by a gross solecism: "Quanto ampliorem honorem habet domus, qui fabricavit illam?" Latin usage requires *domo* (ablative) in place of *domus* (genitive); then the passage becomes intelligible: "How much more honor than a house has he who built it?" At 1 Cor. 6:18 Valla criticized the Vulgate on a similar count—this time for indicating the location of action by using the accusative case, as in the Greek, instead of the ablative of place. If these corrections seem pedantic, one might profitably reflect on the position readers of Latin scripture found themselves in during the Middle Ages and Renaissance. The Vulgate presented the standard text of the New Testament, but was filled with inaccuracies, solecisms, and puzzling passages. From the time of the Venerable Bede until the fifteenth century, no more than a handful of westerners possessed the skills required to explain the Vulgate's eccentricities or to suggest improved translations. One must consider Valla's work in this context. His notes had the capacity to dispel confusion and open the door to understanding for all those who could read the Latin, but not the Greek New Testament.

Furthermore, his notes on translation were by no means limited to inquiries into the fine points of style, nuance, and grammar, but were sometimes freighted with heavy implications for the exegesis of the New Testament or the theology that arose from it. Thus his comments at 1 Cor. 15:51, where he exposed an astounding mistranslation of the Greek. The Greek and Vulgate texts of the passage read as follows:

LORENZO VALLA

GREEK TEXT:
πάντες οὐ κοιμηθησόμεθα, πάντες δὲ ἀλλαγησόμεθα.
(We shall not all sleep [i.e., die], but we shall all be changed.)

VULGATE:
Omnes quidem resurgemus, sed non omnes immutabimur.
(We shall all rise, but we shall not all be changed.)

Valla discussed this passage in both redactions of his notes, though his comments differ somewhat. In the *Collatio* he suggested a cause for corruption in the Latin text: a scribe altered an originally accurate translation, he said, in order to harmonize it with John 5:29, which in contrast to the Greek at 1 Cor. 15:51, implies that all men will die, then be resurrected into either eternal life or eternal judgment. He omitted this point from the *Adnotationes*, perhaps in an effort to avoid providing ammunition for his enemies by emphasizing too openly scripture's liability to corruption.[23] But in both redactions he suggested a more accurate translation: "Non omnes quidem dormiemus, omnes autem immutabimur"—"We shall not all sleep, but we shall all be changed." And in both redactions he defended his translation by showing its harmony with other statements on resurrection at Luke 20:35, 1 Cor. 15:52, and 1 Thess. 4:14-17. Valla's attention to the Greek text therefore led to a vastly improved understanding of New Testament teachings on resurrection.

Valla's comment to another Corinthian text illustrates how

[23] This is not a purely speculative suggestion. Valla commented on Luke 1:29 in both redactions of his notes, reporting corruption in the Vulgate both times. In the *Adnotationes*, however, he explicitly declined the opportunity to discuss the cause of corruption, "lest I should seem to doubt the reliability of scripture." Very likely the controversy with Poggio explains once again why Valla refrained from plain speech about scriptural corruption.

revised translations might impinge on theology at sensitive points. At 1 Cor. 15:10 St. Paul admits laboring more productively than the other apostles, then identifies who is responsible for his success:

GREEK TEXT:

. . . οὐκ ἐγὼ δὲ ἀλλὰ ἡ χάρις τοῦ Θεοῦ ἡ σὺν ἐμοί.

(. . . not I, however, but the grace of God that is with me.)

VULGATE:

. . . non ego autem, sed gratia Dei mecum.

(. . . not I, however, but the grace of God along with me.)

The Vulgate's slight mistranslation seems insignificant, but on the strength of this text, scholastic theologians established their category of "cooperating grace" (*gratia cooperans*), a special kind of grace that, according to St. Thomas Aquinas in his exposition of this passage, helped an individual to make best use of "infused grace" (*gratia infusa*), which in turn rendered the individual's works worthy of salvation. In the *Collatio* Valla simply corrected the Vulgate's translation, proposing in its place his own: ". . . non ego autem, sed gratia Dei quae est mecum"—". . . not I, however, but the grace of God that is with me." He repeated the point in the *Adnotationes*, but added to it his assessment of the theological implications: the Greek text does not speak of God's grace *cooperating* with St. Paul, but attributes *all* his success to the work of grace.

Valla's evaluation of the Vulgate complemented well the work of his Florentine contemporary, Giannozzo Manetti. For a two-year period (1453-1455), the two men held positions as apostolic secretaries at the court of Pope Nicholas V. Manetti soon left Rome, however, and went to Naples at the invitation of Valla's own former patron, King Alfonso the

Magnanimous. During his Neapolitan sojourn (1455-1457) he produced his fresh translation of the Greek New Testament into Latin. Unfortunately, there is no sign that the men cooperated or collaborated in their work, nor even any evidence that Manetti consulted Valla's notes to the New Testament. It is inconceivable that Manetti was not acquainted with Valla and his work, given that he held his secretarial post in Rome just as Valla prepared his *Adnotationes*, and that he then joined the circle of scholars and humanists in Naples where Valla had produced the *Collatio*. Perhaps the two men did not get along well. In any case, New Testament scholarship suffered for their failure to pool their considerable talents. But the similarity of their efforts to refurbish the Latin scriptures emphasizes in striking fashion the general humanist disenchantment with the Vulgate and with New Testament studies undertaken in ignorance of the Greek language.

For despite differences of emphasis, their efforts reveal significant areas of common interest.[24] Manetti's translation deserves a more thorough analysis and study than is possible here, but a brief excursus on Manetti's work will help place Valla's in proper context. Thus I propose here to compare Manetti's translations with those suggested by Valla at several of the passages discussed above. The comparison will illuminate the character of both Valla's and Manetti's works. Like Valla, Manetti sought to improve on the Vulgate's style. At Acts 9:7 he retained the Vulgate's *fiducialiter*, where Valla had preferred *fidenter* or *constanter*; but he agreed with Valla at Mark 4:41, where he replaced the Vulgate's *alteruter* with a more idiomatic *adinvicem*. Manetti repeatedly violated Valla's

[24] The literature on Manetti's translation of the New Testament includes Trinkaus, *In Our Image and Likeness*, 2:571-78; and Garofalo, "Gli umanisti italiani del secolo XV e la Bibbia," pp. 364-65. See also A. de Petris, "Le teorie umanistiche del tradurre e l'*Apologeticus* di Giannozzo Manetti," *Bibliothèque d'humanisme et Renaissance* 37 (1975):15-32.

chief principle of translation—avoid rhetorical variety, and translate a given Greek word consistently with the same Latin word. He opted for flexibility instead of rigid consistency in translating πρεσβύτερος as both *presbyter* and *senior* (at Acts 15:2 and 1 Pet. 5:1, respectively), and νοῦς as both *intellectus* and *mens* (at Rom. 12:2 and 1 Cor. 14:14-15). But in general, like Valla, he strove to present a version of the New Testament more accurate and sensitive than the Vulgate. Thus he agreed with Valla at Rom. 1:17, where he replaced the present-tense verb, *vivit*, with the future, *vivet*; at 1 Tim. 6:10, where he replaced the Vulgate's vague term, *cupiditas*, with the more specific *avaricia*; and at Heb. 3:3, where he avoided the Vulgate's solecism and presented a fresh translation of the entire passage. Perhaps the greatest surprises in his translation occur at two sensitive points discussed above. At 1 Cor. 15:51, where Valla corrected an egregious error in the Vulgate, Manetti presented a conflated and self-contradictory version, including both the traditional Latin text and a translation of the Greek: "Omnes quidem resurgemus, sed non omnes immutabimur. Omnes non dormiemus, omnes autem immutabimur." And at 1 John 5:7-8, Manetti included the *comma Johanneum*, with its report of the three heavenly witnesses, in his translation.

It is impossible to know how Manetti might have justified his translations, since he did not equip his version with explanatory notes. No doubt he would have agreed with Valla's observations at many points; he perhaps would have considered Valla hypercritical, or even pedantic, at other points. In any case, his work stands alongside Valla's as a testimonial to the conviction, quite generally held by Renaissance humanists, that scholars properly versed in linguistic and philological matters could produce a translation of the Latin scriptures much more accurate and meaningful than the Vulgate.

Exegesis

Valla's new methods of biblical study—consultation of the Greek text and the application of philological criticism—therefore significantly advanced New Testament scholarship. His methods enabled him to identify and solve hitherto baffling problems in the Greek and Vulgate texts of the New Testament, and further to suggest more accurate translations of many passages for the benefit of those who read Latin but not Greek. These accomplishments by themselves would have earned Valla an important position in the history of scholarship. Yet Valla's methods entailed implications for exegesis as well as textual criticism and translation: they enabled him to offer an improved understanding of the meaning of New Testament writings and to explain them with reference to their proper historical context.

Perhaps the most distinctive feature of Valla's exegesis in his notes was not his constructive attempt to clarify the meaning of the New Testament, but rather his savage criticism of medieval exegetes who based their commentary on the Vulgate and ignored the Greek New Testament. Valla most often attacked Haimo of Auxerre, a prominent teacher in the ninth-century school at Auxerre. (Valla called him "Remigius," another important figure of the school of Auxerre to whom Haimo's works have often, though mistakenly, been attributed.)[25] But Valla also stalked bigger game. St. Augustine came under fire at Mark 14:3, John 18:28, and John 21:20. One of Valla's bitterest outbursts occurs at 1 Cor. 9:13 in the *Adnotationes*, where he described Haimo and St. Thomas Aquinas[26] as

[25] C. Spicq, *Ésquisse d'une histoire de l'exégèse latine au Moyen Age* (Paris, 1944), pp. 50-51; Eduard Riggenbach, *Die ältesten lateinischen Kommentare zum Hebräerbrief* (Leipzig, 1907), pp. 41-201.

[26] For Valla's views on St. Thomas Aquinas, see two excellent articles: Hanna H. Gray, "Valla's *Encomium of St. Thomas Aquinas* and the Humanist Con-

men not truly refined nor well versed in good letters. But since they were utterly ignorant of the Greek language, I am amazed that they dared to comment on Paul, who spoke Greek, especially in the wake of so many Greek and Latin expositors who were experts in that language. Now, it is said that after Thomas had completed his commentary, Paul himself appeared to him saying he had been comprehended by no one better than by Thomas. Surely Thomas did not understand him better than Basil, Gregory Nazianzen, and Chrysostom? Why mention only Greeks? Surely no better than Hilary, Ambrose, Jerome, and Augustine? May I perish if this old tale is not a lie! Otherwise, why did Paul not advise him of his shortcomings, including among other things, his ignorance of the Greek language?

Thus knowledge of Greek was for Valla the indispensable prerequisite for New Testament exegesis. He intended for his notes primarily to evaluate the Vulgate as a translation of the Greek New Testament, not to provide a new handbook of exegesis. Yet his correction of the Vulgate's errors and his attempt to represent in Latin the sense of the Greek New Testament often involved Valla directly in an explanation of the literal sense of scripture. And his comments not infrequently helped to eliminate confusion and to explain puzzling passages of the Vulgate New Testament. At Matt. 6:27, for example, Valla found the Vulgate's rhetorical variety positively misleading. The Greek verb μεριμνάω ("to be anxious") occurs twice in this passage; the Vulgate represents it first with *cogito* ("to think"), then with *sollicitus esse* ("to be wor-

ception of Christian Antiquity," in *Essays in History and Literature Presented by the Fellows of the Newberry Library to Stanley Pargellis*, ed. H. Bluhm (Chicago, 1965), pp. 37-51; and John W. O'Malley, "Some Renaissance Panegyrics of Aquinas," *RQ* 27 (1974):174-92.

ried"). After pointing out the discrepancy, Valla continued (in the *Collatio*) by briefly expounding the passage: Jesus taught his disciples here not to ignore the necessities of life, but to avoid sorrow, anxiety, and worry. Recourse to the Greek text enabled Valla also to make sense of a knotty passage at Acts 28:11. Many Vulgate manuscripts say St. Paul boarded a ship bearing a "figurehead of camps" ("insigne castrorum")—a reading that makes no sense. The Greek text suggests the correct reading: "insigne Castorum"—"figurehead of the Castors," i.e., of Castor and Pollux, twin sons of Jove. Valla then continued (in the *Adnotationes*) by explaining that ancient mariners considered Castor and Pollux useful guides through storms.

Valla limited his exegesis to explanation of the literal sense of scripture; other, more speculative modes of exegesis held little interest for him. He acknowledged in his dialogue *On the True and False Good* that scripture harbors "enigmas and allegories," but denied that men living in the flesh could accurately perceive such incorporeal and sublime things. As the eye is blinded by the sun, he said, so the human mind is overpowered by the ineffable, divine mysteries enfolded by the scriptures.[27] This attitude governed Valla's commentary in his notes to the New Testament.

Yet Valla spoke occasionally, in the *Collatio* at least, of the *interior sensus* of scripture. What can this interior sense mean, if not the allegorical, tropological, or anagogical senses commonly expounded by medieval exegetes? Valla never explained clearly what he meant by this term, but his treatment suggests that he thought the *interior sensus* lay fairly close to the surface of the scriptures. Once again the dialogue *On the True and False Good* helps to clarify Valla's attitude toward exegesis. There he argued that scripture must be understood above all else as

[27] *De vero falsoque bono*, ed. M. de P. Lorch (Bari, 1970), III, 19 (p. 120).

a personal document through which God speaks directly to individual men. Reading the scriptures should result in the elevation of one's soul, the experience of an inexplicable calm, the recognition of God's love for the individual.[28] Expressing the *interior sensus* of scripture therefore called not for traditional medieval modes of spiritual exegesis, but rather for a sort of rhetorical recasting of scriptural teachings in such a way as to appeal to the individual's emotions. This brand of exegesis thus resembles what Charles Trinkaus has called the *theologia rhetorica* of the Renaissance humanists. The humanists cared less to construct static, scientific theological systems than to move men to acts of charity, to persuade them to share their faith, to inculcate morality, and to do all this not by means of painful pedagogy but rather of delightful discourse.[29] The best illustration of what it means to express the *interior sensus* of scripture comes from Valla's comment in the *Collatio* to 1 Cor. 14:14-15:

> When I sing [Psalm 1:1] "Blessed is the man who does not walk in the counsel of the impious," I do not dwell with barren imagination on the external sense—that the man who does not walk in the counsel of the impious is blessed. Instead I refer this passage to myself; I refer it to Jesus. Christ's reverence and love so warm my heart and so inflame my will that my mind will not go unrewarded.

Valla did not set out in his notes to expound the New Testament, so comments of this sort occur only rarely in his work. The *Collatio*'s warm discourse at 1 Cor. 14:14-15 was itself followed by a series of strictly philological observations. Nevertheless, that comment better than any other illustrates

---

[28] *De vero falsoque bono*, III, 18 (pp. 119-20).
[29] *In Our Image and Likeness*, 1:126-50, 299-307; 2:647-50, 770.

what Valla probably meant by exegesis of the *interior sensus* of scripture.

In both redactions of his notes Valla found passages where philological and historical considerations led to an exegesis of the Greek New Testament that undermined traditional doctrine based on the corresponding Vulgate translation. At 2 Cor. 7:10 he criticized the use of *poenitentia* as a translation for μετάνοια. The Latin word, he observed, connotes weariness or annoyance and does not accurately reflect the more positive sense of the Greek word, "reconsidering one's judgment," or "concern to become better." The text in question suggests that a kind of moral grief (ἡ κατὰ θεὸν λύπη, translated in the Vulgate as *tristitia*—"sadness") is closely related to the concern to improve oneself (μετάνοια, translated in the Vulgate as *poenitentia*—"penance"). Behind this philological point there stood an important theological implication: "They jabber nonsense," Valla argued, "who, disputing at this point whether sadness (*tristitia*) is the same thing as [the sacrament of] penance (*poenitentia*), maintain that penance is tripartite, composed of contrition, confession, and satisfaction. Since it is false, this opinion contributes nothing to the elucidation of Paul's teaching." Valla therefore dealt a severe blow to the complicated Latin theology concerning the sacrament of penance—a theology that looked anachronistic and untenable in the light of an accurate understanding and exegesis of the Greek New Testament. In comments to three other passages—2 Cor. 9:7 (in the *Collatio*), 2 Cor. 8:19, and Phil. 3:14 (both in the *Adnotationes*)—Valla argued further that the Greek New Testament lays no foundation for elaborate theories of divine predestination, or for a distinction between predestination (whereby God selects individuals to be saved) and foreknowledge (whereby God simply knows but does not select those to be damned, and so is spared responsibility for consigning them to hell).

An even clearer example of this sort of historically sensitive exegesis appears in Valla's discussion of Dionysius the Areopagite at Acts 17:22-34. Tradition identified this Dionysius, converted by St. Paul on the Areopagus, with the Pseudo-Dionysius, author of several works of Neoplatonic theology and a supremely influential figure for medieval theologians and exegetes. In both redactions of his notes Valla introduced a wide range of historical and philological arguments contesting—indeed, disproving—this identification. In the first place, he argued, the Areopagus was not a philosophers' forum but a law court; the original Dionysius would therefore not have been a philosopher or theologian, but a judge or lawyer. Furthermore, as a Neoplatonist, the Pseudo-Dionysius would have fit awkwardly in the philosophical environment of St. Paul's time, when the Stoics, Peripatetics, and Academic Sceptics— Valla neglected to mention the Epicureans—predominated. Valla then turned on the Pseudo-Dionysius himself. Valla considered his works a patent forgery because they spoke of the eclipse at Jesus' death (Matt. 27:45) occurring also at Athens, though no other ancient witness recorded it outside Judea. Finally, Valla pointed out, the Pseudo-Dionysius' works were mentioned by no author earlier than Pope Gregory the Great (A.D. 590-604), and even Gregory did not identify the Pseudo-Dionysius with Dionysius the Areopagite.

The legend of the Pseudo-Dionysius thus received its first sound, solid trouncing by the author, fittingly, of the treatise on the Donation of Constantine. The task of historical criticism appealed strongly to Valla, especially destructive criticism. He proved that Constantine did not grant the Donation and that the Pseudo-Dionysius was an impostor, but he seemed uninterested in the more complicated task of determining who in fact did forge the Donation and who masqueraded as the Areopagite. He ventured nothing on his own, but mentioned (in the *Adnotationes* only) that certain "exceptionally learned

Greeks"—meaning no doubt Cardinal Bessarion and his circle—considered the heretic Apollinarius the author of the Pseudo-Dionysius' works. Thorough constructive historical criticism lay beyond the talents of Valla or any other Renaissance humanist, but Valla's fearless destructive criticism by itself deeply influenced the development of scholarship. The application of his broad erudition and acute critical faculty to musty old legends rendered him famous—sometimes infamous—and exhibited to the scholarly world the interesting yields brought forth by the cultivation of philological and historical criticism.

Conclusion

Valla's notes to the New Testament did not elicit universal admiration in his own day, nor even in more recent times. Valla himself responded to the accusations of his bitter enemy, Poggio Bracciolini, that Valla's notes scorned scripture, defamed St. Jerome, and cast darts at Christ. "Why then did I compare the Latin stream with the Greek fount of the New Testament?" Valla asked.[30]

> In order that, like Porphyry, I might impugn the New Testament itself? That I might destroy our religion? That I might through this work engage Christ in war? Or rather that I might serve him and bring into his temple at least goat's hair (as they say) if I am not able to offer better things?

In the next century, Valla's work came under the attack of conservative critics such as Cardinal Guglielmo Sirleto and Frans

---

[30] For Poggio's accusations see his *Opera*, 1:199-200, 210, 231-34, 248. For Valla's responses see his *Opera*, 1:268-70, 339-41. The quotation comes from 1:341.

Tittelmans, to be discussed in the last chapter, who defended
the Vulgate as accurate, reliable, and authoritative scripture.
Even in our own century, one scholar has faulted Valla for
not adhering to a medieval exegetical standard. "Lorenzo nib-
bled at the crust of the biblical text," says Salvatore Garofalo.[31] But

> St. Thomas bit into it and enjoyed its nourishment. Hu-
> manism and the Renaissance surpassed the Middle Ages
> in critical philology, but they remained clearly inferior in
> the realm of exegesis. Valla knew well how to scrutinize
> syllables, to the point that he lacked the strength to un-
> dertake a solid and accomplished exposition. Exegesis was
> not bread for his teeth, and in the rare cases when he
> ventured an exegesis, he promptly backed off, lest he be
> accused of lacking faith in the Bible.

Garofalo was certainly right to emphasize the philological
nature of Valla's notes to the New Testament. While alert to
the religious and theological implications of his analysis—as
Fois, Camporeale, and Trinkaus have shown[32]—Valla prepared for the *Collatio* and *Adnotationes* approximately 2,000
comments of a strictly philological character. But surely this
effort deserves a more positive interpretation than Garofalo
was willing to provide. In order to assess accurately the significance of Valla's notes to the New Testament, one must
consider his work in the context of New Testament studies in
the late Middle Ages. Valla found New Testament scholarship
dominated by commentators who knew no Greek, used an
inferior translation as their basic text, and recognized broad
hermeneutic value in Aristotelian philosophy and scholastic
theology. Valla rejected this approach to scriptural studies and

---

[31] "Gli umanisti italiani del secolo XV e la Bibbia," pp. 352-53.
[32] See note 1 above.

effected a sort of paradigm shift in the realm of New Testament scholarship. He insisted that students of the scriptures learn Greek and base their work on the Greek text of the New Testament. He rejected scholastic theology, alien to the early Christian world, and allowed philological and historical criteria to govern his analysis. Proceeding in this manner, he was able to show that Greek and especially Latin manuscripts of the New Testament were riddled with corruption, that the Vulgate presented an inaccurate and inadequate translation of the Greek New Testament, and that medieval exegetes sometimes offered badly skewed explanations of the scriptures. But he was also able to show by manifold example how scholars might restore the New Testament's text to a more accurate state, recapture its spirit in a more precise translation, and recover its original meaning in a more pertinent exegesis—all this by taking proper account of the philological, linguistic, grammatical, and historical realities that lay in and behind the Greek text of the New Testament.

Thus he opened the door not on a new exegesis or theology so much as on a new brand of scholarship that stood prior to both exegesis and theology. I have no wish to deny Valla's importance as a religious thinker: his dialogues *On the True and False Good, On Free Will*, and *On Monastic Vows* stand out as some of the most original religious documents of the entire Renaissance, not to mention his *Sermon on the Mystery of the Eucharist* and *Encomium of St. Thomas Aquinas*. Some of Valla's works—most notably the dialogue *On Free Will*—influenced theology and moral philosophy over the next several centuries because of their doctrine or their novel approach to traditional problems. Valla's notes to the New Testament also influenced theology, but they did so as a result of their method, not their specific teachings. At least a few of his contemporaries recognized the value of Valla's philological scholarship: Cardinal Bessarion appreciated and encouraged Valla in his studies, Pope Nicholas V praised the *Collatio*, and Cardinal Nicholas of Cusa requested a personal copy of the work.[33] And as a later chapter will show, Erasmus was so deeply influenced by the *Adnotationes* that he devoted much of his career to the task of developing, refining, and extending Valla's methods. Valla's notes to the New Testament perhaps invited the attention of reformers or polemicists in the short run, but their most important function over the long term was to inaugurate the philological tradition in New Testament scholarship.

[33] See the note to John 21:20 in the *Adnotationes* and Valla's *Opera* 1:340.

THREE

The Complutensian New Testament

O N 10 JANUARY 1514 the colophon was placed on the
single most important scholarly publication of the Spanish Renaissance: the New Testament volume of Complutensian Polyglot Bible. The Complutensian Bible presented to
the world the first printed edition of the Greek New Testament. It was not the first *published* edition: Erasmus' edition,
published in 1516, claims that honor. The Complutensian editors were unable to obtain a license to bind and distribute
their work until 1520; by then Erasmus was already at work
on his third edition of the Greek New Testament. But the
Complutensian New Testament emerged from the press almost two years before printing began on Erasmus' first edition. Though eclipsed by the fame of Erasmus' work, the world's
first printed Greek New Testament must obviously figure significantly in any study of early modern scholarship.

A magnificent, multilingual edition of the Bible, the Complutensian Polyglot was only one product of the creative
imagination of Cardinal Francisco Ximénez de Cisneros.
Archbishop of Toledo, Primate of Spain, scourge of the Mus-
lim, twice regent of Spain—Ximénez was perhaps the central
figure of Spanish ecclesiastical and political life in the late fifteenth and early sixteenth century.[1] More than a politician and

---

[1] The most judicious account of Ximénez's life and work is that of Marcel

churchman, however, Ximénez was also an important patron of humanist culture. About 1498 he decided to found a new university that would foster humanist studies, especially in the three biblical languages, Latin, Greek, and Hebrew. His motive was largely pious. Ximénez was devoted to the scriptures, and he hoped the study of languages would lead to a revival of interest in the scriptures, and eventually to widespread reform in the Spanish Church. Construction on the university began in 1502 near Madrid, at Alcalá de Henares (= Complutum in Latin, whence the adjective, Complutensian), and the institution opened its doors in July of 1508. The heart of the new university was the trilingual College of San Ildefonso. Humanist professors at Alcalá thus offered instruction in the three biblical languages well before Jerome Busleiden provided for the Trilingual College at Louvain (1517) and Francis I decided to hire the trilingual *lecteurs royaux* at Paris (1530).[2]

It is not clear exactly when Ximénez decided to organize the publication of a Polyglot Bible. His earliest biographer, Juan de Vallejo, recorded that Ximénez conceived the project during the summer of 1502. All the principal prelates and nobles of Spain were then gathered at Toledo to celebrate the confirmation of Prince Philip the Handsome (of Austria and Burgundy) and Doña Juana (later called "la loca") as successors to the Catholic Kings, Ferdinand and Isabella. Ximénez avoided the festivities, according to Vallejo, and kept to his

---

Bataillon, *Erasmo y España*, trans. A. Alatorre, 2nd ed. (Mexico City, 1966), pp. 1-71.

[2] Of the many studies of the early University of Alcalá, the best are those of Bataillon, *Erasmo y España*, pp. 10-22; and Antonio de la Torre y del Cerro, "La Universidad de Alcalá. Datos para su historia," *RABM*, 3rd ser. 20 (1909):412-23; 21 (1909):48-71, 261-85, 405-33. Readers of English may consult Basil Hall, "The Trilingual College of San Ildefonso and the Making of the Complutensian Polyglot Bible," in *Studies in Church History*, ed. G. J. Cuming, vol. 5 (Leiden, 1969), pp. 114-46, though this article is not without its errors.

palace, where "minding his duty as a true prelate and pastor," he developed his plan for the Polyglot Bible. Upon returning to his permanent residence at Alcalá (September 1502), Ximénez began to recruit Greek and Hebrew scholars to the University of Alcalá to serve on the erudite editorial team that would produce the monumental edition.[3] Vallejo's manuscript memoir of Ximénez's life served as the primary source of information for Alvar Gómez de Castro, who in the mid-sixteenth century prepared the massive biography that remains the basic narrative source for Ximénez's life. Gómez therefore appropriated Vallejo's account of the Polyglot's origin and publicized it much more widely than Vallejo's biography, which lay unpublished until 1913.[4] As a result, this account of the Polyglot's origin has survived well into the twentieth century.[5]

More recently, however, it has been doubted that Ximénez developed his plans so completely as early as Vallejo thought.[6] Perhaps Ximénez supported a coterie of humanists and biblical scholars from about 1502, but probably the idea of publishing a Polyglot Bible emerged only around 1510. Earlier records from Alcalá mention no such project. Furthermore, the Greek and Hebrew editors of the Polyglot gathered at Alcalá in a most leisurely way: the noted Greek scholars, Elio Antonio de Nebrija and Hernán Núñez, arrived only in 1513.

---

[3] Juan de Vallejo, *Memorial de la vida de fray Francisco Jiménez de Cisneros*, ed. A. de la Torre y del Cerro (Madrid, 1913), pp. 56-57.

[4] Alvar Gómez de Castro, *De rebus gestis a Francisco Ximenio Cisnerio, archiepiscopo toletano, libri octo* (Alcalá, 1569), fol. 37^r (MS. fol. 76^r-77^v). The citation in parentheses refers to Gómez's manuscript of the biography. I shall occasionally cite the manuscript specifically, since it sometimes presents more detailed accounts than the published edition of the biography. The manuscript is entitled "De rebus gestis Francisci Ximenii de Cisneros" and is preserved as MS. 105-Z of the Archivo Histórico Universitario (hereafter, AHU), Universidad Complutense de Madrid.

[5] Mariano Revilla Rico, *La Políglota de Alcalá* (Madrid, 1917), pp. 5, 10; Felix G. Olmedo, *Nebrija* (Madrid, 1942), p. 30.

[6] Bataillon, *Erasmo y España*, pp. 22-24, 38-39.

72

In any event, it is difficult to see why fifteen long years would be required to complete the project. (The last volume of the Polyglot left the press in 1517.) But in 1510 there appeared clear signs that Ximénez seriously intended to publish a Polyglot Bible. In that year he induced Arnao Guillén de Brocar, the famous craftsman who printed the Polyglot, to move his shop from Logroño to Alcalá. In the next few years he searched intensively for good manuscripts of the scriptures. Meanwhile, Greek and Hebrew scholars arrived in Alcalá. In 1513 printing began, and by 10 January 1514 the New Testament volume of the Polyglot Bible was completed. In the next three years Brocar printed a Hebrew-Aramaic-Latin lexicon and four volumes of the Old Testament in the original Hebrew, along with the Aramaic, Greek, and Latin versions.

There is less uncertainty about Ximénez's purposes in publishing the Polyglot than about the project's early chronology: Ximénez's motives were threefold. Alvar Gómez said Ximénez was disturbed because medieval scholastic philosophers abandoned the biblical theology of the Church Fathers and increasingly took their intellectual cues from Aristotle. This unfortunate development led to clerical ignorance concerning the elements of true theology, thence to the corruption of popular morals. By the sixteenth century, so Ximénez thought, the scriptures were alien books to most Christians. Thus he decided to imitate Origen, collect all the most important texts and translations of the scriptures, and publish them in one magnificent edition, in the hope that the work would inaugurate a general moral reform of Christendom.[7] Unlike Alvar Gómez, the prefaces to the Complutensian Bible emphasized philological concerns. An edition of the scriptures in their original languages would help scholars to understand their messages more accurately. Each language has its own force,

---

[7] *De rebus gestis*, fol. 37ʳ (MS. fol. 77ʳ).

and no translation can precisely represent the peculiar features of another tongue. Furthermore, a reliable edition of the scriptures in Greek and Hebrew would help to solve textual problems. Latin manuscripts and editions often present irreconcilable readings; only the original languages can lead scholars to the solution of such problems.[8] Finally, Ximénez no doubt looked on the Polyglot as a tool for use in his efforts to bring about religious unity in Spain. He waged a vigorous missionary campaign attempting to provide a common religious denominator for the multilingual, multicultural society that was Spain in the early sixteenth century. From this point of view, his support for the Complutensian Bible stood alongside his revision of the Mozarabic Ritual and (in a less positive vein) his persecution of the Moors. Thus three motives help to explain why Ximénez sponsored the Polyglot Bible: his desire to encourage piety, his recognition of the need for accurate texts of the scriptures, and his urge to unify the disparate religious and cultural elements of early modern Spain.

The Editors

Ximénez was unable to edit a Polyglot Bible himself. Though he understood Greek, Hebrew, and Aramaic, he was a busy man with little time to devote to scholarship. Furthermore, his knowledge of languages probably did not run deep enough to enable him to prepare a sophisticated edition of the scriptures in their original tongues. He therefore entrusted the actual editing of the Complutensian Bible to a team of professional scholars at the University of Alcalá. Unfortunately, it has never been possible to determine precisely which scholars

---

[8] See especially Ximénez's letter of dedication to Pope Leo X prefaced to the first four volumes (i.e., the Old Testament volumes) of the Complutensian Polyglot Bible, vol. I, fol. + iii^r.

served on the team and what role they played in the enterprise. The difficulty arises from confusion in the earliest sources. Juan de Vallejo mentioned the names of only five editors: Pablo Coronel, Alfonso the physician of Alcalá, Elio Antonio de Nebrija, Diego López Zúñiga, and Hernán Núñez.[9] Alvar Gómez added to this list the names of Alfonso de Zamora, Demetrius Ducas, and Juan de Vergara.[10] To complicate matters further, five scholars contributed gratulatory verses to the New Testament volume of the Complutensian Bible, suggesting at least the possibility that they collaborated in its production. The five are Demetrius Ducas, Nicetas Fausto, Juan de Vergara, Hernán Núñez, and Bartolomeo de Castro.[11]

How does one make sense of this confusing array of names and assign each scholar to his proper role? The task is difficult, but it is not impossible to obtain a reasonably clear idea of how the editorial team was constituted and who were its most important contributors. The Old Testament fell into the hands of the three *conversos*, Pablo Coronel, Alfonso the physician, and the esteemed Hebrew scholar, Alfonso de Zamora. Historians agree on this point. Furthermore, there is Alvar Gómez's testimony that Juan de Vergara and other unnamed Complutensian students prepared a Latin translation of the Septuagint, under the supervision of Hernán Núñez and Demetrius Ducas.[12] Hernán Núñez and Ducas were both eminent Greek scholars, and both lived in Alcalá as the Septuagint was being readied for the press, between 1514 and 1516. Most likely they themselves took charge of preparing the Greek text of the Septuagint and oversaw a Latin translation by their better students of Greek, including Vergara.

[9] Vallejo, *Memorial*, p. 56.
[10] *De rebus gestis*, fol. 37ᵛ-38ʳ (MS. fol. 77ᵛ-78ᵛ).
[11] See fol. MM viiiʳᵛ of the New Testament volume, the fifth in the set of the Complutensian Polyglot Bible.
[12] *De rebus gestis*, fol. 38ʳ (MS. fol. 78ʳᵛ).

When one turns to the New Testament, however, the difficulties increase. There is no suggestion other than their gratulatory verses that Nicetas Fausto, Juan de Vergara, and Bartolomeo de Castro collaborated on the Complutensian New Testament, though each was certainly capable of contributing to the work. Fausto later occupied the chair of Greek at Venice.[13] Vergara was competent enough as a student to be invited to work on the Septuagint. In 1516 Castro compiled an erudite Greek-Latin vocabulary which points out the peculiar forms of ancient Greek dialects.[14] It is at least possible that these three served in some capacity in editing the Greek or Latin New Testament. Yet it seems unlikely that any of them played a major role; otherwise the silence of the contemporary sources is difficult to explain. This is especially true in the case of Vergara, perhaps the most capable of the three. Alvar Gómez praised Vergara's modesty and intelligence and lamented his early death with some feeling; he mentioned Vergara's work on the Septuagint and surely would have discussed his contribution to the New Testament had Vergara figured prominently in the enterprise.[15] Nor does it seem likely that Hernán Núñez played more than a small role in editing the New Testament. Though a celebrated Greek scholar, until 1521 he exhibited more interest in politics than in study. His principle works of scholarship—annotations, emendations, and commentaries to Seneca, Pliny, and Pomponius Mela—began to appear only in the 1530s. In any event, he arrived in Alcalá only in 1513, when the New Testament would have been almost ready to go to press.[16]

[13] Deno J. Geanakoplos, *Greek Scholars in Venice* (Cambridge, Mass., 1962), p. 240.

[14] MS. 7-1-10 in the Biblioteca Colombina (Seville), entitled "Vocabularius verborum graecorum editus a magistro Bartholo Castrensi Rome anno 1516."

[15] *De rebus gestis*, fol. 38ʳ (MS. fol. 78ʳᵛ).

[16] On Núñez's early career, through 1521, see Helen Nader, " 'The Greek Commander' Hernán Núñez de Toledo, Spanish Humanist and Civic Leader,"

This leaves us with the names of three scholars who contributed more significantly to the editing of the Complutensian New Testament: Demetrius Ducas, Diego López Zúñiga, and Antonio de Nebrija. Ducas probably served as chief editor of the Greek New Testament, though it is not easy to reconcile this role with what is known of his career and its chronology.[17] Born in Crete, Ducas established himself at Venice about the beginning of the sixteenth century. There he edited classical Greek texts for the great printer, Aldus Manutius, at least until 1509. Sometime thereafter Ximénez invited him to Alcalá to fill the chair of Greek at the university and to help edit the Greek scriptures. Alvar Gómez says Ducas was the first professor to hold the chair of Greek at Alcalá[18]—and therefore would place Ducas in Alcalá shortly after 1508—but the earliest firm indication of his presence there dates from October of 1513, when the university's account book recorded payment of his salary of 300 reales.[19] If Ducas went to Alcalá only in late 1513, he could have had little to do with the editing of the New Testament.

There are signs, however, that Ducas arrived in Alcalá well before the first record of his presence there. In the first place, the university's account book records that Ducas' whole salary of 300 reales was paid in his name to Guillén de Brocar in payment for "certain Greek books which [Brocar] has printed" for Ducas. This no doubt refers to the anthologies of Greek texts that Brocar produced for Ducas to use in his Greek courses.[20] One can only infer that by October of 1513 Ducas had lived in Alcalá long enough to make complicated arrange-

RQ 31 (1978):463-85. On his classical scholarship see Maria Dolores de Asís, *Hernán Núñez en la historia de los estudios clásicos* (Madrid, 1977).

[17] The best study of Ducas is that of Geanakoplos, *Greek Scholars in Venice*, pp. 223-55.

[18] *De rebus gestis*, fol. 81ᵛ.

[19] Antonio de la Torre, "La Universidad de Alcalá," p. 262.

[20] Ibid., p. 262; Geanakoplos, *Greek Scholars in Venice*, pp. 234-38.

ments both with Brocar and with the university bureaucracy. In the second place, Ducas contributed the first of the series of gratulatory poems published (January 1514) in the Complutensian New Testament. In it he lauded Ximénez as a being worthy of divinity for his efforts in organizing publication of the New Testament.[21] It would be difficult to account for such fulsome praise if Ducas had known Ximénez for only a few months (from October 1513 to January 1514) and had not contributed in some way to the Complutensian New Testament. In the third place, Elio Antonio de Nebrija once let slip the information that Hebrews (i.e., *conversos*) and Greeks were charged with editing, respectively, the Hebrew and Greek scriptures.[22] Ducas was the only Greek to serve on the Complutensian editorial team. (Nicetas Fausto was Italian; all the other figures associated with the Complutensian Bible were Spaniards.) In the fourth place, it looks very much as though Ducas wrote the anonymous preface to the Complutensian New Testament.[23] This preface appeared in the Polyglot in its original Greek and in a Latin translation. The Greek version especially betrays Ducas. Here the author implied having observed certain stone inscriptions in Constantinople—but none of the other Complutensian editors appears to have travelled in the Greek world. Finally, one of the marginal notes to the Complutensian New Testament almost certainly reveals Ducas' influence. This is a textual note to Matt. 6:13 which discusses the authenticity of the clause found at the end of the Lord's Prayer, "for thine is the kingdom, the power, and the glory forever." I defer detailed discussion of the note until

[21] Complutensian New Testament, fol. MM viii[r].

[22] "Epistola del maestro de Lebrija al Cardenal," *RABM*, 3rd ser. 8 (1903):493. Later pages will examine this letter in detail.

[23] Geanakoplos develops this argument in detail in his *Greek Scholars in Venice*, pp. 240-43. See also his *Interaction of the "Sibling" Byzantine and Western Cultures* (New Haven, 1976), p. 207. The preface will be found in the Complutensian New Testament, fol. a ii[rv].

later. For now it is relevant to point out that its author exhibits a precise knowledge of the Greek Church's liturgy. Of the Complutensian editors, only Ducas is likely to have been capable of producing this note. Thus it seems in the highest degree probable that Ducas arrived in Spain well before 1513. Ximénez perhaps invited him to Alcalá shortly after Aldus left Venice and retired to Ferrara in 1509. Ximénez would have heard of Ducas' editorial skills and intended for him to work chiefly on the Polyglot. Later on, impressed with Ducas' talents, he would have found him a post in the University of Alcalá. Though it cannot be documented, this explanation seems the only one to make sense of all the evidence bearing on Ducas' career.

Another important member of the New Testament editorial team was Diego López Zúñiga, better known by his Latin name, Stunica. Almost nothing is known of Stunica until 1519, when he began a series of attacks on the New Testament scholarship of Lefèvre d'Étaples and Erasmus (to be discussed in a later chapter). There can be no doubt, however, that he worked on the Polyglot. Juan de Vallejo and Alvar Gómez both placed him among its editors. Furthermore, in his controversial works Stunica displayed intimate familiarity with the manuscripts used by the Complutensian scholars, as the last chapter will show. Finally, there is his statement that he once collated Greek and Latin manuscripts of the New Testament at Ximénez's instance.[24] It is probably safe to guess that Ducas, the Cretan and editor of Greek classics, took primary responsibility for the editing of the Greek New Testament. Stunica no doubt wielded some influence in the establishment of the Greek text, but accepted the editing of the Vulgate as his principal task.

For a while Elio Antonio de Nebrija aided Stunica in the

---

[24] See his *Annotationes contra Iacobum Fabrum Stapulensem* (Alcalá, 1519), fol. A 3ʳ.

preparation of the Vulgate. It will be worthwhile to discuss Nebrija's work in some detail: he was without doubt Spain's most competent biblical scholar in the early sixteenth century, but I know of no study that analyzes his New Testament scholarship.[25] Nebrija (1441-1522) had long enjoyed a reputation as a distinguished scholar because of his contributions to Latin, Greek, and Hebrew grammar and literature, Spanish language and history, and perhaps above all because of his unremitting battle against barbarism. He counted among his patrons Queen Isabella of Castile and Don Juan de Zúñiga, Archbishop of Seville. In 1495 he decided to give up secular concerns and devote his remaining years to sacred studies. During the next ten years he drew up a set of critical notes on the text and translation of the Bible. These notes unfortunately do not survive, because they aroused the suspicions of the Inquisitor General of Spain, Diego de Deza, who confiscated them. Nebrija was not charged with heresy—he later speculated that Deza seized his work not in order to evaluate it, but rather to intimidate him and forestall further philological analyses of the Bible—but he was unable to proceed so openly as before.[26]

Relief soon appeared, however, in the person of Ximénez. King Ferdinand's court spent the winter of 1505-1506 at Salamanca, where Nebrija held the chair of grammar. Ximénez

[25] On Nebrija's life and works see Bataillon, *Erasmo y España*, pp. 22-39; and Pedro Lemus y Rubio, "El maestro Elio Antonio de Lebrixa," *Revue hispanique* 22 (1910):459-508. These two works supersede Olmedo, *Nebrija*, but neither of them attempts to probe Nebrija's scholarly works on the New Testament and identify the methods and principles that governed his studies.

[26] The only account of this confrontation survives in Nebrija's "Argument to the Reader," found only in a late edition of his *Apology* entitled *Apologia earum rerum quae illi obiiciuntur* (Granada, 1535), fol. A i^v-A ii^r. The "Argument" may be considered trustworthy, even though it appeared thirteen years after Nebrija's death. This edition of the *Apologia* was published by Nebrija's sons, who had access to his papers and would in any case have been familiar with his brush with the Inquisition.

and Nebrija met there, perhaps for the first time, and discussed biblical problems. In 1507 Ximénez succeeded Deza as Inquisitor General, and the way was clear for Nebrija to work more freely than before. The earliest surviving products of his work are an *Apologia* for his brand of biblical studies and an impressive analysis of fifty scriptural problems entitled the *Tertia quinquagena*. The *Apologia* was composed about 1504-1506, though it remained unpublished until 1516.[27] Nebrija dedicated the work to Ximénez; the spirited defense of his biblical studies suggests he was looking for a protector. In the letter of dedication Nebrija argued that he had been persecuted without warrant, an obvious reference to his troubles with the Inquisition. If he had limited himself to the production of poetic trifles or historical fables, he said, the learned world would have lauded his work. Instead he subjected scripture to careful analysis and suffered persecution.[28] The body of the work opened with a clear statement of the basic "rules of criticism" (*regula vero viaeque castigandi*). Nebrija succinctly presented the rules: "that whenever in the New Testament there appear variant readings in Latin books, we should have recourse to the Greek; that whenever in the Old Testament there is some difference among Latin books or between Latin and Greek, we should seek reliable information from the truth of the Hebrew source."[29] Nebrija then illustrated the value of these rules by using them to dissolve difficulties in several passages of scripture (to be examined below, since they were repeated in the *Tertia quinquagena*). He disposed of a popular medieval notion that Latin manuscripts are more accurate than

[27] Nebrija, *Apologia cum quibusdam sacrae scripturae locis non vulgariter expositis* (Alcalá, 1516). On its dating see Lemus y Rubio, "El maestro Elio Antonio de Lebrixa," p. 473. Lemus y Rubio finds traces of an earlier edition, now lost, of Logroño, 1508; see p. 474, n. 1.

[28] Nebrija, *Apologia* (1516), fol. a ii^rv.

[29] Ibid., fol. a ii^v.

81

Greek and Greek more accurate than Hebrew. And he strongly asserted the right of grammarians and philologists to treat scriptural problems having to do with language, words, and their meanings.[30]

The published edition of the *Apologia* closed with a letter to Ximénez much more confident in tone than the letter of dedication. The reason is not far to seek. Nebrija again recalled his day of persecution. Though he had striven for ten years to explain scriptures, he said, he held his peace when ecclesiastical superiors silenced him. But now all has changed. He addressed Ximénez as "official judge" (*publicus censor*), which dates the letter to no earlier than 1507, the year Ximénez became both Cardinal and Inquisitor General. Nebrija remembered Ximénez's encouragement in his time of trouble and hinted that now he expected better fortune than in the recent past. As a sign of appreciation for Ximénez's support, he sent his protector a work that presented fifty passages of scripture, not ineptly expounded.[31]

In fact this letter did double duty as dedicatory epistle for the *Tertia quinquagena* as well as parting shot of the *Apologia*. The two works complement each other quite well: the *Tertia quinquagena* applied in individual cases the principles described in the *Apologia*. Nebrija addressed fifty problems—actually forty-nine, since misnumbering resulted in the omission of one problem—drawn from both the Old and New Testaments. Since the New Testament discussions by themselves render a clear picture of the *Tertia quinquagena*'s character, the following discussion is limited to them as more relevant to the subject of this study.

Nebrija devoted a number of discussions to the problem of orthography. This may seem a minor worry, but one must

[30] Ibid., fol. a ii[v]-b ii[r].
[31] Ibid., fol. b ii[rv]. The letter is reprinted in the *Tertia quinquagena* (Alcalá, 1516), fol. a i[v].

remember that many confusing and misleading spellings appeared in the Latin translations of scripture. Thus Nebrija considered it worthwhile to point out the difference between *drama* (δρᾶμα, "theater"), *dragma* (δράγμα, "a bundle"), and *drachma* (δραχμή, a Greek coin). Unless these words are consistently spelled correctly, readers will be confused at Luke 15:8-10, where the old woman of Jesus' parable searches her house for ten lost *drachmas*.[32] Nebrija also corrected the spelling of the pool mentioned at John 5:2: it was Bethesda, meaning "house of effusion," not Bethsaida, as the Vulgate reads, meaning "house of combat."[33] He showed that at Acts 28:1 Paul found himself shipwrecked on the island of Malta ("Melita," Μελίτη), not, as some texts read, at Mytilene (on the island of Lesbos), Melitus (an ancient Ionian city), or even Melitene (a Cappadocian city on the Euphrates River!).[34] If these clarifications seem not very advanced today, it is because editors, translators, and publishers have long since learned to take care in their work. For sixteenth-century readers of scripture who had no Greek, these discussions could spell the difference between confusion and understanding.

More important for the history of scholarship, however, were those discussions that solved problems in the Latin scriptures by examining their base in the Greek text. Here Nebrija emerged as a scholar whose importance paralleled that of Lorenzo Valla. In fact he occasionally made points very similar to Valla's in his own discussions. At Matt. 1:19, for example, Nebrija explained the peculiar significance of the verb *traducere* in much the same way Valla had done. Reference to the Greek counterpart, παραδειγματίσαι, enabled him to show the correct meaning of the text: "Joseph . . . did not wish to embarrass [Mary] publicly," instead of a common medieval misinterpre-

---

[32] Nebrija, *Tertia quinquagena*, fol. b ii^v-b iii^r.
[33] Ibid., fol. a iiii^rv.
[34] Ibid., fol. c ii^rv.

tation, "Joseph . . . did not wish to take [Mary] as his wife."[35] At Acts 28:11 Nebrija argued from the Greek text, again like Valla, that the medieval reading "castrorum" is a corruption for "castorum." The text therefore says the ship that Paul took from Alexandria presented Castor and Pollux on its figure-head.[36]

Whether Nebrija knew Valla's work on the New Testament when he composed the *Tertia quinquagena* remains an open question. It is at least possible that he did. A manuscript copy of Valla's *Collatio* found its way to the Cathedral Library at Valencia sometime after 1478, when it was copied at Naples; and a copy of his *Adnotationes* arrived at Alcalá in the very early sixteenth century, in time to be bound together with a set of manuscript annotations to the New Testament, soon to be discussed in some detail.[37] It can hardly be doubted that Nebrija avidly read Valla as soon as he encountered his notes to the New Testament, but it looks to me as though the composition of the *Tertia quinquagena* preceded that encounter. Nebrija never referred to Valla's work in his biblical studies. So far as I know, he never visited Valencia, where he might have met with the manuscript of the *Collatio*. Apart from his Italian sojourn (1460-1470), Nebrija spent almost all his life in Castile and Andalusia. Finally, he probably began work on the *Tertia quinquagena* well before Erasmus published Valla's *Adnotationes*, in 1505, and he certainly introduced philological techniques into biblical studies before then. In his own account of his clash with the Inquisition, Nebrija says Diego de Deza confiscated one set of biblical annotations, but over-

---

[35] Ibid., fol. d iv^v-d v^v; cf. Valla's *Collatio* and *Adnotationes* to Matt. 1:19.

[36] Nebrija, *Tertia quinquagena*, fol. a vi^rv; cf. Valla's *Collatio* and *Adnotationes* to Acts 28:11.

[37] A. Perosa describes the manuscript of the *Collatio* in his introduction to Valla's *Collatio novi testamenti* (Florence, 1970), pp. xv-xvii. The *Adnotationes* are bound with several manuscripts in MS. 117-Z-1 of the AHU.

looked another set of comments which Nebrija hid until more liberal times.[38] If the *Tertia quinquagena* is intended here, its genesis long antedated Nebrija's acquaintance with the published edition of Valla's notes, since his troubles with the Inquisition occurred about 1504 or 1505. In any case, this piece of information, together with the evidence of the *Apologia*, suggest that Nebrija developed his philological skills independently and did not need Valla to provide his analytical cues.

This makes it all the more remarkable that Nebrija employed methods so similar to those of Valla. He made points like Valla's even when discussing passages that Valla did not treat. At Mark 5:41, for example, he took up a problem caused by confusion of Aramaic words and their transliteration into Greek. Many Vulgate manuscripts present Jesus' Aramaic command as "tabitha cumi," which makes no sense in the context: if translated from the Aramaic, it would mean something like "rise up, gazelle." The problem dissolves upon recourse to the Greek text, which presents ταλιθὰ κοῦμ, "talitha cum"— "little girl, rise."[39] Later Nebrija discussed the nature of the hurricane mentioned at Acts 27:14. The Vulgate says the storm arose from the wind named "Euroaquilo," but this is a difficult term to explain. "Euro" comes from the Greek Εὖρος, meaning southeast wind; "aquilo" is a Latin word meaning north wind. Nebrija solved the problem of the "southeast-north wind"—which he noted had baffled Nicholas of Lyra, Hugh of St. Cher, "and almost everybody else who expounded this passage"—by looking into the Greek text, where he found εὐροκλύδων, meaning a storm or tempest from the east.[40] As it happens, Nebrija's neat explanation of this text is not entirely accurate, as will be seen in discussion of Erasmus'

---

[38] See the *Apologia* of Granada, 1535, fol. A ii[r].
[39] Nebrija, *Tertia quinquagena*, fol. d iii[v]-d iv[r].
[40] Ibid., fol. b iv[rv].

treatment of the term "Euroaquilo." Yet it remains method-ologically important, since Nebrija attacked the problem with the proper philological tools: a thorough knowledge of the Greek language and ancient meteorological works.

Nebrija made other errors, too, in the *Tertia quinquagena*. He thought the word *artemon* at Acts 27:40 signified a pulley instead of a sail.[41] He became thoroughly confused at Apoc. 1:15. He suggested (correctly) that the Greek word χαλκο-λίβανον ("glowing brass") be rendered as *chalcolibanum* ("glowing brass") instead of the Vulgate's *aurichalcum* ("bright brass"). But he suggested as its meaning "strong frankin-cense," not "glowing brass."[42] Cardinal Ximénez himself led Nebrija astray at another point. Nebrija wondered why the disciple Simon is called "son of Jonah" ("Bar Iona") in some places (e.g., Matt. 16:17), but "son of John" ("Simon Ioan-nis") in others (e.g., John 21:15-16). Nebrija related in the *Tertia quinquagena* that he had very nearly decided that Jonah and John were two forms of the same name when Ximénez "filled my mouth with shame" by producing a Greek manu-script in which Simon was called "son of Jonah" in John's as well as Matthew's gospel.[43] In fact this reading is obviously the emendation of a copyist who wanted to harmonize the gospels. Yet it is worth noting that even in his errors Nebrija contributed positively to New Testament scholarship. In all these errors he worked on sound principles by examining the original language of the New Testament whenever he noticed a difficulty in the Latin text. His mistakes were due not to his method, but rather to deficiencies in the textual and lexico-graphical information at his disposal.

The *Apologia* and *Tertia quinquagena* were not the only works

[41] Ibid., fol. a ii^v-a iii^r.
[42] Ibid., fol. a iii^v-a iv^r.
[43] Ibid., fol. b vii^r.

of New Testament scholarship Nebrija produced, but they were the most important. He compiled also a massive dictionary of proper names and place names found in the Bible.[44] And he published a set of scholia to biblical readings recited on holy days. The work is not without interest: Nebrija based many of his observations on the original texts of scripture, and he occasionally even noted differences between the Greek text and the Vulgate.[45] Vestiges survive also of two other works, now lost, that Nebrija devoted to the scriptures. After Nebrija's death, his son, Sebastian, inventoried the works Nebrija left at the College of San Ildefonso. Among them he reported a set of "Annotations of holy scripture" and a "Vocabulary of holy scripture bound in parchment."[46] The annotations would be especially interesting for the modern scholar: they would probably make possible a more direct comparison between Nebrija and Valla, Erasmus, and other New Testament scholars. As things stand, however, there survives no complete review by Nebrija of the Greek text of the New Testament, no new translation of the Greek text, nor even comments on the whole New Testament.

Enough information does survive, however, to make it clear Nebrija belongs in the humanist camp of New Testament scholars. In the *Apologia* he argued strenuously for the introduction of philological criteria into biblical scholarship; in the

[44] Nebrija, *Nebrissensis biblica*, ed. P. Galindo Romeo and L. Ortiz Muñoz (Madrid, 1950). This is the second of four projected volumes of Nebrija's biblical works. The other three volumes unfortunately never appeared. For the editors' original plans, see their edition of Nebrija's *Gramática castellana* (Madrid, 1946), esp. p. 295.

[45] Nebrija, *Segmenta ex epistolis Pauli, Petri, Iacobi, & Ioannis, necnon ex prophetis quae in re divina leguntur per anni circulum tam in diebus dominicis quam in sanctorum festis & profestis* (Alcalá, 1516). For examples of the more interesting comments see the scholia to Acts 3:10; 2 Cor. 4:6, 8; 1 Tim. 1:17; 1 Tim. 6:10; and Heb. 1:11-12 in this work at fol. m v^r, i ii^v, b vi^r, i v^v, and b iii^r, respectively.

[46] Lemus y Rubio, "El maestro Elio Antonio de Lebrixa," pp. 482-83.

Tertia quinquagena he demonstrated that knowledge of ancient language and literature could solve problems that pre-
viously had defied explanation. Nebrija therefore confirmed
Lorenzo Valla's achievement by showing that philology was
the unavoidable prerequisite for one who would properly understand the scriptures.

Yet Nebrija played but a small role in the preparation of
the Complutensian New Testament. He occupied the chair of
grammar at Salamanca from 1505 until mid-1513, when he
resigned after a dispute. Only in 1513 was Ximénez able to
attract Nebrija to Alcalá, and then only at the cost of a handsome salary.[47] Nebrija and Ximénez got along famously at
Alcalá. Alvar Gómez reported that Ximénez often stopped at
Nebrija's house (near Brocar's printing shop) where the two
men held long talks leaning on Nebrija's windowsill.[48] In fact,
these conversations had the potential to become rather festive
occasions, as one might surmise from a note Gómez included
in the collection of raw materials which he gathered in preparation for his biography of Ximénez:[49]

Antonio de Nebrija lived near the printer's shop, and
whenever the Cardinal went to the college, he walked by
there and spent some time talking with him, he in the
street and Antonio at his window. The Cardinal arranged

[47] Contrary to some reports that Nebrija was professor of rhetoric at Alcalá
from its earliest days. On the date and circumstances of Nebrija's move to
Alcalá, see Antonio de la Torre, "La Universidad de Alcalá," pp. 267-71.

[48] *De rebus gestis*, fol. 87ʳ (MS. fol. 185ʳᵛ). The manuscript account provides
a bit more detail here than the printed edition.

[49] This piece of gossip appears in Alvar Gómez's manuscript collection of
notes entitled "Memoriales para la historia de Cisneros." It is preserved as
MS. 106-Z-22 of the AHU. This report appears on fol. 214; the Spanish
text reads as follows: "Antonio de Nebrissa morava par de la imprenta, y
siempre que el cardenal yva al colegio encaminava por alli, y estavase en rrato
hablando con el, el en la calle, y Antonio en su rexa. Estava concertado el
cardenal con su muger que entre dia no le dexase bever vino."

with [Nebrija's] wife that he should not be allowed to
drink wine during the day.

Nebrija unfortunately got along less grandly with the other
members of the Complutensian editorial team. No detailed
information survives concerning the team's internal workings
and conflicts. What little is known comes from a letter of Nebrija to Ximénez by which he resigned his post as a Complutensian editor; and the sketchy information provided there does
more to tantalize than to satisfy the desire to understand the
inner dynamics of the editorial team.[50] Writing in late 1514
or early 1515, Nebrija came quickly to the burden of his message: "I have determined to participate no longer in the emendation of the Bible which your holy lordship desires to publish." He explained his decision by reviewing two disputes
between himself and the other Complutensian scholars. The
first concerned Nebrija's role in editing the Latin scriptures
for the Complutensian Bible. Nebrija said he went to Alcalá
intending to carry out a thorough revision of the Vulgate and
bring it in line with the Hebrew and Greek scriptures. When
he presented his emended Latin translations, however, the other
Complutensian editors charged him with abusing his man-
date. Ximénez himself resolved the issue by instructing Nebrija to follow the general principle established for all the
Complutensian editors, to introduce into the standard texts
no changes except those witnessed in old manuscripts. The
second controversy served as the immediate cause of Nebrija's resignation. At issue were the explanations of Hebrew,
Aramaic, and Greek names to be appended to the Polyglot.
The editorial team planned to include the interpretations of

[50] What follows is based on the "Epistola del maestro de Lebrija al Cardenal," pp. 493-96. On the letter's date, see Bataillon's powerful arguments,
Erasmo y España, p. 35, n. 48.

Remigius of Auxerre, the ninth-century biblical scholar and commentator. Nebrija objected, but Ximénez approved; and the sixth volume of the Complutensian Bible presents a list of etymological explanations much like that of Remigius.

To Nebrija these decisions must have seemed tantamount to willful obscurantism. With no small relish he repeated half a dozen stories in his letter to Ximénez about ignorant friars, preachers, professors, and others who unwittingly spread gross misinterpretations of the scriptures because they used false etymologies or did not properly understand biblical languages. Nebrija regarded Remigius' interpretations as one of the most dangerous works of biblical scholarship available. It shed darkness, not light; it blocked the way to understanding. Worse, its malignant influence passed from the classroom to the pulpit, thence to the crowd. Nebrija did not suggest an alternative to Remigius' work in his letter to Ximénez, but he no doubt would have replaced it with a philologically accurate work like his own dictionary of proper names and place names found in the scriptures.[51]

Granting the justice of Nebrija's complaints on this issue, one must acknowledge that Ximénez held a strong position on the question of the Latin scriptures to be published in the Complutensian Bible. Nebrija had good reason to be impatient with the Vulgate and to envision a revised Latin translation of the scriptures. He no doubt thought his humanist talents, his comprehension of philological problems, and his proficiency in biblical languages would all go to waste unless he was allowed to revise the Vulgate. Nor can there be much doubt that he was capable of vastly improving the Vulgate, clarifying its language, and rendering it more faithful to the Hebrew and Greek scriptures. But Ximénez, in many ways a man devoted to tradition, had other plans. He wanted the

---

[51] *Nebrissensis biblica*, cited above, n. 39.

Polyglot to include the best edition that could be made of the Vulgate itself—and it bears pointing out that this too was a thoroughly legitimate scholarly enterprise. Manuscripts and early printed editions of the Vulgate presented so many variant readings and other textual problems that it was almost impossible to know the original Vulgate's text. Renaissance scholars needed a reliable edition of the Vulgate. Ximénez's project would not allow Nebrija to exercise his talents to the full, but it remained a thoroughly respectable piece of scholarly business that demanded attention.

Nebrija's experience tells us much about the Polyglot. The scholars of Alcalá were in every case capable students of biblical languages; in most cases they were also competent philologists, able to analyze and solve textual problems. But they were also, like Ximénez, conservative men who appreciated the medieval Christian tradition. Their Bible reflects their values.

The Edition

The Complutensian Polyglot Bible is a work magnificent to behold. Six folio volumes make the set. The first four present the Old Testament in Hebrew, Greek, and Latin. A general preface to the first volume explained why the Vulgate appears in the center of the three columns printed on each page: the Hebrew original and Greek Septuagint surround the Latin as the two thieves hung on either side of Jesus at the crucifixion. The Hebrew and Greek texts of the Old Testament were evidently tainted in Ximénez's mind by association with the infidel Jews and schismatic Greek Christians. The first volume also presents at the foot of each page the Targum of Onkelos, an Aramaic paraphrase of the Pentateuch, together with a Latin translation. The sixth volume provides various introductory

materials for the study of the Hebrew Old Testament, including a Hebrew-Aramaic-Latin lexicon; Remigius' interpretations of Hebrew, Aramaic, and Greek names found in scripture; and a short Hebrew grammar.

The following section focuses on the fifth volume of the
set, which presents the Greek and Vulgate New Testaments
in parallel columns. The Greek type is particularly impressive:
one scholar went so far as to call it "undoubtedly the finest
Greek fount ever cut"[52]—a judgment that no doubt seemed
less extravagant in 1900, when the author wrote, than today.
The letters are large, open, and elegant in their simplicity. The
Greek type is a bit odd, however, in one respect: it omits all
breathing marks and most accents. Only the acute accent appears in the Greek New Testament, and that only in polysyl-
labic words. The preface to the New Testament (probably
Ducas' work) explained the reasons for this peculiarity: ancient Greeks used no such marks; lack of the marks does not
hinder understanding for those well versed in Greek; it is fitting to present the New Testament in its original form. The
reasoning will perhaps not seem compelling, but the overall
majesty of the Complutensian Greek fount more than com-
pensates for the inconvenience caused by omission of breathing marks and accents. The preface pointed also to one other
unusual feature of the Complutensian New Testament. For
readers without an advanced knowledge of Greek, the editors
included small index letters matching Greek and Latin words
as closely as possible.

The preface unfortunately had little to say about the manuscripts used in preparing the New Testament.[53] Those used

---

[52] Robert Proctor, *The Printing of Greek in the 15th Century* (Oxford, 1900),
p. 144. A more balanced appreciation of the Complutensian Greek type may
be found in Victor Scholderer, *Greek Printing Types, 1465-1927* (London,
1927), p. 10.

[53] On the problems of the Complutensian manuscripts, see Jerry H. Bent-

for the Hebrew scriptures, the Septuagint, and the Vulgate
have been identified despite the reticence of the Complutensian prefaces, but there survive only the traces of those used
for the Greek New Testament. The preface to the New Testament claimed great antiquity and accuracy for them, but
troubled to mention only a single one, lent to Ximénez by
Pope Leo X from the papal library. It is certain, however, that
other Greek texts were available to the New Testament editors. Two early inventories of the library of the College of San
Ildefonso list, among other Greek books, three New Testament manuscripts: one of the four gospels, another of the
Apocalypse and Matthew's gospel, and a third of the Book of
Acts.[54] Stunica spoke highly of yet another manuscript, a
"Codex Rhodiensis" of the apostolic epistles, sent to Ximénez
from the Isle of Rhodes. Stunica described it as an ancient
and accurate manuscript and said further that Ximénez depos-
ited it in the Complutensian library.[55] If these manuscripts
still survive, they have not been identified. The remnant library of the College of San Ildefonso includes no manuscript
of the Greek New Testament, though the manuscripts used
for the Complutensian editions of the Hebrew scriptures, the
Septuagint, and the Vulgate are still preserved there.[56] Nor
have exhaustive searches and collations led to the sure identification of any text the Complutensian editors used in preparing their Greek New Testament.[57]

---

ley, "New Light on the Editing of the Complutensian New Testament," *Bibliothèque d'humanisme et Renaissance* 42 (1980):145-56.

[54] The inventories are dated 1523 and 1526; they survive in the Archivo
Histórico Nacional (Madrid), sección de universidades y colegios, libro 1091
F, fol. 9ᵛ; libro 1092 F, fol. 29ᵛ.

[55] See Stunica's *Annotationes contra Erasmum Roterodamum in defensionem
tralationis novi testamenti* (Alcalá, 1520), fol. G iiʳ, I viʳᵛ, K iᵛ, K iiʳ.

[56] The collection is catalogued in José Villa Amil y Castro, *Catálogo de los
manuscritos existentes en la biblioteca del noviciado de la Universidad central* (Madrid, 1878). For Greek manuscripts see pp. 5-8.

[57] Bentley, "New Light," pp. 145-47.

Furthermore, unlike Erasmus, the Complutensian editors did not equip their New Testament with extensive notes discussing textual and philological problems. They published hundreds of skimpy notes in the margins of their editions, notes which clarified verb tenses and moods, defined unusual words, and identified quotations and allusions to other parts of scripture. In only four cases, however, did they address serious textual problems in longer, more detailed annotations. Two of these relied on St. Jerome, not Greek manuscripts, as their source of textual information. At 1 Cor. 13:3 the Complutensian editors presented the readings καυθήσομαι and *ardeam* as their text—"If I hand over my body so that I might burn. . . ." In their note they merely call attention to an alternate reading on Jerome's witness: καυχήσομαι, *glorier*—"If I hand over my body so that I might be glorified. . . ." At 1 Cor. 15:51 the editors presented conflicting Greek and Latin texts, as follows:

> πάντες μὲν οὐ κοιμηθησόμεθα, πάντες δὲ ἀλλαγησόμεθα.
>
> (We shall not all sleep, but we shall all be transformed.)

> Omnes quidem resurgemus, sed non omnes immutabimur.
>
> (We shall all rise, but we shall not all be transformed.)

In their notes to this passage they did not attempt to explain the discrepancy between Greek and Latin texts as Lorenzo Valla had done, but only cited an alternate reading in the Greek text reported by Jerome:

> πάντες μὲν οὖν κοιμηθησόμεθα, ἀλλ' οὐ πάντες ἀλλαγησόμεθα.
>
> Omnes quidem igitur dormiemus, sed non omnes immutabimur.

(We shall all therefore sleep, but we shall not all be transformed.)

In a third note the Complutensian editors depended not on
Jerome, but on St. Thomas Aquinas as their textual authority.
They made an unwise decision in this case, for unlike Jerome,
St. Thomas offers reliable textual information for neither the
Greek nor the Latin New Testament. As a result, the editors
went badly astray in their treatment of the text in question,
the *comma Johanneum* at 1 John 5:7. Most Vulgate, but only
four Greek manuscripts include the passage, which mentions
the "three heavenly witness" (Father, Word, and Spirit) to
Christ's truth. Yet Latin Christians since the early Middle Ages
had considered this passage the clearest scriptural proof of the
doctrine of the Trinity. The Complutensian editors decided to
err on the side of orthodoxy. They quoted St. Thomas at length
and accepted his argument that anti-Trinitarian heretics suppressed the passage in many old manuscripts. What is more,
on their own initiative they added the passage to their Greek
text! Assuming the Vulgate to be more accurate than their
Greek manuscripts, they translated the *comma* from Latin into
Greek, as follows:

Quoniam tres sunt qui testimonium dant in celo: pater,
    verbum, et spiritus sanctus, et hi tres unum sunt.
ὅτι τρεῖς εἰσιν οἱ μαρτυροῦντες ἐν τῷ οὐρανῷ, ὁ
    πατὴρ καὶ ὁ λόγος καὶ τὸ ἅγιον πνεῦμα, καὶ οἱ
    τρεῖς εἰς τὸ ἐν εἰσι.
(There are three witnesses in heaven, the Father and the
    Word and the Holy Spirit, and the three are one.)

There can be no doubt the Complutensian editors translated
from Latin to Greek. They had access to none of the four
Greek manuscripts that present the passage, and their text agrees
with that found in none of the four. Futhermore, in a famous

dispute on the issue, Stunica could not cite manuscript evidence for the Greek text, but only assert stubbornly that Latin manuscripts were more reliable than Greek at 1 John 5:7.[58]

The three annotations so far discussed do not reveal great acuity or independence of judgment on the part of the Complutensian editors. The fourth note, however, that to Matt. 6:13, helps at least partly to salvage their reputations as competent critics. This note, which clearly exhibits Demetrius Ducas' influence, addressed a textual problem at the end of the Lord's Prayer. Most Greek manuscripts include a clause not found in the Latin text: "for thine is the kingdom, the power, and the glory forever." The note cast doubt on the authenticity of the clause; it suggested that the clause crept into Greek New Testament manuscripts by way of the Greek mass, where it occurs in the liturgy. Their critical approach to Greek manuscripts served the Complutensian editors well in this case, if not in that of the *comma Johanneum*. In fact, they improved on Lorenzo Valla's analysis of this passage. Valla assumed that Greek manuscripts are always better than Latin, and blinded by this prejudice, he assailed the Vulgate for omitting "a good chunk of the Lord's Prayer." The Complutensian editors understood better than Valla that Greek as well as Latin manuscripts are liable to corruption, and they were able to explain more accurately than Valla the problem of the clause in the Lord's Prayer. Modern scholars agree that the original gospel of Matthew did not present this clause, that liturgical adaptation of the Lord's Prayer influenced later Greek manuscripts,

---

[58] On the manuscript evidence for the passage, see Bruce M. Metzger, *Textual Commentary on the Greek New Testament*, 3rd ed. (New York, 1971), pp. 716-18. The most complete study of the problem remains August Bludau's somewhat dated work: "Der Beginn der Controverse über die Aechtheit des *Comma Johanneum* (1 Joh. 5, 7.8.) im 16. Jahrhundert," *Der Katholik*, 3rd ser. 26 (1902):25-51, 151-75. See pp. 151-57 for the Complutensian Polyglot. For Stunica's argument see his *Annotationes contra Erasmum Roterodamum*, fol. K ii[r].

and that the Latin text reflects the original Greek better than late Greek manuscripts themselves.[59]

On the evidence of these annotations, it is possible to return at least a preliminary verdict on the scholarly quality of the Complutensian New Testament. Only the last of the four notes suggests that the Complutensian editors possessed the independence of judgment usually associated with critical philological scholarship. On the other hand, all four notes betray a deep respect for the Vulgate: in no case did the editors tailor the Vulgate to fit the Greek text, though in two cases (Matt. 6:13 and 1 John 5:7) they altered the Greek to make it conform to the Vulgate. They had good reason to emend the Greek at Matt. 6:13, even though they apparently had no manuscript supporting the text they printed. At 1 John 5:7, however, they abandoned critical methods and without warrant accepted the Vulgate as the authoritative text of the New Testament. The four notes therefore yield a portrait of the Complutensian editors as extremely conservative philologists. They commanded impressive linguistic skills, and they were capable of explaining complicated textual problems, witness the analysis of Matt. 6:13. But they declined to employ their talents except in the service of traditional Latin orthodoxy. As a result, they did not advance understanding of the scriptures as much as they might have, had they less timidly applied sound philological methods.

Lack of reliable information has long stymied Complutensian scholarship. Since the New Testament manuscripts have escaped identification, scholars have had little more than the four notes discussed above to guide them in evaluating the quality of Complutensian New Testament scholarship. Those four notes may seem a slender base for the preliminary verdict just returned; indeed, it would not be easy to argue otherwise,

[59] Metzger, *Textual Commentary*, pp. 16-17.

especially in the light of most previous assessments. Earlier students have given the Complutensian editors high marks for their care and diligence in editing the Greek New Testament. Frederick Henry Scrivener, an exacting critic, was able to discover only fifty printer's errors in the Polyglot Greek New Testament, besides a few other minor problems, including 224 iotacisms and a handful of errors in spelling and usage.[60] The most appreciative student of the Complutensian Bible, Mariano Revilla Rico, concluded his account with fulsome praise for the Polyglot Greek New Testament: "among editions prepared in the sixteenth and seventeenth centuries, the Complutensian must be considered, if not the best, at least one of the most excellent."[61] Such favorable evaluations have been possible partly because scholars have been unable to consult the Complutensian manuscripts to see what textual problems the editors encountered and how they solved them. In order to confirm or challenge judgments like Revilla Rico's, one must gain more information on the Greek and Latin readings available to the Complutensian editors and learn how the editors appraised these readings. Only then might one accurately evaluate the quality of the Complutensian scholars' editorial work.

Fortunately, it is now possible to resort to a hitherto unused source that provides the sort of information needed, and that renders more secure the preliminary verdict returned above. The source is a set of unpublished manuscript annotations to the Complutensian New Testament. It survives in the remnant library of the College of San Ildefonso, now maintained by the University of Madrid.[62] The notes are bound together with

[60] *A Plain Introduction to the Criticism of the New Testament* (Cambridge, 1861), p. 293.

[61] *La Políglota de Alcalá*, p. 135.

[62] The annotations survive in MS. 117-Z-1 of the AHU. Revilla Rico first called attention to them, though he did not present a thorough study of them: *La Políglota de Alcalá*, pp. 167-71.

a copy of the Vulgate New Testament revised in the light of the Greek (to be discussed later), a copy of Lorenzo Valla's *Adnotationes* to the New Testament (edition of 1505), and an interpretative list of Hebrew, Aramaic, and Greek names found in the New Testament. The manuscript works lack titles, prefaces, and dedications, but the sixteenth-century binding describes its contents as the translation and annotation of the Complutensian New Testament: "TRANSLAT. ET ANNOT. COMPLUTENS. NOV. T." The two manuscript works—the annotations to the Complutensian New Testament and the revised translation of the Vulgate—are both unsigned and undated. The identity of their author(s) remains unknown, but both works were beyond doubt related intimately to the editing of the Complutensian New Testament.

The annotations are especially important for the following analysis, for they look very much like a set of philological notes drawn up by one or more of the Complutensian editors as they prepared the text of the New Testament itself. As I have argued before, peculiar readings cited in the manuscript annotations suggest that the annotations predated the printing of the Polyglot New Testament. The annotations survive in one fair copy. In comments on many passages, the annotations present Greek texts significantly different from those of the Polyglot New Testament. In comments to a few of these passages (discussed in more detail below) a second hand introduced marginal notes citing readings in the Greek text that agree with the Polyglot. It is extremely difficult to explain why the author(s) of the original annotations—who were clearly associated with the Complutensian editorial team—would not accept the Polyglot's readings as a standard text, if they were available.[63] It thus appears that the manuscript annotations were a sort of working copy of philological notes prepared by

[63] Bentley, "New Light," pp. 148-52.

one or more of the Complutensian scholars as they edited the Polyglot New Testament. As such, the manuscript annotations become one of the few sources to yield reliable insights into the editorial thinking of the Complutensian scholars.

The main purpose of the manuscript annotations was to point out differences between the Greek New Testament and the Vulgate, but without suggesting so pointedly as Lorenzo Valla that the Vulgate presented an inaccurate translation of the Greek. The annotations diligently noted passages where the Vulgate omitted something found in the Greek or added something not found in the Greek. Like Valla, they reported at Apoc. 4:8 that their Greek manuscripts repeated the word ἅγιος ("holy") nine times, where the Vulgate presented *sanctus* only three times. At 1 Tim. 1:17 and Jude, v. 25 the annotations pointed to an omission that later would figure importantly in Erasmus' controversies on New Testament scholarship. In both places the Vulgate offers praise "to the only God" (*soli deo*), where the Greek speaks of "the only wise God" (μόνῳ σοφῷ θεῷ).

Unlike Valla, however, the annotations refrained from casting aspersions on the Vulgate New Testament. In fact, in many places the annotations apparently sought to shield the Vulgate from criticism. The annotations repeated verbatim, for example, the better part of the note on the Lord's Prayer (Matt. 6:13) found in the margin of the Complutensian Bible, and like the Polyglot, the annotations openly charged the Greek text with error and by implication absolved the Vulgate of responsibility for corruption. The annotations defended the Vulgate also by distinguishing between the original Vulgate and later, corrupted copies of it. A substantial minority of the notes reported that readings in early Vulgate manuscripts ("in Bibliis nostris antiquis") agree with the Greek text, though the commonly accepted Vulgate text, presumably that found in later manuscripts, disagreed. In the gospel of Matthew, for example, the annotations noted 352 differences between the Greek text and the Vulgate; but in 59 cases they found agreement between the Greek text and early Vulgate manuscripts. The annotations therefore reinforce the suggestion offered above: the Complutensian editors often chose to employ their philological talents in such a way as to protect the reputation of the Vulgate.

Their eagerness to defend the Vulgate led the Complutensian editors to an important insight regarding corruption in the Latin text of the New Testament. In several notes to passages in the synoptic gospels they showed that corruption sprang not from faulty translation, but from the problem of assimilation. They recognized, in other words, that scribes sometimes carelessly added to one passage a word, phrase, or even a whole sentence that properly belongs to a different, though similar passage. At Matt. 24:42 they found a whole sentence not witnessed in the Greek, but derived instead from Luke 17:34: "Duo in lecto: unus assumetur et unus relinquetur"—"[That night there will be] two people in bed; one will be taken and one left behind." Similarly, they noticed a long clause at Matt. 27:35 witnessed neither in the Greek nor in early Vulgate manuscripts, but adapted from the parallel text at John 19:24. At Luke 12:31 they found words creeping in from the parallel text at Matt. 6:33. The Complutensian editors were not always right in suspecting assimilation as the cause of corruption.[64] Nevertheless, these notes offer further

[64] At Matt. 17:2 and Luke 23:39 the annotations suggested assimilation as the explanation for differences between Greek and Vulgate texts. Modern editions, however, present readings rejected by the Complutensian editors, "sicut nix" ("like snow") and "latronibus" ("thieves"), respectively, as the original texts of the Vulgate, though they do not accurately represent the Greek. Even here, though, the annotations made a reasonable case: "sicut nix" could easily have been assimilated from Mark 9:3 and "latronibus" from Matt. 27:44 or Mark 15:27. It is only the extensive knowledge of Vulgate manuscripts, un-

evidence that the Complutensian editors were competent philologists, especially when serving the cause of tradition and orthodoxy.

So far analysis of the manuscript annotations has concentrated on points that the author(s) intentionally made in the individual notes. The annotations also harbor much unintentional evidence, however, that sheds light on the editorial work of the Complutensian scholars. The annotations often—in fact, almost always—mentioned the readings found in the Complutensian Greek and Latin manuscripts. The annotations therefore provide at least some of the information scholars have lacked because of their inability to identify the Complutensian manuscripts of the Greek New Testament. Collation of these readings with those published in the Polyglot is a tedious business, but it can reveal interesting things about the editing of both the Greek and the Latin New Testaments.

The Greek texts cited in the annotations usually agree with those published in the Polyglot, but in some cases, especially in the gospels, the two works present significantly different readings. In eight cases the annotations almost enable us to reconstruct the editing of the Polyglot Greek New Testament. The original annotations to the eight texts, all in the gospels of Matthew and Mark, presented Greek readings that differ significantly from those found in the Polyglot. But after the annotations were prepared in fair copy, a second hand noted alternate Greek readings in the margins beside the eight notes. In every single case the reading reported in the margin supports the Vulgate. In every single case, too, the Polyglot presents the reading reported in the marginal note, not that originally cited in the annotations. Table 1 lists the texts and the different readings found in the original notes and marginal notes of the manuscript annotations. What does all this mean?

---

available in the sixteenth century, that proves the Complutensian editors wrong in these notes.

Table 1

Texts in the gospels of Matthew and Mark where marginal notes in the manuscript annotations offer significantly different Greek readings from those found in the original notes.

Text	Original Reading in the Annotations (disagrees with the Polyglot and Vulgate)	Marginal Reading in the Annotations (agrees with the Polyglot and Vulgate)
Matt. 13:22	ἀγάπη	ἀπάτη
Matt. 16:3	γὰρ ὁ οὐρανός	γὰρ στυγνάζων ὁ οὐρανός
Matt. 16:27	'εν τῇ δόξῃ	ἐν τῇ δόξῃ τοῦ πατρὸς
Matt. 25:29	καὶ ὃ ἔχει	καὶ ὃ δοκεῖ ἐχεῖν
Matt. 26:26	καὶ εὐχαριστήσας	καὶ εὐλογήσας
Matt. 26:71	τοῦ γαλιλαίου	τοῦ ναζαραίου
Mark 4:24	μετρηθήσεται ὑμῖν	μετρηθήσεται καὶ προστεθήσεται ὑμῖν
Mark 7:22	ἀσέλγεια, ὑπερηφανία	ἀσέλγεια, ὀφθαλμὸς, πονηρός, βλασφημία, ὑπερηφανία

The Polyglot's editors must originally have assumed one reading—that originally noted in the annotations—to be the true text in these eight passages. Later they noticed another reading that offered the advantage of supporting the Vulgate. A conscientious member of the editorial team introduced the new reading into the margin of the annotations, and the editors brought the Polyglot Greek text in line with their new information. The Complutensian editors were therefore disposed to establish a Greek text of the New Testament that supported the Vulgate.

By no means did the Complutensian editors always alter the Greek text in order to harmonize it with the Vulgate. Their Greek and Vulgate texts diverge at hundreds of points. Yet besides the eight mentioned above, it is possible to cite many other passages where the Polyglot Greek text differs from that cited in the annotations, and where the Polyglot reading supports the Vulgate. In the gospel of John alone I find eight more cases fitting this pattern. Table 2 lists the texts and different readings found in the manuscript annotations and the Complutensian New Testament. In none of these new cases do the annotations cite a variant reading, either in the original note or in a marginal note. It is therefore impossible to say for sure whether or not the Complutensian editors had manuscript support for the readings they published in the Polyglot at these passages. On the other hand, it is certain that the editors established their Greek text in a conservative way. The annotations came from the circle of New Testament scholars at Alcalá, and the editors unquestionably knew the readings cited in them. Yet they chose different readings in preparing their Greek text—readings that had the attraction of agreeing with the Vulgate.

The annotations shed even more light on the editing of the

Table 2

Texts in the gospel of John where the manuscript annotations present Greek readings significantly different from those published in the Complutensian New Testament.

Text	Reading in the Annotations (disagrees with the Vulgate)	Reading in the Polyglot (agrees with the Vulgate)
John 1:31	omit: κ'αγὼ οὐκ ᾔδειν αὐτόν	add: κ'αγὼ οὐκ ᾔδειν αὐτόν
John 4:1	ὁ κύριος	ὁ Ἰησοῦς
John 6:1	τῆς θαλάσσης τῆς τιβεριάδος	τῆς θαλάσσης τῆς γαλιλαίας τῆς τιβεριάδος
John 6:14	ὁ ἐποίησεν	ὁ ἐποίησεν σημεῖον
John 6:15	ἀνεχώρησεν εἰς τὸ ὄρος	ἀνεχώρησεν πάλιν εἰς τὸ ὄρος
John 6:71	omit: εἷς ὢν ἐκ τῶν δώδεκα	add: εἷς ὢν ἐκ τῶν δώδεκα
John 12:47	καὶ πιστεύσῃ	καὶ μὴ φυλάξῃ
John 14:3	omit: καὶ ἐὰν πορευθῶ καὶ ἑτοιμάσω ὑμῖν τόπον	add: καὶ ἐὰν πορευθῶ καὶ ἑτοιμάσω ὑμῖν τόπον

Vulgate than on the preparation of the Greek New Testament, because they provide information on variant Vulgate readings and the Complutensian editors' assessments of them. It is possible to know many readings the editors accepted as the standard text of the Vulgate, for they appear at the head of the individual notes in the annotations. It is also possible to know many readings they considered better or older than the standard texts, for the annotations often record variant readings found in early Vulgate manuscripts ("in Bibliis nostris antiquis"). It is possible to know finally which passages the editors considered to conflict with the Greek New Testament, for the main purpose of the annotations was to point out differences between the Greek and Latin New Testaments. By examining the Polyglot edition of the Vulgate New Testament—bearing in mind all this information from the annotations—one may develop some reliable judgments regarding the scholarly quality of the Complutensian Vulgate.

Though Antonio de Nebrija wanted to publish a thoroughly revised Latin New Testament, as seen above, the Polyglot presented the Vulgate. The editors of the Vulgate, perhaps led by Stunica, largely refrained from altering traditional readings, even where they conflicted with the Greek New Testament. The annotations point out hundreds of differences, both small and large, between Greek and Latin New Testaments; in the large majority of cases the Polyglot Vulgate agrees with the standard text of the Vulgate cited in the annotations. The editors therefore left the commonly accepted text of the Vulgate largely intact; they simply did not see it as their duty to revise the Vulgate, or to improve it, or to bring it into line with the Greek New Testament. Thus far their editing of the Vulgate is easy enough to understand.

Upon analysis of those passages where they did introduce changes into the standard text of the Vulgate, however, their editing becomes more difficult to explain. In fact, I think we can only say that they treated the Vulgate in a most erratic way. The editors occasionally corrected the standard Vulgate text by readings they found in early manuscripts. At 1 Cor. 1:10, for example, they changed *scientia* ("knowledge") to *sententia* ("opinion"), and at Eph. 3:4 they changed *ministerio* ("ministerial office") to *mysterio* ("mystery"). In both cases the annotations report the latter reading in early Vulgate manuscripts; in both cases they find the latter reading a better reflection of the Greek text; and in both cases the Complutensian editors presented the latter, older, and better reading in their edition of the Vulgate. The editors also took minor corrections from early Vulgate manuscripts at many other passages.[65]

This does not mean, however, that the editors attempted systematically to recover the earliest possible text of the Vulgate. More often than not, the Polyglot retains standard Vulgate readings, even where Greek texts and early Vulgate manuscripts agree in a different, and often better reading. The editors thus included in their edition an opening clause at John 14:1 which they found neither in Greek nor in early Latin manuscripts, but only in recent Vulgate manuscripts: "Et ait discipulis suis, . . ."—"and he said to his disciples, . . ." At 2 Cor. 4:9 the editors included an entire sentence on the strength of similar evidence: "Humiliamur, sed non confundimur"—"We are abased, but not confounded." Modern editors agree with many readings in the Polyglot Vulgate, but on the basis of evidence cited in the annotations these readings must be considered the inferior variants.[66] Certainly the

[65] For example, they presented *plebi* for *plebis* at Luke 1:68; Iona for Ioanna at John 1:42; *principes sacerdotum* for *principes* at John 7:32; and they added *dicentes* at John 9:2—all of this on evidence from early Vulgate manuscripts.

[66] The Polyglot for example offers the following standard Vulgate readings in the face of opposition from both Greek and early Vulgate manuscripts: Israel for Jerusalem at Luke 2:38; *spiritu sancto* for *spiritu* at John 3:5; *ambulat* for *ambulabit* at John 8:12; inclusion of Thoma at John 20:29; inclu-

Complutensian editors had adequate reason to correct the standard readings of the Vulgate when they found early Vulgate manuscripts and the Greek text allied against them. Apparently they were so deeply committed to preserving the integrity of the traditional text that they decided to keep emendations to a minimum.

And yet—the editors in a few places emended the Vulgate on the strength of the Greek text alone! Such corrections occur only rarely in the Polyglot Vulgate, and they never involve important changes in text or message. The emendations remain significant, however, because of the editorial principle they presume. In most cases they find support in no Vulgate manuscripts whatever, so that only conscious alteration on the basis of the Greek text can account for their presence in the Polyglot. Most of these emendations concern verb tenses. At John 7:31 the Polyglot Vulgate presents *fecit* ("he made") instead of *facit* ("he makes"). Twice the editors changed *audivimus* ("we have heard") to *audimus* ("we hear"), at Acts 2:8, 11. Three times they changed *vivit* ("he lives") to *vivet* ("he will live"), at Rom. 1:17, Gal. 3:11, and Heb. 10:38: "The just man will live by faith." At 2 Cor. 4:4 the editors added a word to the Vulgate, *eis* ("in them"); they were evidently unaware that many Vulgate manuscripts present *illis* ("in these") here, a word that also satisfies the requirements of the Greek.[67]

In general, then, anarchy reigned over principle in the editing of the Polyglot edition of the Vulgate New Testament. The Complutensian editors seem to have followed no principle consistently in this part of their work. Perhaps the most

---

sion of *interpretationes sermonum* at 1 Cor. 12:28; inclusion of the phrase *in hac parte* at 2 Cor. 11:21; Cephae for Petro at Gal. 2:14.

[67] They may have been unaware also of manuscripts which present *in eum* at John 4:41 and *in te* at Mark 14:29. In both cases the annotations point out the lack of the phrase in the Vulgate; in neither case do the annotations cite the phrase in early Vulgate manuscripts; in both cases the Polyglot presents the phrase.

baffling passage in the Polyglot Vulgate is John 12:8: "For you always have paupers with you, but you will not always have me." The Greek text twice presents the verb ἔχετε ("you have"); the Complutensian manuscripts of the Vulgate twice present *habebitis* ("you will have"). (More accurate Vulgate manuscripts read *habetis*—"you have.") The annotations twice note that ἔχετε calls for *habetis* (present tense), not *habebitis* (future tense). But the Polyglot presents the first verb in the present tense and the second in the future! One can conclude only that the editing of the Polyglot Vulgate was a haphazard, not to say a sloppy affair.

In the lack of the Complutensian manuscripts of the Greek New Testament, the manuscript annotations alone provide the bits of information that make it possible to evaluate the scholarly quality of the Complutensian editors' work. Unfortunately, the annotations do little more than that. Only a few notes proceed from textual annotation to exegesis, and those few never stray from a basic, literal explanation of the passage in question. Unlike Lorenzo Valla, the Complutensian scholars preferred not to allow philological considerations to undermine traditional interpretations. In no case do the annotations develop a point like Valla's at 1 Cor. 15:10, for example, where he rejected the scholastic category of cooperating grace on the basis of the Greek text. The Complutensian scholars knew Valla's thought on this passage, but did not appreciate it: in the copy of Valla's *Adnotationes* bound with the Complutensian manuscript annotations, an angry hand blotted out Valla's entire note to 1 Cor. 15:10. In the manuscript annotations themselves there appears only a brief note which points out the Vulgate's slightly inaccurate translation and corrects it by the addition of two words, here italicized: "Non ego autem, sed gratia dei *quae est* mecum"—"Not I myself, but the grace of God *that is* with me."

As in textual criticism and exegesis, so also in translation the Complutensian scholars remained conservative. As Revilla Rico pointed out long ago, there is a manuscript Latin translation of the New Testament, not the Vulgate, bound together with the manuscript annotations. The translation was based on the Polyglot Greek text, but it is not the fresh, independent version Revilla Rico thought.[68] It is instead a slightly revised Vulgate, perhaps the sort of work Antonio de Nebrija intended to prepare for the Polyglot Bible. The translation is closely related to the manuscript annotations: in most places where the annotations find differences between Greek and Latin New Testaments, the translation offers a Latin text that more accurately reflects the Greek. Language and word order remain so close to the Vulgate, however, that it is misleading to call this work a fresh Latin translation of the New Testament. In fact, the manuscript translation preserves standard Vulgate readings in many places where the author(s) of the annotations considered them inaccurate representations of the Greek. At Luke 1:28 the annotations suggest "Gaude gratia plena"—"Hail ye, full of grace"—as the best translation of the Greek: χαῖρε, κεχαριτωμένη. The manuscript translation, however, repeats the Vulgate's "Ave gratia plena." This is of course a translation highly honored by time and liturgy, but the manuscript translation follows the Vulgate also at less sensitive points. At Heb. 3:3, for example, the manuscript annotations agreed with Lorenzo Valla that the Vulgate presented a confusing translation. The annotations suggest rewording: "Quanto ampliorem honorem habet ille qui fabricavit domum magis quam ipsa domus?"—"How much more honor does he have who has built a house than the house itself?" The manuscript translation, however, repeats the Vulgate, only changing the case of the word *domus* ("house") from genitive to ablative: "Quanto ampliorem honorem habet domo

---

[68] Revilla Rico, *La Políglota de Alcalá*, pp. 168-69.

[Vulgate: *domus*] qui fabricavit illam?"—"How much more honor than the house has he who built it?"

Thus do the manuscript annotations and translation draw the veil from the Complutensian editors' work, and the New Testament scholars emerge from their previous obscurity as an extremely conservative scholarly circle. When confronted with variant readings in the Greek New Testament, they selected those that agreed with the Vulgate. At 1 John 5:7 they took it on themselves consciously to alter the Greek text so as to bring it in line with the Vulgate and medieval Latin theology. The Vulgate itself appears in sullied form in the Polyglot, since the editors consistently employed no editorial principle, but haphazardly followed first one, then another. Sometimes they followed early Vulgate manuscripts; but often they rejected their early texts in favor of standard Vulgate readings; and on occasion they emended the Vulgate on the strength of the Greek text alone. In short, the Polyglot editions of the Greek and Latin New Testament did not result from careful, professional editorial scholarship.

Nevertheless, students from the sixteenth to the twentieth century have praised the Polyglot—not entirely without reason. The Complutensian editors, after all, took on an arduous, intricate, complex task; and at the time of the printing (1514-1517) their editions of the Hebrew, Greek, and Latin scriptures were probably the finest scholars could use. As pioneers, the Complutenisan editors may be excused if their work does not meet the exacting standards of modern New Testament scholarship. Upon completion of the Polyglot Bible, Alcalá swelled with pride, according to Alvar Gómez, and no one was more pleased than the Polyglot's chief patron, Cardinal Ximénez. The last volume of the Old Testament bears a colophon dated 10 July 1517. Ximénez had by this time fallen gravely ill; indeed his death came soon thereafter, 8 November 1517. But when the completed Polyglot reached him, so

Alvar Gómez reported, the Cardinal was overcome with joy. Of all his accomplishments, he announced, the edition of the scriptures was the most praiseworthy, since it made available to all the sources of the Christian religion.[69]

The Complutensian New Testament was indeed a magnificent work, even if it does not warrant the exaggerated praise of Revilla Rico and others. For the historian of scholarship it is a work of no little significance. Like Lorenzo Valla's notes on the New Testament, it illustrates the slow and painful process by which sound philological criteria came to govern modern scholarship. Valla assumed too quickly that any Greek manuscript presented a better New Testament than any Latin text. The Complutensian scholars assumed too quickly that differences between the Greek and Vulgate New Testaments resulted from corruption in the Greek tradition. Beginning with Erasmus, later scholars would improve on the work of both Valla and the Complutensian editors because they appreciated better the qualities and limitations of both Latin and Greek textual traditions, they recognized more complicated problems than their predecessors, and they devised more sophisticated methods for solving those problems. Later advances must not be allowed to obscure the achievements of Valla and the Complutensian circle, however, for without their example successors might never have appeared.

[69] *De rebus gestis*, fol. 38ᵛ (MS. fol. 79ʳ).

FOUR

Desiderius Erasmus: Christian Humanist

F EW EUROPEAN intellectuals have enjoyed such general prestige and influence as did Erasmus of Rotterdam about 1516. On this frail scholar men hung their hopes for the revival of learning and good literature, the restoration of pristine Christian piety, and the reform of Church, state, and society. There were detractors, too, of course: the theologians of Paris and Louvain, for example, wanted no part of revival, restoration, and reform, at least not along the lines envisioned by Erasmus. But in 1516 these men could almost be ignored. They lacked Erasmus' personal charm, his powers of persuasion, and his influence with popes, princes, and prelates. Northern humanism stood at high tide in 1516, the year More published his *Utopia* and Erasmus his *Education of the Christian Prince* and his editions of Seneca and St. Jerome.

It was also the year Froben's press completed Erasmus' edition of the Greek New Testament, the first and one of the most influential ever published. In 1633 the Elzevir brothers published a slightly revised version of Erasmus' text and called it the *textus receptus*, the standard or commonly received text, which dominated studies on the Greek New Testament until

112

the nineteenth century.[1] In view of the long-term significance of Erasmus' work, it is surprising that scholars have not examined its composition, except superficially. They have studied almost every other important aspect of Erasmus' life and work: they have presented marvelous biographies,[2] for example; analyses of his religious thought and theology;[3] studies of his reaction to the Reformation;[4] investigations of his political thought and observations;[5] researches into his reputation in later ages;[6] and even a report on his skeleton,[7] to mention only a few subjects explored by Erasmus scholars. The full extent of scholarship on Erasmus can be appreciated only by consulting Jean-Claude Margolin's three thick volumes of bibliography.[8] Yet in all this massive body of literature on Erasmus' career, the interested reader will not find an adequate study of the philological foundations of his New Tes-

[1] Bruce M. Metzger, *The Text of the New Testament*, 2nd ed. (New York, 1968), pp. 95-146.

[2] Roland H. Bainton, *Erasmus of Christendom* (New York, 1969); James D. Tracy, *Erasmus: The Growth of a Mind* (Geneva, 1972); Jan Huizinga, *Erasmus and the Age of Reformation*, trans. F. Hopman (New York, 1957).

[3] Georges Chantraine, *"Mystère" et "philosophie du Christ" selon Érasme* (Namur, 1971); Ernst-Wilhelm Kohls, *Die Theologie des Erasmus*, 2 vols. (Basle, 1966); Marjorie O'Rourke Boyle, *Erasmus on Language and Method in Theology* (Toronto, 1977).

[4] Karl Heinz Oelrich, *Der späte Erasmus und die Reformation* (Münster, 1961); C. Augustijn, *Erasmus en de Reformatie* (Amsterdam, 1962).

[5] Hans Treinen, *Studien zur Idee der Gemeinschaft bei Erasmus von Rotterdam* (Saarlouis, 1955); James D. Tracy, *The Politics of Erasmus* (Toronto, 1978).

[6] Andreas Flitner, *Erasmus im Urteil seiner Nachwelt* (Tübingen, 1952); Bruce Mansfield, *Phoenix of His Age: Interpretations of Erasmus, c. 1550-1750* (Toronto, 1979).

[7] A. Werthemann, *Schädel und Gebeine des Erasmus von Rotterdam* (Basle, 1928-1929).

[8] *Quatorze années de bibliographie érasmienne (1936-1949)* (Paris, 1969); *Douze années de bibliographie érasmienne (1950-1961)* (Paris, 1963); *Neuf années de bibliographie érasmienne (1962-1970)* (Paris, 1977).

tament scholarship.[9] Erasmus' Greek text dominated New Testament research for three centuries, but the methods, principles, and reasoning that governed its preparation remain unexamined. The long chapter to follow I think requires no further apology.

[9] The most complete study remains A. Bludau's long dated work, *Die beiden ersten Erasmus-Ausgaben des Neuen Testaments und ihre Gegner* (Freiburg-im-Br., 1902). Bludau limits his study to the first two editions of Erasmus' New Testament; he makes no attempt to analyze Erasmus' methods of scholarship; his strong point is to set the New Testament in the context of Erasmus' movements, correspondence, and controversies. Most other studies of Erasmus' New Testament concentrate on his exegesis. See the following studies: John B. Payne, "Erasmus and Lefèvre d'Étaples as Interpreters of Paul," *ARG* 65 (1974):54-82; and "Erasmus: Interpreter of Romans," *Sixteenth Century Essays and Studies* 2 (1971):1-35; C.A.L. Jarrott, "Erasmus' Biblical Humanism," *Studies in the Renaissance* 17 (1970):119-52; and Albert Rabil, *Erasmus and the New Testament: The Mind of a Christian Humanist* (San Antonio, 1972). For analysis of Erasmus' philological scholarship, see my preliminary studies: "Erasmus' *Annotationes in Novum Testamentum* and the Textual Criticism of the Gospels," *ARG* 67 (1976):33-53; and "Biblical Philology and Christian Humanism: Lorenzo Valla and Erasmus as Scholars of the Gospels," *SCJ* 8 no. 2 (1977), pp. 9-28. H. J. de Jonge has recently argued that Erasmus' main purpose in publishing his New Testament was to present a more accurate version of the Latin scriptures than that found in the Vulgate, and that his Greek text was intended to play only a minor role in the project as a whole. See his "Novum testamentum a nobis versum. De essentie van Erasmus' uitgave van het Nieuwe Testament," *Lampas* 15 (1982):231-48. While agreeing with one of de Jonge's major points—that scholars have not generally recognized the importance Erasmus attached to preparing an accurate Latin translation of the New Testament—I must point out two considerations that make it difficult to accept his thesis in its entirety. In the first place, Erasmus did not present his own translation in the first edition of his New Testament. In 1516 he published a revised Vulgate alongside his Greek text; his own fresh version appeared only in 1519, in the second edition of the New Testament. In the second place, I believe de Jonge underestimates the amount of time and energy Erasmus expended on the Greek text of the New Testament. Following pages will demonstrate that Erasmus recognized the need for a Greek New Testament as early as 1507 and that from 1511 onward he carefully studied and collated more Greek manuscripts of the New Testament than has been generally realized. Erasmus clearly regarded his edition of the Greek text as a work of primary importance.

Development and Sources of Erasmus' Work

Despite his massive correspondence, the genesis of Erasmus' New Testament scholarship remains shrouded in obscurity. As early as 1501 he reported himself hard at work on a commentary (*enarratio*) on the Pauline epistles.[10] He soon found his progress stymied by lack of Greek—which he began to study only in 1500—but not before turning out, "in one quick assault, as it were," four volumes on the Epistle to the Romans alone.[11] These early commentaries seem not to have survived, except insofar as Erasmus might have included excerpts from them in his later works. They cannot be identified with Erasmus' *Annotations* to the New Testament: the *Annotations* depend upon a thorough knowledge of Greek; and in any case, other information dates their origin at least a decade later than the commentaries of 1501. Furthermore, John Payne argues convincingly that the early commentaries cannot be identified with Erasmus' *Paraphrases* on the New Testament either: Erasmus always distinguished between a commentary and a paraphrase, and as late as 1522—five years after the *Paraphrases* began to appear—he promised his readers a complete commentary on Paul. No such commentary ever appeared, and in 1527 Erasmus withdrew his promise.[12]

Thus Erasmus' earliest New Testament scholarship lies beyond retrieval. One might safely hazard the guess, however,

[10] *EE*, no. 164 (1:374-75). This letter is composed of excerpts from Erasmus' *Enchiridion militis christiani*, which is itself cast in the form of a long epistle. The best critical edition of the work is that found in Holborn. See esp. p. 135.

[11] *EE*, no. 181 (1: 404), a letter of December 1504, where Erasmus described events of three years earlier. Erasmus first mentioned his study of Greek in a letter to his friend James Batt in March of 1500, *EE*, no. 123 (1:285).

[12] Payne, "Erasmus: Interpreter of Romans," pp. 4-6.

that its character differed considerably from his surviving works. In 1501 Erasmus was held in thrall not by philological criticism, but rather by the allegorical method of exegesis. In his early manual of theology, the *Enchiridion militis chrisitiani*—where he first announced his Pauline commentary—he urged the reader to study exegetes who "go as far as possible beyond the literal sense." He cited Jesus, Paul, Origen, Jerome, Ambrose, and even the Pseudo-Dionysius as those exegetes who most fruitfully developed the spiritual senses of scripture.[13] Erasmus' early commentaries more than likely reflected this deep interest in allegorical exegesis.

His surviving New Testament scholarship took its inspiration from a very different attitude. In the summer of 1504, while working in the library of the Abbey of Parc, near Louvain, Erasmus encountered by serendipity a manuscript of Lorenzo Valla's *Adnotationes* to the New Testament. From that point one can trace the development of Erasmus' New Testament scholarship in its characteristic form. In December of 1504 he wrote to John Colet saying he intended to devote the rest of his life to the study of scripture.[14] In April of the next year he published Valla's *Adnotationes* in Paris at the press of his friend, Josse Bade. The letter of dedication (to Christopher Fisher) did not conceal Erasmus' excitement at discovering a philologist (*grammaticus*) who took such a fresh, critical approach as Valla to the manifestly corrupted Vulgate.[15] Probably in 1505, but in any case before 1506, Erasmus began his own new translation of the Greek New Testament. His scribe, Peter Meghen, prepared fair copies of the translation in several large, handsome volumes, most of which bear colophons dated 1506 or 1509.[16] Erasmus published this

[13] Holborn, pp. 28-38, 67-88, esp. pp. 33, 71.
[14] *EE*, no. 181 (1:404-405).
[15] *EE*, no. 182 (1:406-12).
[16] Heinz Holeczek argues that Erasmus prepared his translation while in

translation only in 1519, when he used it as a replacement for the Vulgate in the second edition of his New Testament, but Meghen's manuscripts prove that Erasmus had set his hand to the improvement of the Latin scriptures long before then.

Meanwhile, by 1507 Erasmus began to see the need also for a reliable text of the Greek New Testament. On 28 October of that year he wrote Aldus Manutius, the Venetian printer, asking among other things why Aldus' long-promised edition of the Greek New Testament had been delayed.[17] I doubt that Erasmus planned his own edition as early as 1507, as one recent scholar has suggested.[18] He had consulted Greek manuscripts in preparing his Latin translation of the New Testament, but there is no evidence at that early date that he compared and collated manuscripts with an eye toward editing the Greek New Testament.

That work began in late 1511 or early 1512. In August of 1511 Erasmus went to Cambridge to begin lecturing on Greek. He addressed his first letter from Cambridge to his old friend,

---

England in 1505 and 1506: *Humanistische Bibelphilologie als Reformproblem bei Erasmus von Rotterdam, Thomas More und William Tyndale* (Leiden, 1975), pp. 101-13. This dating seems likely enough, though it cannot be proved beyond doubt. The manuscripts containing Erasmus' translation are the following, listed in chronological order of their preparation with their contents: British Library, Reg. 1. E. V. 2 (Apostolic Epistles, 1 Nov. 1506); Cambridge, University Library, Dd. VII. 3 (Matthew and Mark, 8 May 1509); British Library, Reg. 1. E. V. 1 (Luke and John, 7 Sept. 1509); Hatfield House, Cecil Papers, MS. 324 (Acts and Apocalypse, undated). The last cited manuscript probably was written later than the others. See J. B. Trapp, "Notes on Manuscripts Written by Peter Meghen," *The Book Collector* 24 (1975):89, no. 9. Meghen later produced even more manuscript copies of Erasmus' Latin New Testament, at least one of which survives in Oxford, Corpus Christi College, MSS. E. 4. 9-10. Trapp suggests this copy was prepared between 1514 and 1520: pp. 88-89, no. 8. Father Henri Gibaud has recently completed work on an edition, soon to be published, of Erasmus' early translation of the New Testament into Latin.

[17] *EE*, no. 207 (1:437-39).

[18] Louis Bouyer, "Erasmus in Relation to the Medieval Biblical Tradition," *CHB*, 2:496, 498.

Colet, who had lectured on the Pauline epistles in the 1490s. Almost as a postscript he told Colet of his plans: "I shall perhaps take on also your man, St. Paul. Behold the daring of your friend Erasmus."[19] Erasmus soon found Greek manuscripts at Cambridge—at least one of them identifiable, as later pages will show—and after a year (in the autumn of 1512) he reported his intention to complete an emendation (*castigatio*) of the New Testament.[20] Some months later he wrote Colet (11 June 1513) that he had finished a collation (*collatio*) of the New Testament and planned to start work on Jerome.[21] This chronology matches the testimony of Erasmus' famous letter to Servatius Roger, prior of Erasmus' home monastery at Steyn. In this letter (8 July 1514) Erasmus diplomatically refused Servatius' command to return to the cloister, and he justified his life in the world by pointing to his accomplishments of the past two years. Among other things he mentioned his editorial labors on the scriptures: "After collation of Greek and other ancient manuscripts, I have emended the whole New Testament, and I have annotated over a thousand passages, not without benefit to theologians."[22] News of this work spread quickly. As early as April 1514, Jan Becker wrote Erasmus almost panting for a copy of the revised New Testament and annotations.[23]

Printers also learned of Erasmus' work. Bade hoped to publish it,[24] but Johann Froben eventually got the contract. Erasmus went up the Rhine in the summer of 1514; in August he arrived at his destination, Basle, where he intended to see a new edition of the *Adages* through Froben's press. He was

---

[19] *EE*, no. 225 (1:466).
[20] *EE*, no. 264 (1:517).
[21] *EE*, no. 270 (1:527).
[22] *EE*, no. 296 (1:570).
[23] *EE*, no. 291 (1:558).
[24] *EE*, no. 434 (2:272).

cordially greeted, not to say flattered, by the humanists of upper Germany, with whom he developed close relations.[25] Yet he delayed making a firm decision on a publisher for his New Testament, and some have argued that he wanted the famed house of Aldus to do the job.[26] Indeed, as late as April of 1515 Erasmus had not made up his mind where to publish his work: in that month Beatus Rhenanus wrote twice on behalf of Froben, who desperately wanted Erasmus' Greek New Testament, and promised to match any offer to get it.[27] It looks to me, however, as though Erasmus had never excluded the possibility of entrusting his work to Froben. In August of 1514 he wrote Johann Reuchlin, requesting the loan of an important manuscript of the Greek New Testament—MS. 1, to be discussed below—and asking further that Reuchlin allow Froben access to it.[28] Over the next six months Erasmus labored over this and other manuscripts at Basle.[29] More than once in that period he mentioned the New Testament in the same breath as other works intended for Froben's press, especially the *Adages* and the editions of Seneca and St. Jerome.[30] And already by January of 1515 Jan Becker had word from Erasmus and others that Erasmus would leave the New Testament with printers at Basle, before departing on a trip he planned (but did not make) to Italy.[31] Though inconclusive, the evidence thus suggests that Erasmus always regarded Froben as a prime candidate for publisher of his New Testament. One might even surmise from Beatus Rhenanus' pleas

[25] James D. Tracy, "Erasmus Becomes a German," *RQ* 21 (1968):281-88.

[26] Rabil, *Erasmus and the New Testament*, p. 90; Basil Hall, "Erasmus: Biblical Scholar and Reformer," in *Erasmus*, ed. T. A. Dorey (London, 1970), p. 95.

[27] *EE*, nos. 328, 330 (2:63, 65).

[28] *EE*, no. 300 (2:4-5).

[29] *EE*, no. 322 (2:47).

[30] *EE*, nos. 305, 307 (2:23, 26).

[31] *EE*, no. 320 (2:44).

of April 1515 that Erasmus delayed his decision in order to gain from Froben the best possible terms!

In any case, Froben received the commission that he so dearly desired. Erasmus predicted in May of 1515 that he would publish his work very soon—"next summer"—and by 30 August he was able to report that his Greek New Testament, Latin translation, and annotations were in the press.[32] They cannot have been very far into production, for on 11 September Nikolaus Gerbel, one of Froben's employees, addressed a letter to Erasmus raising questions about the format of the edition and advising specifically that the Greek and Latin texts be printed separately.[33] Erasmus eventually had his way—the texts appeared in parallel columns—but his difficulties were not yet at an end. Printing was interrupted later in September for lack of proofreaders, Erasmus wearily reported, but was resumed by 2 October.[34] Several months later Erasmus explained further problems in a letter to Guillaume Budé. During the printing of his New Testament, he said, he came under the pressure of certain unnamed people—meaning no doubt Gerbel, Johannes Oecolampadius, and Beatus Rhenanus, all then employed by Froben and assigned to work on the New Testament—who urged him to revise and expand his work on the spot. Thus, even as both the New Testament and the edition of Jerome went through the press, he augmented his annotations and introduced corrections into the text of the Vulgate—which appeared instead of Erasmus' own Latin version in the edition of 1516—besides undertaking final checking of the proofs.[35] The chaos of Froben's shop during those months hardly bears thinking about. Yet it does not seem that Erasmus exaggerated in his letter to Budé: in his biography

[32] *EE*, nos. 334, 348 (2:78, 137).
[33] *EE*, no. 352 (2:140-42).
[34] *EE*, nos. 356, 360 (2:146, 149).
[35] *EE*, no. 421 (2:253-54).

of Erasmus (1540), Beatus Rhenanus recalled that Erasmus hastily revised and expanded his annotations as the New Testament went through the clattering press.[36] Somehow amid the din and clangor the New Testament emerged. On 3 February 1516 Erasmus wrote that "the New Testament rushes toward completion."[37] And finally, 7 March, he was able to announce proudly to Urban Regius: "Novum Testamentum editum est."[38] To be a little more precise, the colophon to the text of Erasmus' New Testament bears the date February 1516; that to the *Annotations*, 1 March 1516.

Erasmus titled this *editio princeps* of the Greek New Testament the *Novum Instrumentum*, a nomenclature he explained only in 1527. A *testamentum* is a will or covenant, he said, which might or might not be written; an *instrumentum* is the written document that establishes the terms of various pacts or agreements. There was an Old Testament long before Moses wrote the Pentateuch, he continued; there was no written New Testament when Jesus offered his disciples the cup of the new covenant. Thus Erasmus considered it more accurate to refer to the scriptures as *instrumenta*, the documents that describe the Hebrew and Christian covenants, or *testamenta*. He adduced support for this usage from the writings of St. Jerome and St. Augustine, but still found himself confronted with detractors who objected to the novelty of the term *instrumentum*.[39] This no doubt explains why he published all subsequent editions of his New Testament under the traditional title, *Novum Testamentum*.

The *Novum Instrumentum* was hardly off the press before Erasmus began to express his dissatisfaction with this first edition. More than once he admitted in a famous phrase that

---

[36] Beatus' biography of Erasmus appears as *EE*, no. IV (1:64).
[37] *EE*, no. 385 (2:187).
[38] *EE*, no. 394 (2:209).
[39] *EE*, no. 1858 (7:140).

"the New Testament was rushed out rather than edited"—
"Novum Testamentum praecipitatum est verius quam aedi-
tum."[40] By June of 1516 Erasmus planned a second edition
and solicited advice from William Latimer and Guillaume
Budé.[41] He began work on the second edition no later than
mid-1517; in the summer of 1518 he spoke of himself revis-
ing the *Annotations* "from head to foot"; and by the next December printing had progressed up to the Pauline epistles.[42]
The colophon for the second edition was placed in March of
1519, and Erasmus soon spread the news of its publication.[43]
Similar announcements heralded the appearance of three more
editions—published in 1522, 1527, and 1535—of Erasmus'
Greek New Testament.[44] The fifth edition of his Greek text,
Latin translation, and *Annotations*—the last that Erasmus himself worked on—was reprinted twice in collected editions of
Erasmus' works, the first edited by Beatus Rhenanus (1540-
1541), the second by Jean LeClerc (1703-1706). I shall ordinarily cite Erasmus' New Testament according to LeClerc's
edition—still the standard one for most of Erasmus' works—
but I shall also refer at times to the original sixteenth-century
editions in order to illustrate the development of Erasmus'
scholarship.[45]

[40] *EE*, nos. 402, 694 (2:226; 3:117).

[41] *EE*, nos. 417, 421 (2:248, 254).

[42] *EE*, nos. 597, 694, 695, 847, 848, 856, 860, 904 (3:4, 117, 120, 340-
41, 359-60, 381-82, 445). For the revision of the *Annotations* see Erasmus'
Apologia qua respondet duabus invectivis Eduardi Lei in Ferguson, p. 245.

[43] *EE*, no. 950 (3:552).

[44] For the editon of 1522 see *EE*, nos. 1030, 1174, 1218, 1235, and 1267
(4:92-93, 425, 541, 583; and 5:32). For the edition of 1527 see *EE*, nos.
1415, 1571, 1581, 1744, 1755, and 1818 (5:393-94; 6:68, 91, 403, 417;
and 7:59). For the edition of 1535 see *EE*, nos. 2951 and 3096 (11:13, 283).

[45] LeClerc's edition claims the whole sixth volume of *LB*. Short-title citations of the sixteenth-century editions, all published by Froben, are as follows: *Novum Instrumentum omne, diligenter ab Erasmo Roterodamo recognitum
& emendatum* (Basle, 1516); *Novum Testamentum omne, multo quam antehac
diligentius ab Erasmo Roterodamo recognitum, emendatum ac translatum* (Basle,

The chief source for this study will be Erasmus' *Annotations* to the New Testament, an indispensable mine of information on the character and quality of his New Testament scholarship. The *Annotations* reveal the scholar's thinking much more fully than Valla's philological observations or the Complutensian editors' sketchy notes. In the first edition of Erasmus' Greek New Testament the *Annotations* already claimed 294 folio pages. Erasmus almost doubled their size for the second edition, and he continued to expand them in later editions. By the fifth editon of 1535, they filled a fat, 783-page folio volume.

Erasmus explained the purposes of this work in a lengthy epistle "to the pious reader" prefaced to the *Annotations*. There he described his work not as a commentary, but rather as a collection of brief notes (*annotationculas*) designed to illuminate the text of scripture and, perhaps more importantly, to justify in advance Erasmus' reasons for editing and translating the New Testament just as he did. Erasmus predicted that some people would object to his work, since he altered many traditional readings and translations; he hoped the *Annotations* would forestall criticism and make it more difficult for future scholars to corrupt what he had corrected with great effort. He pointed out four general types of problems addressed in the *Annotations*. Where he found textual corruption, he restored the original reading, explaining his reasoning in the *Annotations*. Where he found obscure or ambiguous passages, he illuminated them and suggested a probable understanding. Where he found an inaccurate or ungrammatical Latin translation, he replaced it with one that better reflected the Greek while observing the rules governing good Latin

1519); *Novum Testamentum omne, tertio iam ac diligentius ab Erasmo Roterodamo recognitum* (Basle, 1522); *Novum Testamentum, ex Erasmi Roterodami recognitione, iam quartum* (Basle, 1527); *Novum Testamentum iam quintum accuratissima cura recognitum a Des. Erasmo Roter.* (Basle, 1535).

expression. Finally, with the aid of Johannes Oecolampadius, he compared New Testament quotations from the Septuagint with the original Hebrew text of the Old Testament. Erasmus readily admitted that many notes addressed apparently minute problems of language and grammar. Far from apologizing, however, he vigorously defended his work and asserted its absolute necessity, since apparently minute problems had often led unwary theologians into grave error.[46]

This preface to the *Annotations* expressed quite well the scholarly tasks Erasmus took on during the preparation of his New Testament. But Erasmus also had a larger purpose in mind for his work, one revealed more clearly in other prefaces to the New Testament. In his letter of dedication to Pope Leo X, for example, Erasmus succinctly outlined his thinking. The surest method of reforming Christendom, he said, would be to instill evangelical and apostolic doctrine in all individual Christians, but this doctrine works most effectively when drawn from the fount and source instead of muddy ponds and rivulets; hence the edition of the Greek New Testament and revision of the Latin against its standard.[47] The goals of personal transformation, social reform, and religious renewal—which Erasmus so passionately advocated in the *Paraclesis* and other works—thus stood behind his technical scholarship on the New Testament. There will be some occasion in the following pages to see how Erasmus kept his larger purpose in view even when addressing the smaller problems of New Testament text, translation, and explanation.

THE AIMS and chronological development of Erasmus' New Testament scholarship are therefore much better documented than those of Valla and the Complutensian editors. The same holds true for manuscripts. It is impossible to identify with

[46] *EE*, no. 373 (2:164-72).
[47] *EE*, no. 384 (2:181-87).

certainty a single Greek codex used by Valla or the Complutensian scholars, but several of Erasmus' Greek and Latin manuscripts survive, enabling us to evaluate his scholarly judgments with greater precision and accuracy than is possible for his predecessors. This good fortune does not arise from Erasmus' own general statements about his manuscripts, however, for these are sometimes misleading through their lack of precision. In the *Apologia* prefaced to the editions of the Greek New Testament, for example, Erasmus said he used four Greek manuscripts in preparing his first edition and five in the second.[48] Yet on the basis of readings cited in the *Annotations*, it can be demonstrated that he consulted many more than four manuscripts for his first edition. Part of the explanation for the discrepancy may lie in the definition of "manuscript" (*codex* in Erasmus' parlance). Scholars today consider MS. 817 of the gospels and MS. 7 of the Pauline epistles (both discussed below) as New Testament manuscripts, though the books present their texts only as the subject of commentaries. Erasmus made heavy use of both volumes, but never cited either as a *codex*. In the *Annotations* he referred to them instead, respectively, as "Vulgarius" (i.e., Theophylactus, the commentator) and "Graeca scholia" (a set of anonymous comments on the Pauline epistles). Thus one must resort to the *Annotations* in order to gain the most reliable information about Erasmus' manuscripts of the Greek New Testament.

By 1516 Erasmus had consulted many Greek manuscripts, though he probably had not thoroughly collated more than a few. He had based his fresh Latin translation (1505-1506) on Greek manuscripts; but his extant writings make no mention of them, and they remain unidentified. Fortunately, he volunteered more information about the manuscripts he used in editing the Greek New Testament. In several places he pointed

[48] Holborn, p. 166.

out to his critics that he based his Greek text on manuscripts from Britain, Brabant, and Basle.[49] The British manuscripts no doubt refer to those Erasmus collated during his Cambridge sojourn (1511-1514). Their number is unknown, but it is sure that among them was MS. 69, sometimes called the Codex Leicesterensis, which includes the entire New Testament with minor gaps.[50] This is an extremely important witness to the Greek New Testament, a prime member of a closely related and highly valued group of manuscripts known as Family 13; the entire group in turn is thought to be related to the third-century text used by Origen in Caesarea. Erasmus did not esteem the manuscript so greatly as modern textual critics: Family 13 had yet to be identified in Erasmus' day, and he may be excused for not recognizing the special importance of this manuscript. But it is certain that he consulted MS. 69 because he cited—and rejected—readings peculiar to it in the *Annotations*.[51] Other manuscripts Erasmus collated at Cambridge remain unidentified.

Far more important in any case were the manuscripts Eras-

[49] *LB*, 9:277 A, 308 C, 333 A, 986 F.

[50] Now housed in Leicester, County Record Office. The literature on MS. 69 includes J. Rendel Harris, *The Origin of the Leicester Codex of the New Testament* (Cambridge, 1887); and Kirsopp and Silva Lake, *Family 13 (The Ferrar Group)* (London, 1941).

[51] Johann Jakob Wettstein first pointed out this connection in the Prolegomena to his *Novum Testamentum graecum*, 2 vols. (Amsterdam, 1751-1752), 1:53, 120. There he mentioned sixteen passages where he thought Erasmus' *Annotations* presumed knowledge of MS. 69. I have compared MS. 69 and the *Annotations* at all these passages. In two of them (Mark 14:41 and John 7:26) I do not find a clear reference to MS. 69 in the *Annotations*. There remain at least fourteen passages, however, where Wettstein found Erasmus citing readings, some of them very rare or peculiar, found in MS. 69. The fourteen include Luke 18:7, John 11:47, Acts 14:19, and eleven passages in the gospel of Mark: 3:14, 3:16, 4:21, 4:30, 4:40, 5:33, 6:3, 8:11, 8:26, 9:11, and 14:36. Furthermore, I have myself noticed citations of readings that probably came from MS. 69 in Erasmus' notes to the following passages: Mark 3:18, 8:10, 8:14; Acts 8:10. Thus it is safe to infer that Erasmus had carefully examined and collated MS. 69.

mus used at Basle. These manuscripts are in general quite well known, though they can be made to yield new information on the character and development of Erasmus' textual scholarship. They went to Basle in the train of John of Ragusa, one of the leaders of the Council of Basle (1431-1439). He lingered in Switzerland after the Council, died in Lausanne in 1443, and bequeathed his library to the Dominicans in Basle.[52] Erasmus consulted some of Ragusa's manuscripts of the Greek New Testament at the Dominicans' library, but Johann Reuchlin had already borrowed others when Erasmus arrived in Basle (August 1514) and began to prepare copy for his edition. Erasmus borrowed them temporarily and returned them to Reuchlin, who retained them until his death in 1522. Most of Ragusa's books were then returned to Basle, though some were scattered elsewhere. The Reformation closed the Dominicans' house in Basle in 1529, and the University of Basle benefited by its library; the manuscripts remain even today in (to give it its proper name) the Öffentliche Bibliothek der Universität Basel. (In the following pages I indicate in parentheses the modern shelf mark after the first citation of each manuscript.)

Erasmus based his editions largely on two codices now regarded as inferior witnesses to the Greek New Testament: MS. 2 of the gospels (A. N. IV. 1) and MS. 2 of Acts and the apostolic epistles (A. N. IV. 4). Both date from the twelfth century. Erasmus used the manuscripts themselves as printer's copy, and one may still consult the observations and corrections he introduced into them.[53] The codex of the gospels especially required his attention: sloppily copied, it abounds

---

[52] On Ragusa's library see André Vernet, "Les manuscrits grecs de Jean de Raguse (d. 1443)," *Basler Zeitschrift für Geschichte und Altertumskunde* 61 (1961):75-108.

[53] K. W. Clark, "Observations on the Erasmian Notes in Codex 2," *Texte und Untersuchungen zur Geschichte der altchristlichen Literatur* 73 (1959):749-56.

with inaccurate additions and omissions, many of which Erasmus was able to correct because of his collation of other Greek manuscripts. For the Apocalypse Erasmus had only one manuscript, the Codex Reuchlini (MS. 1 of the Apocalypse).[54] The manuscript unfortunately had lost its final leaf already in the sixteenth century, and scholars have never forgiven Erasmus for his (let us call it) creative method of recovering the last six verses of the book: he translated the Vulgate back into Greek and printed the result as his Greek text. He admitted the deed in the *Annotations*, but disingenuously suggested that all Greek manuscripts lacked the verses.[55] Only in the fourth edition (1527) of his New Testament did Erasmus print a more reliable text, on the authority of the Complutensian Polyglot.

Erasmus also made much use of three other Basle manuscripts in preparing the first edition of his Greek New Testament: MS. 817 of the gospels (A. III. 15), MS. 7 of the Pauline epistles (A. N. III. 11), and MS. 4 of Acts and the apostolic epistles (A. N. IV. 5). MS. 817 includes the text of the gospels along with the commentary of the eleventh-century Archbishop of Bulgaria, Theophylactus; MS. 7 presents an important text of the Pauline epistles together with a set of anonymous scholia; MS. 4, an undistinguished work, served as a source of corrections for Erasmus' text. The binding of MS. 817 describes its contents only as "Vulgarius Archiepiscopus super Evangelia quattor." Erasmus did not recognize "Vulgarius Archiepiscopus" as Theophylactus, Archbishop of Bulgaria, and fell into the embarrassing error of citing the

---

[54] Now at Schloss Harburg, Öttingen-Wallersteinische Bibliothek, I, 1, 4, 1. The most complete study I know of this manuscript remains Franz Delitzsch, *Handschriftliche Funde*, 2 vols. (Leipzig, 1861-1862).

[55] See the beginning of his last note to the Apocalypse in the 1516 edition of the *Annotations*: "Quanquam in calce huius libri, nonnulla verba reperi apud nostros, quae aberant in Graecis exemplaribus, ea tamen ex latinis adiecimus," fol. 675 of the *Novum Instrumentum*.

author of the commentary as "Vulgarius" in the first two editions of his *Annotations*. Frequent reference to this "Vulgarius" and his variant readings proves that Erasmus consulted
MS. 817 in preparing the first edition of the Greek New Testament. In fact, evidence soon to be cited suggests strongly
that he used it as his chief source of corrections for MS. 2 of
the gospels. As for the Pauline epistles, F. H. Scrivener long
ago suggested that Erasmus consulted MS. 7 on the basis of
some twenty peculiar readings found in his New Testament.[56]
There is no need to argue by inference, however, for the *Annotations* again prove that Erasmus used this codex. He quoted
the scholia of MS. 7 verbatim many times in the *Annotations*
to the Pauline epistles, beginning at Rom. 1:4; and in notes
to some passages (e.g., Rom. 4:9, 1 Cor. 15:31, and 2 Thess.
4:16) he openly cited the "Graeca scholia" as the source of
variant readings. The *Annotations* do not speak so much of
MS. 4 as of MSS. 817 and 7, but evidence cited in the following pages suggests that Erasmus used MS. 4 as his main source
of emendations while editing the Book of Acts and the apostolic epistles.

There remain two important Basle manuscripts that Erasmus did not consult, or at least did not use much in establishing his Greek text. He evidently did not even know of the
great uncial MS. E of the gospels (A. N. III. 12), despite
C. C. Tarelli's wistful suggestion to the contrary.[57] MS. E be-
longed to the Dominicans at Basle like the other books from
John of Ragusa's library, so that no physical obstacle pre-
vented Erasmus from seeing it. But not a shred of evidence
supports the notion that he used it. Erasmus never mentioned

---

[56] See his personal letter to Franz Delitzsch, quoted in the latter's *Studien
zur Entstehungsgeschichte der Polyglottenbibel des Cardinal Ximenes* (Leipzig,
1871), p. 3, n. 1.

[57] C. C. Tarelli, "Erasmus's Manuscripts of the Gospels," *Journal of Theological Studies* 44 (1943):155-62, esp. p. 159.

an uncial manuscript of the New Testament, though he often described the peculiar features of his codices. Furthermore, the one reading that Tarelli cites in support of his suggestion (ταχύ at Mark 16:8) is present also in MS. 2, the main source of Erasmus' Greek text. (Incidentally, Tarelli's further speculation, that Erasmus might have consulted MS. Δ of the gospels—Codex Sangallensis, then as now housed in St. Gall—must be utterly rejected.)[58]

Nor—again despite Tarelli—did Erasmus make extensive use of an extremely important minuscule manuscript at Basle, MS. 1 of the whole New Testament, except the Apocalypse (A. N. IV. 2). This is a fine, carefully copied and corrected codex dating from the twelfth century.[59] It stands at the head of Family 1, a group of manuscripts closely related to Family 13 and consequently to the type of text Origen used at Caesarea in the third century. Erasmus, however, harbored grave doubts about MS. 1. He considered it "more pretty than accurate" and feared that it had been corrected to the Vulgate's standard.[60] Most students of Eramus' New Testament have recognized that he made little use of MS. 1.[61] Tarelli has argued otherwise, however, that Erasmus' agreements with MS. 1 against MS. 2 are "too numerous to be accidental," and that

[58] Ibid., p. 162. There is no evidence that Erasmus even visited St. Gall. He enjoyed only a cool relationship with St. Gall's chief humanist and reformer, Vadianus, who was perhaps best placed to inform Erasmus of MS. Δ. Vadianus did not even trouble to meet Erasmus at Constance in 1522, even at the urging of Erasmus' friend and host, Johann Botzheim. See Ernst Gerhard Rüsch, "Erasmus in St. Gallen," in his *Vom Heiligen in der Welt* (Biel, 1959), p. 57. Nor is there any extant correspondence between Erasmus and Vadianus. There is no reason therefore to think Erasmus knew or even suspected an important manuscript to be at St. Gall.

[59] Kirsopp Lake, *Codex 1 of the Gospels and Its Allies* (Cambridge, 1902).

[60] He leveled this charge in an *Apologia contra quosdam monachos hispanios* published in 1528 (*LB*, 9:1049 CE).

[61] E.g., Clark, "Observations on the Erasmian Notes in Codex 2," pp. 751, 754; Bo Reicke, "Erasmus und die neutestamentliche Textgeschichte," *Theologische Zeitschrift* 22 (1966):259.

Erasmus' text, "where it disagrees with 2, very commonly agrees with 1."[62] In support of this thesis he cited seventeen passages where he thought Erasmus corrected MS. 2 by MS. 1. Possibly Erasmus did indeed draw some of these corrections from MS. 1; but it bears pointing out that at five of Tarelli's seventeen passages—Matt. 9:5; Mark 7:2; Luke 1:36, 14:15, and 22:47—Erasmus' corrections find support in MS. 817 (which Tarelli did not examine) as well as MS. 1.

More damaging for Tarelli's thesis are Erasmus' own notes in MS. 2, the book that served as printer's copy for his first edition of the Greek New Testament. Most of these notes simply correct iotacisms or errors in spelling, but in MS. 2 of the gospels Erasmus introduced sixty textual emendations as well. The corrections did not always find their way into Erasmus' edition: some of them the printers either ignored or modified, possibly on later instructions of Erasmus or his collaborators, Gerbel and Oecolampadius. In any case, one may easily collate Erasmus' handwritten emendations with his manuscripts and learn to what extent he relied on various codices. Of the sixty emendations he introduced into MS. 2 of the gospels, there are only four cases—Matt. 27:35, Mark 11:8, Luke 2:43, and Luke 14:27—where Erasmus' emendation agrees with MS. 1 against every other manuscript he is known to have used. But at twenty-five passages his emendation agrees with MS. 817 against all his other codices, including MS. 1, while in only nine cases do Erasmus' emendations conflict with the reading of MS. 817.[63] Still other signs suggest that Erasmus did not even examine MS. 1 very closely. At Matt. 6:13,

[62] Tarelli, "Erasmus's Manuscripts of the Gospels," pp. 157-58.

[63] The twenty-five passages include Matt. 1:7-8, 2:11, 10:34, 19:9, 20:31, 21:7, 23:26, 23:30; Mark 4:4, 6:55, 7:2, 8:15, 9:7, 10:11, 10:24, 10:43, 12:23, 16:9; Luke 23:29; John 1:39, 5:9, 7:41, 12:34, 13:32, 19:38. The nine passages where Erasmus' notes and MS. 817 disagree include Matt. 5:27, 14:12, 16:3, 20:31, 27:35; Mark 11:8; Luke 2:43, 6:26, 14:27.

for example, he observed in the *Annotations* (in all editions from 1516 forward) that *all* Greek manuscripts include the apocryphal clause at the end of the Lord's Prayer, "for thine is the kingdom, the power, and the glory forever." But MS. 1 does not present the clause. Again, as Tarelli himself pointed out, at Luke 1:35 Erasmus said *all* Greek manuscripts lacked a phrase (ἐκ σοῦ—"from you") that MS. 1 preserves. The conclusion is inescapable: Erasmus did not think highly of MS. 1, did not closely examine it, and did not use it extensively in correcting MS. 2. As his chief source of emendation for the gospels he probably used instead MS. 817, a codex that, so far as I know, New Testament textual experts have never carefully studied.

The case is not so clear for the remainder of the New Testament as for the gospels. Erasmus introduced corrections also into MS. 2 of Acts and the apostolic epistles, but not nearly so frequently as in MS. 2 of the gospels. Furthermore, many of his emendations in MS. 2 of Acts and the apostolic epistles have been lost or rendered illegible through trimming of the manuscript's pages. The fragmentary character of his notes in this manuscript thus will not allow so sure a conclusion for the Acts and epistles as for the gospels. Such evidence as survives, however, points toward MS. 4 as the source of Erasmus' corrections. Thirteen of his emendations survive in MS. 2 of Acts and the epistles, of which four—at Acts 15:34, 17:5, 24:6, and 26:26—agree with MS. 4 against his other codices. None of the thirteen agrees with MS. 1 against the others.

Erasmus did not rest content with the manuscript information he developed for the first edition of his New Testament, but continued for the rest of his career to extend his knowledge of manuscripts and their variant readings. He consulted several new manuscripts while preparing the second edition of the New Testament, published in 1519; he no doubt had these in mind when he spoke of the manuscripts he examined in Brabant.[64] His correspondence shows that he collated Greek manuscripts during the first half of 1517, while traveling in the Low Countries and preparing the text for his second edition.[65] Chief among these was MS. 3 of the gospels, Acts, and apostolic epistles, which Erasmus borrowed from the Augustinians at Corsendonck, near Turnhout. Erasmus considered it a particularly faulty book, but recorded on its title page the fact that he used it in his second edition.[66] Other Greek manuscripts he consulted in the Low Countries included one lent by Cuthbert Tunstall and a codex of the gospels obtained from the monastery of Agnietenberg, near Zwolle.[67] I am not aware that he ever described them or took new readings from them. In fact, when he explicitly cited his manuscripts from Brabant, it was usually to support texts he had already established on the strength of other authorities.[68] He evidently did not consider them significant enough to serve as the basis of a thoroughly revised text.

For his third edition (1522) Erasmus consulted the Aldine edition (1518) of the Greek New Testament.[69] Though little more than a reprint of his own first edition, Erasmus occasionally cited the Aldine text as an independent witness in his discussions of textual problems (e.g., in the *Annotations* at Luke 1:35, Acts 8:37, Rom. 11:6, 1 Cor. 13:11, and 2 Cor. 4:4). More significant for the third edition was Erasmus' use of the Codex Montfortianus (Evv. 61, Acts 34, Paul. 40, Apoc. 92,

---

[64] *LB* 9:277 A, 333 A, 986 F.

[65] *EE*, no. 597 (3:4). See also Erasmus' *Apologia qua respondet* in Ferguson, p. 241.

[66] MS. 3 is now housed at the Nationalbibliothek in Vienna (Suppl. gr. 52). For Erasmus' judgments on its worth see his *Annotations* at 2 Cor. 8:5 and his *Responsio* to Frans Tittelmans's attack on his New Testament (*LB* 9:972 CF).

[67] See the *Apologia qua respondet*, Ferguson, p. 241, and *EE*, nos. 504, 515 (2:422, 432).

[68] *LB* 9:277 A, 333 A.

[69] See Erasmus' *Apologia* prefaced to the New Testament, Holborn, p. 166.

now at Dublin, Trinity College). Erasmus never saw this manuscript himself, but on its witness he included the *comma Johanneum* (1 John 5:7) in his third edition. (I defer until later a detailed discussion of Erasmus' thought on this passage.) In his fourth edition (1527) Erasmus made use of the Complutensian New Testament.[70] From it he drew his text for Apoc. 22:16-21, in place of his own retranslation from the Vulgate, and several variant readings cited in the *Annotations* (e.g., at Acts 8:37, Rom. 11:6, 1 Cor. 13:3, 1 John 5:7, and Apoc., *passim*).

He collated no new manuscripts for his fifth edition (1535), but this does not mean Erasmus had ceased working on the text of the New Testament. In fact, from the third edition on, Erasmus vastly expanded his collection of textual data from a different kind of textual source—the writings of the Church Fathers. The *Annotations* of the later editions teem with variant readings Erasmus noticed in the Fathers' works, many of which he edited in the 1520s and 1530s. Erasmus also requested and received variant readings in correspondence with friends and scholars. As early as 1518 he consulted William Latimer's annotations on Matthew, which no doubt included textual information based on Latimer's studies.[71] In 1526 he asked Ferry Carondelet to send from Besançon "something in the way of old manuscripts, especially of the gospels and apostolic epistles."[72] He received readings in the Pauline epistles from Johann Faber in Rome.[73] From Rome he also received, through Paolo Bombasio and Juan Ginés Sepulveda, collations of the great uncial MS. B, Codex Vaticanus, the single

[70] Ibid.

[71] *EE*, no. 886 (3:423).

[72] *EE*, no. 1749 (5:411).

[73] *Briefwechsel des Beatus Rhenanus*, ed. A. Horawitz and K. Hartfelder (Leipzig, 1886), p. 305.

most important of all Greek New Testament manuscripts.[74] Erasmus never saw the Vaticanus, but that did not prevent him from using it, and even criticizing it. In correspondence with Sepulveda he voiced the suspicion that MS. B had been corrected against the Vulgate. Somewhere he had picked up a wild tale that in 1435, after the Council of Florence, the Byzantine emperor ordered all Greek New Testament manuscripts to be emended and established the Vulgate as the standard. Sepulveda doubted Erasmus' suspicions and told him so frankly.[75] Erasmus seems finally to have accepted Sepulveda's arguments, but not before he lodged a public charge against the Vaticanus in an addition of 1535 to his *Capita argumentorum contra morosos quosdam ac indoctos*, an apologetic work prefaced to his New Testament in editions from 1519 forward.[76] Still, Erasmus invoked Vaticanus' authority in *Annotations* to several passages (e.g., Mark 1:2-3, Acts 27:16, 1 John 5:7).

Erasmus never devoted so much attention to the Vulgate as to the Greek New Testament. The first edition of his New Testament presented a Vulgate text that Erasmus had rather extensively revised, so as to bring it in line with the Greek text, printed opposite the Vulgate in parallel columns. In all later editions of his New Testament Erasmus published his own fresh Latin translation opposite the Greek. The text of the Vulgate proper appeared again only in the fourth edition (1527). Erasmus included it then in hopes of quelling conservative criticism of his own translation, criticism that in the mid-1520s grew increasingly violent and widespread.[77]

Thus only once did Erasmus undertake to edit the Vulgate

---

[74] *EE*, nos. 1213, 2873 (4:530; 10:307-309).

[75] *EE*, nos. 2905, 2938 (10:355-56, 394-95).

[76] *EE*, nos. 2951 (11:13-14). For the *Capita argumentorum* see *LB*, 6: * * *ʳ, par. 6.

[77] See *EE*, nos. 1571 and esp. 1581 (6:67-69, 91).

itself, but he spent many years searching out and studying good, old Vulgate manuscripts. For the first edition of his New Testament he consulted two manuscripts lent by John Colet from the college library of St. Paul's in London; Erasmus described them in his note to Matt. 1:18 as written in an ancient script; they seem not to have survived the various fires at St. Paul's Cathedral. For the second edition he used a book written with golden ink which he called the *aureus codex* (now in the Escorial) lent him by Margaret of Austria; a Latin manuscript from Corsendonck (now in Berlin); a codex of the gospels (now lost) provided by the Abbot of St. Bavo's at Ghent; and some unidentified manuscripts supplied by the Amorbach brothers of Basle. For the third edition he consulted at least four manuscripts from the college library of St. Donatian's Cathedral in Bruges, and he described them in his note to Matt. 3:16: some he said were 800 years old; one contained the entire New Testament; the oldest was mutilated and preserved only a few of the epistles. All apparently perished in the fire that destroyed St. Donatian's. Erasmus mentioned all these manuscripts of the Vulgate in his preface to the *Annotations* or in his *Apologia* (1525) responding to Petrus Sutor's criticism of his fresh Latin translation.[78] The *Annotations* and other works show that he examined other Latin manuscripts as well. In the third edition he cited readings (at 1 Pet. 2:2 and 1 John 5:7) from a manuscript owned by the Franciscans at Antwerp. For the same edition he relied also on a manuscript from the college library at Anderlecht, near Brussels, where he spent the summer of 1521 as the guest of Canon Peter Wychman.[79] Finally, for the fourth edition he

[78] *EE*, no. 373 (2:166). See also *LB*, 9:766 E–767 A, and many points in the *Annotations* where Erasmus mentioned these manuscripts (e.g., at Matt. 1:3, 1:18, 3:16; 1 Cor. 8:6; Phil. 2:1).

[79] See the *Annotations* at Phil. 4:8-9; also *LB*, 9:340 CD. Allen evidently was unaware that Erasmus cited this codex, but he knew Erasmus used it because of a manuscript note acknowledging the fact. See his headnote to *EE*, no. 373 (2:165).

used several manuscripts (now lost) from Constance shown to Erasmus by his friend Johann Botzheim.[80]

Erasmus inspected his Vulgate manuscripts closely. In the *Annotations* to 1 Cor. 8:6 and Phil. 2:1 he pointed out that someone had erased the original (and correct) readings and replaced them with inferior texts in the manuscripts of St. Paul's and Constance. Erasmus found his extensive research into the Vulgate's text useful, even though he edited the Vulgate only once. He often cited the authority of old manuscripts in the *Annotations* as support for his own Latin translation, on the assumption, largely accurate, that more recent Vulgate manuscripts exhibited more than their fair share of corruption.

Textual Criticism

Erasmus therefore drew on more sources of textual data, both Greek and Latin, than is usually realized.[81] True, he did not rely consistently on more than a few manuscripts in establishing his text of the New Testament, and the ones he chose to follow were not the best available to him. His Greek text largely reproduces MS. 2, with corrections drawn from other manuscripts, mostly those available to him at Basle. He distrusted the better codices, MSS. B, 1, and 69, which critics today recognize as infinitely superior to MS. 2. If one evaluates Erasmus' New Testament scholarship on the basis solely of the manuscripts he favored and the text he printed, as scholars have thus far done, he cannot help but judge Erasmus an in-

[80] See *EE*, nos. 1761, 1858 (6:425; 7:130-31). See also the *Annotations* at John 21:22, Rom. 13:1, Gal. 3:1, Col. 1:28, Phil. 2:1, 1 John 5:7.

[81] Most scholars say Erasmus consulted only a few manuscripts ready to hand at Basle, without appreciating the true extent of his textual research. Cf. Basil Hall, "Biblical Scholarship: Editions and Commentaries," *CHB*, 3:59-60; Metzger, *The Text of the New Testament*, pp. 99-103; Tracy, *Erasmus: The Growth of a Mind*, pp. 153-54.

ferior scholar—an enthusiastic but incompetent amateur at best, a careless, undisciplined, anti-critical bungler at worst.[82]

The truth, however, is not so simple, for two reasons. First, it makes for thoroughly unhistorical procedure to hold Erasmus responsible for later textual discoveries. Not until the late nineteenth century did anyone know or even suspect that MSS. 1 and 69 figured prominently in manuscript groups (Families 1 and 13, respectively) that derived ultimately from the text current in third-century Caesarea. Only centuries of comparisons, collations, and accumulated insights enabled scholars to evaluate New Testament manuscripts as accurately as they do today. Standing at the beginning of this analytical process, Erasmus and other Renaissance humanists were happy to be able to consult *any* published Greek text of the New Testament. If it turned out faulty, the text could be improved; but in its lack, one could only go to the Vulgate and such Greek manuscripts as one might scrounge.

In the second place, Erasmus' manuscripts and editions by themselves do not reveal the quality of his New Testament scholarship. From at least 1505 forward, Erasmus carefully studied, then collated New Testament manuscripts all over Europe. He noticed thousands of variant readings in both Greek and Latin texts, and he supplemented these with other variants that he found preserved in patristic writings or received through correspondence with friends. It would have made little sense for Erasmus to collect textual data throughout his scholarly career only to ignore it. He did not always deal with

---

[82] Besides works cited in the previous note, see also the following, ranked roughly from the more favorable to the near-slanderous, falling within this spectrum: Roland Bainton, "The Bible in the Reformation," *CHB*, 3:10; Jean Hadot, "La critique textuelle dans l'édition du Nouveau Testament d'Érasme," in *Colloquia erasmiana turonensia*, ed. Jean-Claude Margolin (Toronto, 1972), 2:749-60; Reicke, "Erasmus und die neutestamentliche Textgeschichte"; J. W. Bailey, "Erasmus and the Textus Receptus," *Crozer Quarterly* 17 (1940):271-79; and Delitzsch, *Handschriftliche Funde*.

variant readings as a modern editor would, and he did not always select what we would call the best of the variants for publication in his editions. He did use them, however, to illuminate textual problems, to show how texts become corrupted in transmission and how scholars may recognize and remove that corruption. Only by going beyond the superficial study of Erasmus' manuscripts and editions, by analyzing his thinking on texts and their problems, may one evaluate more accurately the quality of his New Testament scholarship.

The only source that allows this sort of analysis is the *Annotations*, where Erasmus offered his reasons for editing, translating, and explaining the New Testament as he did. The *Annotations* unfortunately remain one of the least studied and least understood of Erasmus' works. Only in the past dozen years have scholars turned their attention to the *Annotations*. Several students have used Erasmus' notes to good effect in clarifying his position on moral, religious, and theological problems.[83] They still contain a vast amount of relatively untapped information, however, for students of Erasmus' New Testament scholarship.[84] The remainder of this chapter will

[83] See Payne, "Erasmus: Interpreter of Romans," and "Erasmus and Lefèvre d'Étaples as Interpreters of Paul"; Georges Chantraine, "Le mustérion paulinien selon les Annotations d'Érasme," *Recherches de science religieuse* 58 (1970):351-82; C.A.L. Jarrott, "Erasmus' Biblical Humanism," pp. 119-52, and "Erasmus's Annotations and Colet's Commentaries on Paul: A Comparison of Some Theological Themes," *Essays on the Works of Erasmus*, ed. R. L. DeMolen (New Haven, 1978), pp. 125-44; Rabil, *Erasmus and the New Testament*, esp. pp. 115-80; André Godin, "Fonction d'Origène dans la pratique exégétique d'Érasme: les Annotations sur l'épitre aux Romains," in *Histoire de l'exégèse*, pp. 17-44; and two articles by M. G. Mara, "L'esegesi erasmiana di alcuni passi della *Lettera ai Romani*," *Studi storico religiosi* 1 (1977):165-82; and "La II Epistola di Pietro: testo e annotazioni erasmiane," *Archeologia classica* 25-26 (1973-1974):376-94.

[84] My preliminary studies anticipate the following analysis: "Erasmus' *Annotationes in Novum Testamentum*," and "Biblical Philology and Christian Humanism." See also Jacques Chomarat's "Les *Annotations* de Valla, celles d'É-

thus rely largely on the *Annotations*. Only there does one find the evidence that allows the reconstruction of Erasmus' methods and principles of textual scholarship; only on that evidence may one accurately evaluate Erasmus as observer and critic of texts.

Erasmus closely followed Lorenzo Valla's lead in his criticism of the Latin text of the New Testament. He understood and thoroughly sympathized with Valla's animus toward scribes who intentionally altered the texts they were charged to transmit. The *Annotations* ring with his indictments of the "audacity of the scribes" who corrupted what they could not comprehend. At 1 Cor. 12:13, for example, he denounced the copyists who took it on themselves willfully to change St. Paul's meaning by writing *vocati sumus* ("we are called") for *potati sumus* ("we drink"). And at Rom. 1:32 he suspected scribes of expanding the Latin text so as to fill out and clarify the meaning of a somewhat obscure passage.

In other ways, too, Erasmus showed himself the student of Valla's *Adnotationes*. Like Valla, he compared the Vulgate and its variant readings with the Greek New Testament—a method that enabled him to explain and remove textual corruption in the Vulgate. He found many places, for example, where simple inspection of the Greek text proved the Latin text corrupted by the confusion of similar-sounding words. Like Valla, he pointed out the confusion of *evertit* ("she overturns") for *everrit* ("she sweeps") at Luke 15:8; *ad* ("to") for *a* ("from") at John 18:28; and *sic* ("so") for *si* ("if") at John 21:22. In each case the Greek text exhibits no significant variant; confusion and corruption are confined to the Vulgate. The Latin near-homonyms manifestly account for that corruption; con-

---

rasme et la grammaire," in *Histoire de l'exégèse*, pp. 202-28, which discusses Erasmus' *Annotations*, but without recognizing that Erasmus far surpassed Valla in the quality as well as the quantity of his observations, as the remainder of this chapter will show.

sulting the Greek text enables the scholar to remove it. Erasmus' explanations of this sort differed from Valla's chiefly in number: Erasmus applied the method more thoroughly than Valla and consequently exposed many corrupt passages that Valla had not discussed. At Luke 8:19, for example, Erasmus showed that the common reading *audire* ("to hear") was a corruption of the original reading *adire* ("to approach") on the strength of the Greek verb συντυχεῖν ("to meet with"). Erasmus' *Annotations* far surpassed Valla's sketchy notes in size and scope, so it is not surprising to find Erasmus shedding much more philological light than Valla on the text of the Vulgate.

Erasmus extended Valla's insights with respect not only to homonyms, but also to the problem of assimilation. He agreed with Valla in diagnosing assimilation at many passages—e.g., at Matt. 27:39-40 and John 7:29-30—but he drew attention to other assimilated corruptions that Valla did not discuss. At 1 Cor. 4:16 Erasmus found a passage in Vulgate manuscripts assimilated from 1 Cor. 11:1 (here italicized in translation): "And so I exhort you to be imitators of me, *just as I am of Christ*." He judged the passage a corruption on the basis of his extensive research in Greek, Latin, and patristic manuscripts. It does not occur in Greek texts, he said, nor in the old Vulgate manuscripts he saw at Constance and St. Donatian's, nor in the commentary of Ambrosiaster (whom Erasmus called "Ambrose" here and throughout his *Annotations*). He admitted finding it in a manuscript at St. Paul's—though only as a marginal addition by a later scribe—and in the commentary of St. Thomas Aquinas. These witnesses, however, cannot overrule the much stronger authority of the Greek text, the early Vulgate manuscripts, and the fourth-century commentary of Ambrosiaster. Erasmus often presented this sort of thorough, well-documented discussion of textual problems in the *Annotations*. His charges of textual corruption therefore convince the reader much more readily than Valla's often correct, but unsubstantiated allegations.

It was in the discipline of Greek textual criticism, however, not Latin, that Erasmus registered his most significant advances beyond Valla's work and that of the Complutensian scholars as well. Valla had reported a few variant readings in the Greek text and expressed opinions about which was better; but only rarely had he attempted to explain how the variants arose, much less devise sophisticated techniques to use in analyzing the Greek text and restoring it to its original purity. The Complutensian scholars had prepared an edition of the entire Greek New Testament; but they had relied on questionable editorial principles, they had selected variants that agreed with the Vulgate, and they had not seen fit to justify their editorial decisions, or even discuss their textual evidence, except in a few cases. Erasmus' advances beyond the scholarship of Valla and the Complutensian circle arose partly because he recognized more clearly that the scriptures were liable to almost infinite corruption. He realized better than the other humanists that the scriptures were human documents, only as reliable as the human beings who transmitted them. At one point he even ventured the daring suggestion that the original authors of scripture themselves introduced error into their work. At Matt. 2:6 the evangelist reversed the meaning of prophecy quoted from Mic. 5:2. In his note to this passage Erasmus attributed the error to a slip of the memory, unlike earlier commentators, who had strived mightily to explain away the evangelist's mistake. If the evangelists themselves could err, how much more likely was it that scribes and copyists would blunder in their transmission of the scriptures! Thus Erasmus possessed a keen sense of scripture's liability to manifold corruption, and an equally keen desire to remove that corruption. A close analysis of the *Annotations* on textual problems will reveal in Erasmus a much more acute observer

and astute critic than any of his predecessors in textual scholarship, including even Origen and St. Jerome, by any odds
the most competent biblical scholars of the patristic age.[85]

Erasmus improved on the methods of his predecessors even
in the relatively simple task of collecting variant readings. He
diligently consulted new manuscripts and obtained textual information through correspondence, as shown above, so that
from one edition to the next the *Annotations* swelled with reports of new textual data. But he did not stop with manuscripts, as his predecessors had done. Instead he extensively
mined the writings of the Church Fathers, especially the Greeks,
who often quoted scripture and preserved readings appearing
rarely or never in New Testament manuscripts. As time went
on, Erasmus apparently trusted the Greek Fathers over manuscripts as witnesses to the New Testament—probably because of his mistaken suspicion that Greek manuscripts had
been corrected against the Vulgate after the Council of Florence. At any rate, from the third edition of the New Testament forward, Erasmus reported variant readings from patristic works, especially those of Chrysostom and Theophylactus,
more than any other source. Modern textual critics rely more
heavily on the better manuscripts than Erasmus, but they still
recognize patristic quotations as an extremely important source
of textual data. The Fathers' works not only preserve some
readings lost in the manuscript tradition, but also suggest how

[85] On the quality and character of Origen's scholarship see Maurice F. Wiles,
"Origen as Biblical Scholar," *CHB*, 1:454-89; and Bruce M. Metzger, "Explicit References in the Works of Origen to Variant Readings in New Testament Manuscripts," in his *Historical and Literary Studies* (Leiden, 1968),
pp. 88-103. On Jerome see Bruce M. Metzger, "St. Jerome's Explicit References to Variant Readings in Manuscripts of the New Testament," in *Text
and Interpretation*, ed. E. Best and R. Wilson (Cambridge, 1979), pp. 179-
90; H.F.D. Sparks, "Jerome as Biblical Scholar," *CHB*, 1:510-41; and K. K.
Hulley, "Principles of Textual Criticism Known to St. Jerome," *Harvard Studies
in Classical Philology* 55 (1944):87-109.

thinly or widely spread a given reading may have been in, say, the early fourth century. Erasmus did not realize all the implications of patristic quotations, nor the problems involved in using them. Yet he was the first New Testament scholar to see the value and begin the accumulation of variant readings recorded by the Church Fathers.[86]

Erasmus also relied on an ingenious method for recovering Greek readings that he found in neither Greek manuscripts nor the works of the Church Fathers—inference on the basis of peculiar translations. He knew well that no proper critic could take Latin readings from Latin translations of the Greek Fathers, for translators often cast the Fathers' scriptural quotations in the familiar language of the Vulgate. Thus he showed in the *Annotations* that Origen's and Theophylactus' translators had altered the exegetes' original readings at Rom. 11:5 and 2 Cor. 15:5, respectively, in order to make them conform to the Vulgate. And in an apologetic work Erasmus scorned Edward Lee for drawing readings from a Latin translation of Chrysostom.[87] Yet he realized the possibility of inferring certain Greek readings from the works of Latin Fathers who used Greek manuscripts. He surmised at 1 Tim. 6:20, for example, that the Greek texts used by Ambrosiaster and the translator of the Vulgate read καινοφωνίας on the basis of the transla-

[86] Bruce M. Metzger underestimates how extensively Erasmus used patristic citations of the Greek New Testament: ". . . instead of drawing upon these Fathers for help in establishing the text, Erasmus quotes them in his exegetical *Adnotationes* which conclude the volume." See his article, "Patristic Evidence and the Textual Criticism of the New Testament," *New Testament Studies* 18 (1971-1972):380-81. In fact, the *Annotations* was not a strictly exegetical work, but one rather where Erasmus discussed myriad textual problems. Furthermore, though he did not often publish readings on the strength of patristic evidence alone, analysis of the *Annotations* shows that by 1535 and the last edition of his New Testament, Erasmus introduced patristic evidence at almost every relevant point when he discussed textual problems in the Greek New Testament.

[87] *LB*, 9:230 D, 230 E.

tion, "vocum novitates"—"new-fangled words." The correct Greek text is κενοφωνίας—"vocum inanitates"—"empty words" or "inanity." At 1 Cor. 13:7 the correct text has πάντα στέγει—"omnia suffert"—"[charity] endures all things." From Cyprian's "omnia diligit" Erasmus postulated the variant reading πάντα στέργει—"[charity] esteems all things." Modern textual critics recognize the value of inference in reconstructing the Greek text of the New Testament, and as a result they have studied all the early translations of the New Testament available to them.[88] Again, Erasmus' work does not approach that of contemporary critics in its extent, complexity, and mastery of the technical problems involved. But he clearly anticipated modern scholars by developing and employing the method of inference. Besides the examples cited above, he inferred Greek variants also at 1 Cor. 2:1, 1 Cor. 14:38, and 1 Tim. 3:1, and in his apology to Latomus he explicitly defended the method.[89]

Erasmus did not even shrink from supposing the existence of variant readings on the strength of sheer conjecture. He conjectured many Greek and Latin variants in his *Annotations*—e.g., at John 12:35, Rom. 4:9, and 2 Pet. 2:18—but perhaps the most striking illustration of Erasmus' use of this method occurs in his discussion of Acts 27:14. Here, as seen above, Antonio de Nebrija solved the problem of the "southeast-north wind" ("Euroaquilo") by consulting the Greek New Testament, where he found εὐροκλύδων ("a storm or tempest from the east"). Erasmus' manuscripts also presented εὐροκλύδων, but he suggested the possibility that the author of Acts originally wrote εὐροακύλων ("Euroaquilo"), combining the Greek Εὖρος ("southeast wind") with the Latin "Aquilo" ("north wind"). In support of his conjecture, Erasmus pointed out that St. Paul elsewhere Hellenized the Latin name Aquila

[88] Metzger, *The Early Versions of the New Testament.*
[89] *LB*, 9:88 DE.

as Ἀκύλα (Rom. 16:3). Erasmus' conjecture may seem rash, since the word he proposed is attested nowhere in Greek literature except at Acts 27:14. Indeed, the very unlikelihood of the word and the prospect of a "southeast-north wind" perplexed scribes and copyists so much that they offered the reading εὐροκλύδων in its place. Yet Erasmus' conjecture was later confirmed by readings in early manuscripts and papyri of the New Testament, and modern editors print εὐρακύλων as their text.[90]

Thus during years of research on the Greek text of the New Testament, Erasmus assembled by one means or another a vast corpus of variant readings. The next step was to solve their problems: explain their origin, eliminate the late arrivals, and select one as the best representative of the original Greek New Testament. Sometimes this task was simple, because Erasmus found manifestly nongenuine material in his manuscripts. At 2 Cor. 8:4-5, for example, he noticed that the dull scribe who copied MS. 3 had introduced a marginal note into the very text: ἐν πολλοῖς τῶν αὐτογραφῶν οὕτως εὕρεται . . .—"in many manuscripts it appears like so . . ."!

Most variant readings posed harder problems. In some cases Erasmus relied simply on the weight of textual evidence to select the best variant. Thus his discussion of the Wandering Doxology (Rom. 16:25-27), so called because it follows Rom. 14:23 in some manuscripts, 15:33 in others, 16:24 in most, and does not even occur in yet others. Erasmus placed it at the traditional point, on the witness of Greek and early Latin manuscripts, Ambrosiaster, and Origen. So also with the longer ending of Mark's gospel (Mark 16:9-20). Erasmus cited Jerome's testimony that few Latin and almost no Greek manuscripts presented this passage. He found it in all his Greek codices, however, and therefore published it in his editions.

[90] Bruce M. Metzger, *A Textual Commentary on the Greek New Testament*, 3rd ed. (New York, 1971), p. 497.

He omitted only a passage he called the *coronis Marci*, an apocryphal addition at Mark 16:14-15. Scholars know it today as the Freer logion because it is witnessed only in the Freer Codex (MS. W, which came to light only in 1906) and in manuscripts reported by Jerome.[91] Erasmus knew of the passage only through Jerome and thus had no direct manuscript support for it. Furthermore, he found it lacking in evangelical gravity, and even considered it redolent of Manichaeism. He therefore discussed the passage in the *Annotations*, but declined to print it as part of his text.

Even more interesting was Erasmus' argument regarding the story of the woman taken in adultery (John 7:53-8:11). He knew that many Greek manuscripts lacked the story, and that others included it at different places. In the *Annotations* he reviewed the evidence of the Fathers: Jerome did not find the passage in all Greek manuscripts; Chrysostom and Theophylactus failed to mention it in their commentaries on John's gospel; Eusebius thought it apocryphal. But Erasmus liked the story! Its themes of forgiveness and repentance no doubt appealed to him, and he badly wanted to consider it genuine. He acknowledged the strong possibility that it was apocryphal, but added that many apocryphal things were also true. He even ventured the wild speculation that John included the pericope only in a late edition of his gospel, thus explaining its presence in some manuscripts and absence in others. In the end he accepted the story as genuine and printed it at the traditional point. He advanced several considerations in the story's favor: many Greek manuscripts included it; Augustine commented on it; Lorenzo Valla presumably found it in his Greek manuscripts, since he did not comment on it; and finally, "the consensus of the Church" approved it as worthy of the gospel.

[91] C. R. Gregory, *Das Freer-Logion* (Leipzig, 1908). See also Metzger, *The Text of the New Testament*, p. 57.

Thus in all three of these important cases Erasmus expressed doubts about traditional texts, but decided to print them, largely on the basis of widespread manuscript support in his own day. Modern editors can hardly do otherwise. With their advanced understanding of manuscripts and textual data in general, most modern critics doubt the genuineness of the Wandering Doxology and regard as utterly spurious the longer ending of Mark and the pericope of the adulteress.[92] Yet editors continue to include the passages in their editions, at least as appendices or variant readings, in order to represent the hundreds of Greek New Testament manuscripts that present the passages. Erasmus did not approach a modern understanding of these passages and their problems. Beyond doubt or question, however, his discussions left sixteenth-century readers well informed with respect to the evidence for and against the texts.

In judging between variant readings, Erasmus did not always rely simply on the amount of manuscript or patristic support that could be mustered for each variant. Most textual problems are soluble only through hard thinking, not the mechanical counting of manuscripts. If the critic can explain the origin of variant readings, he will be well placed to eliminate the corrupt and select the genuine variant. Erasmus understood this truth, and his *Annotations* prove it. Like Valla and the Complutensian editors, he often noticed Greek texts corrupted by assimilation or the confusion of homonyms. He pointed out at 2 Cor. 12:1, for example, that similarity of sound and spelling gave rise to several readings: δεῖ ("it is necessary"), δὴ (the particle, "now"), and δὲ ("on the other hand"). He called attention to other such confusions at Luke 1:4, 1 Cor. 13:3, and 2 Cor. 7:16, among many other passages. As for assimilation, he noticed in his Greek manuscripts at Mark 6:11 an entire sentence imported from Matt. 10:15:

---

[92] Metzger, *Textual Commentary on the Greek New Testament*, pp. 122-28, 219-22, 533-36, 540.

"Verily I say unto you, it will be more tolerable for Sodom and Gomorrah on the day of judgment than for that city." He exposed other assimilated passages at 2 Cor. 2:3 and 2 Cor. 4:4. One of Erasmus' most important codices, MS. 2 of the gospels, itself bears witness to his recognition of assimilation. Among his handwritten corrections in MS. 2 one finds assimilated passages underlined at Luke 12:21 and Luke 14:24. Beside both texts Erasmus wrote in the margins of MS. 2 the word *super*—"above"—indicating that the underlined passages came, respectively, from Luke 8:8 and Matt. 22:14.

In this sort of criticism Erasmus usually agreed with the analyses of Valla and the Complutensian editors, but even here he surpassed them not only quantitatively—by exposing many more corruptions caused by assimilation and the confusion of homonyms than they had recognized—but also qualitatively—by developing more sophisticated insights into the nature of corruption. Take for example the comments of Valla and Erasmus to 2 Pet. 2:18. Valla found in the Vulgate a word, *paululum* ("a little bit") that did not correspond to the reading of his Greek manuscripts, ὄντως ("actually"). He suggested, reasonably enough, that the translator originally wrote *plane* ("certainly"), implying that *plane* could easily have been corrupted to *paululum*. Erasmus cited Valla's reasoning in the *Annotations*, but rejected it in favor of another explanation—one that recognized corruption not only in the Latin, but also in the Greek New Testament. Erasmus thought *paululum* the original Latin translation, but conjectured that the translator's manuscript read ὀλίγως ("a little") instead of the more common reading, ὄντως. The reading ὀλίγως is now widely attested in Greek manuscripts.

Erasmus moved even further beyond his predecessors in his treatment of one especially important type of corruption—that caused by intentional changes which scribes introduced into the Greek text of the New Testament. Valla had spotted intentional alterations of the Vulgate's text, but never recognized, or at least never reported similar corruptions in the Greek New Testament. Nor does any evidence show that the Complutensian editors realized how deeply scribal scruples had affected the Greek text. Granted, they recognized the final clause of the Lord's Prayer (Matt. 6:13) as a nongenuine addition to the Greek text. Far from removing corruption, however, they positively introduced it by intentionally including the *comma Johanneum* (1 John 5:7) in their edition of the Greek New Testament. Erasmus advanced beyond Valla by concentrating his efforts at criticism on the Greek text, not the Vulgate, and he improved upon the work of the Complutensian team by editing the Greek New Testament on the basis of philological criteria, rejecting the Vulgate as an appropriate standard.

Erasmus recognized many reasons why scribes might alter the Greek text before them. At Matt. 15:7-8 he found them adding to the text in order to complete a quotation. The original gospel cited Isaiah's prophecy (29:13) in abbreviated form; the scribe filled out the quotation and harmonized it with the Septuagint. Other places Erasmus found scribes rounding out the sense of New Testament authors themselves. At Rom. 14:6 he noticed in Theophylactus and some Greek manuscripts that scribes sought to provide balance for St. Paul's teachings by adding without warrant the clause here italicized: "He who observes a certain day does so for the Lord's sake, and he who eats meat does so for the Lord's sake, for he gives thanks to God; *and he who does not observe a certain day declines to do so for the Lord's sake,* and he who does not eat meat abstains for the Lord's sake, and he gives thanks to God." Erasmus recognized also the urge felt by many scribes to clarify references that might strike some readers as obscure. At Eph. 3:14, for example, the original author expressed "thanks to the Father." In the *Annotations* Erasmus cited St. Jerome's testimony that

Latin manuscripts specified this Father as "the Father of our Lord Jesus Christ," but that Greek manuscripts remained uncorrupted. "Now the wonder is," Erasmus continued, "that what Jerome said was added in Latin manuscripts I now find in the Greek." Thus he found a sort of progressive corruption of Latin and Greek manuscripts by overzealous scribes. At Matt. 6:13 Erasmus argued that the Greek liturgy induced scribes to add the final clause to the Lord's Prayer: "for thine is the kingdom, the power, and the glory forever." He found the clause, he said, in all Greek manuscripts—in fact, MS. 1 omits it—but in no Latin manuscripts and in no commentaries except those of Chrysostom and Theophylactus. He rejected Valla's charge that Latin Bibles cut out "a good chunk of the Lord's Prayer," but saved his censure for the "temerity of those who fear not to patch their trifles onto so divine a prayer." The clause found its way into the Lord's Prayer, Erasmus said, for the same reason the phrase *gloria patri*—"glory to the Father"—was added at the end of the Psalms: familiar formulas influenced scribes and forced their way into the text. Many of these mutations may seem minor in that they work no positive distortion on the doctrine or teachings of the New Testament. They do lead to textual confusion, however, and Erasmus rightly denounced scribes who willfully altered the texts of scripture.[93]

Even more serious and less excusable in Erasmus' view were alterations introduced because of some apologetic or theological consideration, but he had all too frequent occasion in the *Annotations* to expose texts so corrupted. At 1 Tim. 1:17 he found all Greek manuscripts united in offering honor and glory "to the only wise God"—μονῷ σοφῷ θεῷ. The Vulgate, however, refers simply to "the only God"—*soli Deo*. He found support for the Greek reading in Chrysostom and Theophylactus,

---

[93] He trounced them not only in the *Annotations*, but also in other works, such as the *Apologia* prefaced to the New Testament, Holborn, p. 166.

but widespread support for the Vulgate also in the works of early Latin Fathers, Jerome, Augustine, and Ambrosiaster. This suggested to Erasmus the possibility that σοφῷ (*sapienti*—"wise") was not genuine, but added to Greek manuscripts in order to combat Arian heresy. The adjective would qualify the otherwise stark reference to "the only God" and make it less likely for interpreters to cite the text in an effort to exclude Jesus from the Godhead. Erasmus advanced this suggestion in a remarkable passage that appeared only in the first edition of the *Annotations*.[94] In later editions he suppressed it—an extremely rare practice for Erasmus, who often enlarged but seldom pruned his writings—perhaps in order to avoid charges that he himself sympathized overmuch with the Arians.

Much more significant and controversial was Erasmus' treatment of the *comma Johanneum* at 1 John 5:7. He found the *comma* in no Greek manuscript, few Latin manuscripts of antique vintage, and only rarely in patristic works. He cited with approval the opinion of St. Jerome, that Latin copyists had introduced the passage on their own in order to refute the Arians and provide scriptural support for Trinitarian doctrine. Thus he omitted the *comma* from both Greek and Latin texts in the first two editions of his New Testament. The result was a veritable uproar. Led by Stunica and Edward Lee, critics pounced on Erasmus' treatment of the *comma*, accused him of tampering with the scriptures, and even suggested that his text would bolster Arian heresy. In an apologetic moment,

[94] This passage follows the sentence, "Et ad eum quidem modum legit Chrysostomus, & hunc sequutus Theophylactus, si modo non fallunt codices." The passage itself reads as follows: "Caeterum quoniam id nec apud Hieronymum nec apud Ambrosium, nec apud ullum praeterea reperio, nonnihil suspicor additum adversus Arianos, qui solum patrem vere deum esse volebant. Siquidem & haeretici nonnihil immutabant in litteris sacris, quo suum tuerentur errorem ita compertum locis aliquot, addita quaedam ad orthodoxis ad excludendos aut refellendos etiam haereticorum errores, uti locis aliquot indicavimus."

Erasmus said he would have included the passage in his text if any of his Greek manuscripts had presented it.[95] Such a manuscript quickly came to light—Codex Montfortianus (MS. 61 of the gospels, 34 of Acts and the catholic epistles). In fact, it was almost certainly manufactured by Erasmus' enemies for the express purpose of confuting him. Nevertheless, Erasmus included the *comma* in the last three editions of his New Testament—but only under protest. He added to the *Annotations* a long note where he pointed out the weighty patristic and manuscript evidence against the passage and expressed his suspicions regarding the integrity of the "Codex Brittanicus," as he called the Montfortianus. He even cited in his favor the testimony of MS. B, Codex Vaticanus, whose reading at 1 John 5:7 he had learned through correspondence with Paolo Bombasio.[96]

Erasmus deplored corruptions brought on by apologetic or theological considerations, but texts thus distorted helped him to develop a highly sophisticated tool of textual analysis. I refer to an insight known in the jargon of textual critics as the principle *difficilior lectio potior*—"the more difficult reading is the better"—and in plain English as the principle of the harder reading. When confronted with two or more variant readings of unequal difficulty, so the principle advises, the critic will often do well to select the more difficult as his text. Cogent reasoning stands behind this ostensible paradox: a scribe copying an earlier work is more likely to replace a difficult with an easier reading than to make a difficult reading out of one that is easy to begin with. The more difficult variant

[95] See Erasmus' *Responsio* to Lee's *Annotationes novas*, *LB*, 9:275 BC.

[96] *EE*, no. 1213 (4:530). On this text see H. J. de Jonge, who clarifies several important points in his article, "Erasmus and the *Comma Johanneum*," *Ephemerides theologicae lovanienses* 56 (1980):381-89. See also A. Bludau, "Der Beginn der Controverse über die Aechtheit des *Comma Johanneum* (1 Joh. 5, 7. 8.) im 16. Jahrhundert," *Der Katholik*, 3rd ser. 26 (1902), esp. pp. 167-75.

therefore is more likely the original reading. The principle of
the harder reading is universally recognized by critics as a generally valid guideline of textual analysis, and it still finds its
place in the repertoire of modern textual scholars. To Erasmus' credit as a discerning critic, it is now possible to identify
him as the first scholar to develop the principle of the harder
reading and to employ it regularly in his criticism of the Greek
New Testament.[97]

At Matt. 5:22, for example, the original Greek gospel warned
that "whoever becomes angry at his brother will be held accountable at the judgment." Erasmus found some manuscripts, however, that added a word—εἰκῇ—to qualify this
categorical statement: "whoever becomes angry at his brother
without cause will be held accountable in the judgment." The
addition, he argued, was not genuine, but supplied by someone who wanted to soften the harsh teaching of the original
text. He found another apologetically motivated alteration at
John 7:1. There his Greek manuscripts recorded that Jesus
"did not wish to travel in Judea because the Jews sought to
kill him." In the commentaries of Chrysostom, Cyril, and Augustine, however, he found evidence of another, more difficult
reading: Jesus "*was not able* to travel in Judea because the Jews
sought to kill him." Again Erasmus argued that the harder
reading was more likely original, but had been altered by
someone offended by its suggestion that Jesus lacked the power
to do as he willed. At Matt. 21:37 Erasmus exposed apologetic tampering with similar reasoning—this time with respect
to the Vulgate, however, not the Greek, where the text retains
its integrity.

At other passages Erasmus noticed intentional changes that
arose from advanced theological scruples, and here too he in-

---

[97] For a more thorough discussion see Jerry H. Bentley, "Erasmus, Jean Le
Clerc, and the Principle of the Harder Reading," *RQ* 31 (1978):309-21.

voked the principle of the harder reading in his effort to recover a more pure text of scripture. At Matt. 24:36 the original Greek text teaches that "no one knows about this day and
hour [i.e., that of Jesus' return], neither the angels of the
heavens, nor the son, except the Father alone." The parallel
text at Mark 13:32 reads almost identically. Erasmus' manuscripts, however, lacked the phrase "nor the son" at Matt. 24:36.
He found it in the works of Origen, Augustine, Jerome, and
others who commented on this passage; he had Jerome's testimony to its presence in many Latin manuscripts at Matt.
24:36; and he found it in his own Greek manuscripts of Mark,
which he considered merely a summary of Matthew's gospel.
With this evidence in mind he framed a sophisticated argument that the phrase had originally been included at Matt.
24:36, but had been erased by opponents of the Arians. Pious
scribes or theologians had a motive for suppressing the phrase
at Matt. 24:36, but the commentators and author of Mark
had no reason gratuitously to add a phrase suggesting Jesus
was not omniscient. At 1 John 4:3 Erasmus found another
alteration—this one aimed not at the Arians, but at Docetic
heretics. The original Greek warns that "every spirit that does
not confess Jesus is not of God." Erasmus' Greek manuscripts
slightly expanded on this text: "every spirit that does not confess *that Jesus came in the flesh* is not of God." He apparently
knew no manuscript or patristic evidence for the correct text,
but the Vulgate's rendition raised his eyebrows: "every spirit
that rejects Jesus is not of God." Even without good textual
data he suspected—probably correctly—that his Greek manuscripts had been doctored so as to emphasize Jesus' human
as well as his divine nature.

Perhaps better than his analysis of any other single text,
Erasmus' treatment of 1 Cor. 15:51 reveals how far his textual
scholarship surpassed that of his predecessors. Lorenzo Valla

had called attention to the discrepancy between the Greek and Vulgate texts at this point, and had suggested a revised and improved translation of the Greek. The Complutensian editors had not seen fit to point out the discrepancy—except briefly in their manuscript annotations—and they published conflicting Greek and Latin texts in their edition. In a footnote they cited a variant reading in the Greek text on Jerome's witness, but made no attempt to explain the origin of the variant or in any way to throw further light on the problems of this text.

Erasmus' treatment of 1 Cor. 15:51 is manifestly superior to those of both Valla and the Complutensian circle. Erasmus began his discussion of this passage with a review of the textual data. He found in Greek manuscripts the following text:

πάντες μὲν οὐ κοιμηθησόμεθα, πάντες δὲ ἀλλαγησόμεθα.
(Although we shall not all sleep, yet we shall all be transformed.)

The Vulgate presumed a different Greek text:

Omnes quidem resurgemus, sed non omnes immutabimur.
(We shall indeed all rise, but we shall not all be transformed.)

Erasmus cited Jerome's testimony to Greek manuscripts that presented a text supporting the Vulgate, but he found his own Greek text preserved in the works of many Greek Fathers, including Chrysostom, Theophylactus, and Origen. Besides the two Greek texts, Erasmus found three Latin renderings of the passage. Most widely spread was that of the Vulgate, which he found supported by Ambrosiaster. Augustine also knew the Vulgate text, but reported a second reading in some Latin manuscripts:

Omnes quidem dormiemus, sed non omnes immutabimur.
(We shall all sleep, but we shall not all be transformed.)

Erasmus pointed out further that Pelagius (whom Erasmus called the Pseudo-Jerome) and Thomas Aquinas discussed both these Latin readings in their commentaries and added to it yet a third, one that agreed with the Greek:

Omnes quidem non dormiemus, sed omnes immutabimur.
(We shall not all sleep, but we shall all be transformed.)

This reading he found supported also in the works of Tertullian. Erasmus' own translation differed only slightly from this last:

Non omnes quidem dormiemus, omnes tamen immutabimur.
(We shall not all sleep; nevertheless, we shall all be transformed.)

How does the textual critic make sense of this confusing array of variant readings? Erasmus began with the assumption that the Greek manuscripts preserved the correct text; then he considered the various scruples that might induce a scribe to alter the genuine text. St. Augustine himself had raised questions about the first clause of the Greek text: "We shall not all sleep." He thought this teaching contradictory to what St. Paul wrote only a few lines earlier, at 1 Cor. 15:36: "What you sow is not brought to life unless it first dies." Erasmus dissolved this difficulty by explaining Paul's intention: he did not mean to say at 1 Cor. 15:51 that no man escapes death, but sought rather to offer encouragement to his readers by persuading them that the dead would eventually be restored to life. Erasmus suggested also a second scruple as a possible cause of corruption. The second clause of the passage—"we shall all be transformed"—might suggest to readers that the impious will benefit alongside the pious at the resurrection. This worry, Erasmus thought, moved scribes to alter Paul's teaching and present it in more orthodox form: "We shall indeed all rise, but we shall not all be transformed." In favor of his own Greek reading and his Latin translation of it he cited the widespread consensus of Greek manuscripts and the doctrinal harmony between his texts and St. Paul's other teachings on resurrection at 2 Cor. 5 and 1 Thess. 4. And finally, he invoked the principle of the harder reading: "Whenever the ancients report variant readings, that one always seems to me more esteemed which at first glance seems more absurd, for it is likely that a reader who is either not very learned or not very attentive was offended by the specter of absurdity and altered the text."[98]

Thus, in place of a simple criticism of the Vulgate's translation (as in Valla) or simple report of a variant reading (as in the Complutensian New Testament), Erasmus presented at 1 Cor. 15:51 a sophisticated analysis of both Greek and Latin texts, taking into account the various scruples that might have induced scribes to tamper with the original Greek text.

This pattern is observable time and again not only in the "lower criticism" discussed so far, but also in the "higher criticism," the analysis of problems of composition, authorship, and authenticity of New Testament writings. Lorenzo Valla reported St. Jerome's doubts about the authorship of the catholic epistles, as seen above, and he ventured contradictory opinions concerning the original language of Matthew and the authorship of the Epistle to the Hebrews. The mind of the Complutensian editors on such questions is unclear, since they did not raise issues of higher criticism in their edition of

[98] On Erasmus' note to 1 Cor. 15:51 and its problems see ibid., esp. pp. 317-20.

the New Testament or in their manuscript annotations. Only Stunica openly addressed such issues, and then only in polemical works directed against Erasmus' scholarship, to be examined in the next chapter. Given the generally conservative tenor of Complutensian scholarship, one suspects that Stunica spoke for most of his colleagues in rejecting Erasmus' criticism in favor of traditional teachings.

Erasmus made himself unpopular in some quarters for airing views that challenged tradition. He rejected out of hand the authenticity of the pseudo-Pauline Epistle to the Laodiceans and the apocryphal correspondence between Seneca and St. Paul, both published by Lefèvre d'Étaples as part of his edition of the Pauline Epistles.[99] In a note to Matt. 8:23, Erasmus disputed two other cherished myths: he argued that the gospel of Matthew and the Epistle to the Hebrews were originally composed in Greek, not in Hebrew, as hoary legend maintained. In all these cases he depended chiefly on stylistic arguments. The epistle to the Laodiceans and the Seneca-Paul correspondence he considered frigid in tone, not at all similar to the genuine Pauline writings with their fervent, sometimes impassioned teachings. He found the language of Matthew's gospel so close to that of Mark and Luke especially, and to a lesser extent John, that one could hardly doubt all were originally composed in the same tongue, Greek. He did not develop such a detailed argument for the Epistle to the Hebrews, but merely advanced his opinion that its style too suggested composition in Greek.

Much more controversial in his own day were Erasmus' doubts concerning the authorship of two canonical books of

[99] The spurious Epistle to the Laodiceans and Seneca-Paul correspondence occur in Lefèvre's *Pauli epistolae* (Paris, 1512), fol. 188[r], 226[v]-29[r]. Erasmus rejected the authenticity of the documents in notes respectively to Col. 4:16 and 2 Thess. 2:5. For the Seneca-Paul letters see also *EE*, no. 2092 (8:40-41).

the New Testament, the Epistle to the Hebrews and the Apocalypse. As a matter of convenience Erasmus referred to Paul as the author of Hebrews throughout the *Annotations* to that epistle, but at the end of the letter he presented a long note disputing Pauline authorship. The epistle lacked the subscript found at the foot of several other Pauline letters, he noted, and many Church Fathers entertained doubts about its authorship. More significantly, he found theological discrepancies between Hebrews and other Pauline writings: the author of Hebrews held no hope for baptized Christians who slid back into sin (Heb. 6:4-6), but St. Paul considered eligible for salvation even the man who had slept with his father's wife (1 Cor. 5:1-5). Finally, Erasmus referred, unfortunately without elaboration, to great differences in literary style between Hebrews and genuine Pauline writings. Though unable to prove it, he inclined toward St. Jerome's suggestion that Clement of Rome wrote the epistle and intended it for the Church of Corinth. As for the Apocalypse, Erasmus thought untenable the traditional ascription to John the Evangelist, and he developed his argument in a note to Apoc. 22:20. Again he cited doubts of the Fathers as to the book's author, and he pointed out the obvious stylistic discrepancies between the Apocalypse and the gospel of John. He added his own observation that some Greek manuscripts ascribe the Apocalypse to a certain John the Theologian, not the Evangelist. He admitted the book into the canon of scripture, albeit reluctantly, on the consideration that God would not allow the Church to labor 1,500 years under the deception of false revelation. But he felt uneasy about the bizarre, allegorical riddles of the book, and he openly hinted that it was not a very important part of scripture. And he left the clear impression that John the unimpeachably orthodox Evangelist had nothing to do with its production.

Erasmus did not approach the precision of twentieth-century scholarship in his treatment of these problems, but his application of independent, unbeholden reflection to scriptural problems must be reckoned a crucial step in the emergence of critical New Testament scholarship. In fact, on the evidence of the preceding pages, one can only conclude that Erasmus' scholarship was in general an impressive affair. Modern editors do not always agree with the texts and readings he chose to publish, nor with his analysis of textual problems. But the *Annotations* make it clear that Erasmus devoted an enormous amount of time and effort to New Testament research, considered a staggering amount of evidence, and intelligently evaluated it in proper theological and philological context. The *Annotations* alone should prove sufficient to dispose of a rather silly notion, sometimes still repeated, that Lorenzo Valla and Politian were the only true philologists of the Renaissance.[100] In criticizing the Greek and Latin texts of the New Testament, Erasmus far outstripped his predecessors in philology and textual scholarship. And in doing so he furthered the development of the methods, principles, and insights that later philologists would use in classical and New Testament studies. Modern scholars do not often realize it, but their analytical tools make frequent appearances, at least in embryo, in the *Annotations* of Erasmus.

Translation

As in textual criticism, so in his evaluation of the Vulgate as a translation of the Greek New Testament, Erasmus took his initial cues from Lorenzo Valla's work. Valla had argued that St. Jerome did not translate the Vulgate New Testament, and he attacked the Vulgate itself for poor literary style, in-

[100] E. J. Kenney, *The Classical Text* (Berkeley, 1974), p. 18.

accurate translations, and general obscurity in representing the Greek New Testament. Erasmus heartily endorsed Valla's critical examination of the Vulgate beginning in 1505, when he prepared the *editio princeps* of Valla's *Adnotationes*. But again as in his textual criticism, he did not stop with Valla's achievements. Instead he bolstered all Valla's main points with additional evidence. Furthermore, in two ways he stretched the boundaries of New Testament scholarship insofar as translation is concerned: he produced a fresh Latin translation of the entire New Testament, and he attempted to put philology to practical use by developing the moral and theological implications of his revised translations.

Erasmus argued as early as 1505, in the preface to his edition of Valla's *Adnotationes*, that Jerome could not be held responsible for the Vulgate; and he expanded the argument in a famous apologetic epistle (1514) to Maarten van Dorp.[101] In these places, however, he made his case only in general terms. Many passages of the Vulgate, he said, were marred by solecisms that Jerome, fine stylist that he was, simply would not have allowed into his work. More to the point, perhaps, Erasmus also maintained that Jerome did not prepare the Vulgate on the evidence of his commentaries, where he frequently presented Latin translations more accurate than those found in the Vulgate. But Erasmus reserved for the *Annotations* the real evidence standing behind his argument. There he noted scores of Vulgate passages—e.g., Acts 26:2-3, 1 Cor. 5:6, Gal. 5:7-9, Eph. 1:14, and Eph. 4:29—whose readings conflicted with Jerome's style or commentaries.

This insight no doubt encouraged Erasmus, like Valla, to take a pronouncedly critical attitude toward the traditional Latin scriptures, for rejection of the Vulgate implied no negative judgment on St. Jerome's scholarly abilities. Thus Erasmus

[101] *EE*, nos. 182, 337 (1:410-11; 2:109-110).

freely castigated the Vulgate on many grounds. I cite only a few examples here, since his criticism closely resembles Valla's, even where he treated passages Valla had not discussed. As for style, Erasmus did not hesitate to charge the translator of the Vulgate with bad usage or solecisms, witness his comments to Matt. 22:30, Mark 4:38, Acts 26:2-3, Rom. 2:7, and Rom. 5:3, among many other texts. With Valla he deplored also the Vulgate's rhetorical variety—translation of a given Greek word by several Latin words in order to grace Latin scriptures with a variety absent in the Greek New Testament—citing among other passages Matt. 11:23, Rom. 4:3-8, and 2 Cor. 1:4 on this count. As for accuracy, Erasmus discovered the Vulgate often omitting things found in the Greek text (e.g., at Matt. 27:22, Mark 1:45, and 1 Pet. 1:22), even more often adding things not found in the Greek text (e.g., at Matt. 8:28, Luke 24:36, 1 Cor. 6:20, Eph. 5:15, Phil. 4:8-9, and 1 Tim. 1:2), and perhaps most often failing to represent accurately the nuances and verb tenses of the Greek (e.g., at Matt. 4:4, Mark 13:17, Rom. 1:17, Rom. 10:2, and 1 Thess. 3:6). As for obscurity, Erasmus found no lack of it in the Vulgate. Like Valla, he noticed the translator of the Vulgate abusing Latin cases on the example of the Greek language, which lacks an ablative case and consequently employs the genitive and dative cases in ways foreign to Latin usage. Erasmus clarified many passages clumsily translated as a result of this abuse, among them Rom. 2:15, 1 Cor. 14:18, 2 Cor. 2:13, Heb. 3:3, and Titus 1:5.

Erasmus did not slavishly follow Valla's example in his criticism of the Vulgate. Even with respect to the issues discussed here Erasmus treated problems of scriptural translation independently of Valla. He frequently needled Valla, for example, for quibbling over minute points of grammar and usage—e.g., at Matt. 1:16, Mark 1:4, and Luke 2:23—and there will be opportunity in the pages ahead to notice yet other differences between the two men on the problem of translation.

Erasmus' complete translation of the New Testament no doubt aided him in developing this independent attitude toward Valla's work. He set high standards for his version and made large claims for its value. He strove above all for clarity and fidelity in his translation, according to the *Apologia* prefaced to his New Testament. He was less interested in carping at the Vulgate, he said, than in purifying Latin scriptures. He steered a middle course on the question of linguistic style. He considered it necessary to remove solecisms and stylistic eccentricities from the Vulgate, to turn scriptures into good Latin. But he declined the temptation to exhibit his literary skills. The Greek New Testament was not the product of Attic orators, after all, but rather of simple, straightforward working people. Erasmus saw no need to present the Latin New Testament in fancy literary dress. Thus he made no attempt to achieve Ciceronian standards of eloquence in his translation, but neither did he disdain natural elegance born of simple and pure expression. In the end he defined his purpose not as literary, but instructional. He had no desire to displace the Vulgate, revered by many for its familiar and time-honored renditions, but he ventured the promise that whoever read his translation would understand better the meaning behind the Vulgate.[102]

Thus Erasmus set high standards for his version. The question naturally arises: To what extent did he meet those standards?[103] In some ways Erasmus presented a more literal ver-

[102] See the *Apologia* in Holborn, pp. 167-68, 170, 173.

[103] Though several scholars have taken Erasmus' translation of the New Testament as a topic for their research, none has studied the translation itself. Instead they have discussed chiefly the chronology of Erasmus' translation, the controversies it engendered, or his general thought on Bible study and translation. See Bludau, *Die beiden ersten Erasmus-Ausgaben des Neuen Testaments*, pp. 33-48; Holeczek, *Humanistische Bibelphilologie als Reformproblem*,

sion than the Vulgate. At hundreds of points he altered the traditional reading, without necessarily implying criticism of the Vulgate, in order to represent the Greek text as faithfully as possible. At Gal. 4:1-3, for example, the Vulgate rendered the Greek word νήπιος ("infant") as *parvulus* ("youngster"). Erasmus approved the translation as good Latin, but preferred *puer* ("boy") or *infans* ("infant") as better representations of the Greek; he presented *puer* as his own translation. Similarly, at Acts 5:21 he offered *universum seniorum ordinem* ("whole order of the elders") in place of the Vulgate's *omnes seniores* ("all the elders") as a more accurate translation of the Greek, πᾶσαν τὴν γερουσίαν ("whole council of the elders"). Erasmus knew well that such corrections improved on the Vulgate only marginally, but when it came to language, Erasmus was a fastidious man. He wanted his readers to see as clearly as possible what the Greek text said. As a result, his *Annotations* bristle with observations of the sort mentioned above, observations that suggest a slightly more precise Latin rendering than the Vulgate's of the Greek New Testament.

This does not mean that Erasmus fell into a narrow, mechanical literalism, however, and neglected the sense of the words he translated. Indeed, he frequently chastised the Vulgate for sacrificing the sense of a passage on the altar of the letter. As an example, consider his comment on Matt. 6:10. The Greek presents a somewhat stilted text:

γενηθήτω τὸ θέλημά σου, ὡς ἐν οὐρανῷ καὶ ἐπὶ γῆς.
(Let thy will be done, as in heaven also on earth.)

The Vulgate translates absolutely literally, as follows:

Fiat voluntas tua sicut in caelo et in terra.
(Let thy will be done, as in heaven, also on earth.)

pp. 101-37; and W. Schwarz, *Principles and Problems of Biblical Translation* (Cambridge, 1955), pp. 92-166.

"Though he caught the Greek figure of speech," Erasmus noted, "the translator expressed rather obscurely the meaning" of the passage, which Erasmus explained as follows: "What you [God] will, let it be done on earth, i.e., among your celestial people still living bodily on the earth, just as it is done in heaven, where no one opposes your will." Erasmus' own translation captured this sense more succinctly:

Fiat voluntas tua, quemadmodum in caelo, sic etiam in terra.
(Let thy will be done, as in heaven, so also on earth.)

Again, the *Annotations* reverberate with the charge that the Vulgate badly construed the sense of the Greek New Testament. At Rom. 11:11 Erasmus argued that a more sensitive translation would have obviated the need for St. Thomas Aquinas to propose a complicated fourfold exegesis of the Vulgate. At Acts 20:24 he castigated the translator for misrepresenting the sense of the Greek without even offering an accurate literal version.

He never said it in so many words, but his translation and *Annotations* prove it: Erasmus recognized that the effective translator must possess the quality of flexibility. The translator has no warrant, of course, to distort the letter of the original text; but in order to bring forth a useful work, he must stand prepared at least occasionally to bend his text a little bit, to resort to paraphrastic translations, or to adapt his text to the idiom of the receiving tongue. Erasmus recognized the futility of establishing rigid rules of translation to be mechanically applied. Thus he developed an easygoing, flexible attitude toward variety in translation. Like Valla, he scorned the needless rhetorical variety sometimes exhibited in the Vulgate. Yet he recognized that a single Latin word does not always express all the nuances of a given Greek word. Erasmus therefore resorted regularly to varying translation in his effort to capture as fully as possible the sense of the Greek New Testament. He agreed with Valla that the ambiguous verb παρακαλέω ("to exhort" or "to console") should be translated *consolor* ("to comfort") at 2 Cor. 1:3-7, where it occurs several times. At other places, however, he took account of the word's ambiguity and represented it with different Latin terms. In the synoptic gospels alone he rendered παρακαλέω with seven different Latin translations: *rogo* ("to ask"), *deprecor* ("to pray for"), *obsecro* ("to implore"), *exhortor* ("to exhort"), *consolatio admittere* ("to be comforted"), *consolatio accipere* ("to take consolation"), and *solatio fruor* ("to dwell in consolation").[104]

At 1 Cor. 3:17 Erasmus positively approved the Vulgate's varying translation. As St. Paul teaches here: "Si quis autem templum Dei violaverit, disperdit illum Deus"—"If someone profanes God's temple, God will destroy him." Behind the verbs "violaverit, disperdit" there stands the Greek, φθείρει, φθειρεῖ. Indeed the verb φθείρω means not only "to corrupt" or "to profane," but also "to destroy" or "to lay waste." In his zeal to translate each Greek word consistently with the same Latin word, Valla suggested *destruere* ("to destroy") as an appropriate representation of φθείρω in both clauses of 1 Cor. 3:17. But Erasmus preferred to express as fully as possible the sense of each clause. Since no single Latin word embraces all the nuances of the Greek verb, he had recourse to two Latin words in his own translation: "Si quis templum Dei profanat, hunc perdet Deus." Erasmus disagreed with Valla also, to cite a final example, on the translation of δύναμις ("strength," "might," "power," or "ability"). In notes to Matt.

[104] Erasmus translated παρακαλέω as *rogo* at Matt. 8:31, 8:34, 18:29, 26:53; Mark 5:17, 5:18; Luke 7:4, 8:31, 8:32, 8:41, 15:28; as *deprecor* at Mark 1:40, 5:10, 5:12, 5:23, 6:56, 7:32; as *obsecro* at Matt. 8:5, 14:36, 18:32; Mark 8:22; as *exhortor* at Luke 3:18; as *consolatio admittere* at Matt. 2:18; as *consolatio accipere* at Matt. 5:4; and as *solatio fruor* at Luke 16:25.

7:22, Matt. 24:30, and Luke 1:48, Valla insisted on translating the word consistently as either *potentia, potestas,* or *vis* ("power" or "strength"). In the gospels Erasmus usually translated δύναμις as *virtus,* explaining at Matt. 7:22 and Luke 1:17 in the *Annotations* that he used *virtus* in the sense of "divine power," not "virtue" as opposed to vice. But he used different translations at some places in the gospels: *potentia* ("power") at Matt. 6:13, *facultas* ("ability") at Matt. 25:15, and *potestas* ("power") at Luke 4:36 and Luke 9:1. In two passages where the word occurs twice—Mark 13:25-26 and Luke 21:26-27—Erasmus translated it first as *virtus,* then as *potestas.* In the Pauline epistles Erasmus' practice differed even more markedly. There he rarely translated δύναμις as *virtus,* the word he used thirty-two times in the gospels, but instead resorted ordinarily to *potentia,* sometimes *potestas,* occasionally *vis,* and once *fortitudo* ("strength").[105]

The passages discussed so far help to illuminate the principles that guided Erasmus' translation of the New Testament. The revisions he proposed in these texts have few implications for Christian doctrine, theology, morality, or piety, but they demonstrate beyond doubt that Erasmus sought to prepare a version that was both faithful to the letter and sensitive to the spirit of the Greek New Testament.

Erasmus did not look on his translation, however, as a purely objective, purely scholarly exercise. To the contrary, in fact, much more than Lorenzo Valla, his predecessor in criticizing

---

[105] He translated δύναμις as *virtus* in the Pauline epistles at 1 Cor. 4:19-20, 2 Cor. 4:7, 2 Cor. 12:9 (*bis*), 2 Cor. 13:4 (*bis*), Gal. 3:5, Col. 1:29, 1 Thess. 1:5, Heb. 2:4, and Heb. 6:5. He preferred *potentia* at Rom. 1:4, 1:6, 1:20, 9:17, 15:13, 15:19 (*bis*); 1 Cor. 1:18, 1:24, 2:4, 2:5, 6:14, 12:10, 15:43, 15:56; 2 Cor. 6:7, 12:12; Eph. 1:19, 3:7; Phil. 3:10; Col. 1:11; 2 Thess. 1:7, 1:11, 2:9; 2 Tim. 1:7, 1:8; Heb. 1:3, 7:16. He resorted to *potestas* at Rom. 8:38; 1 Cor. 5:4, 12:28; 12:29, 15:24; and Eph. 1:21. He used *vis* at 1 Cor. 14:11; 2 Cor. 1:8, 8:3 (*bis*); Eph. 3:20; 2 Tim. 3:5; Heb. 11:11, 11:34. He used *fortitudo* at Eph. 3:16.

the Vulgate, and unlike Giannozzo Manetti, his predecessor as a translator of the Greek New Testament into Latin, Erasmus kept in view the practical possibilities and doctrinal implications of his fresh version. In preparing his translation he found abundant opportunity to cast important or specially revered passages in new literary form. And in the *Annotations* he often took the occasion to draw moral lessons or develop theological points suggested by his revised and improved translation of the Greek New Testament.

Thus at Matt. 3:2 Erasmus discussed John the Baptist's message: μετανοεῖτε—"repent." The Vulgate translates his teaching as "poenitentiam agite"—"do penance"—which many Latin theologians took as a reference to the sacrament of penance. Erasmus deplored this sort of distorted exegesis based on a faulty translation. In his note to the passage he stressed not the legal, but the moral element of John's teaching. The Greek injunction μετανοεῖτε does not demand that one perform an act of penitence so much as it encourages one to transform his thinking and behavior. Erasmus suggested as a better translation "resipiscite"—"return to your senses." In his own translation he retained the traditional language—"poenitentiam agite"—at Matt. 3:2, where John the Baptist preached repentance. But at Matt. 4:17, where Jesus began his preaching with the same exhortation, μετανοεῖτε, Erasmus provided a new translation: "resipiscite." At Luke 1:28 Erasmus altered another traditional formula, the angelic salutation of the Virgin at the Annunciation: "Ave gratia plena"—"Hail, ye full of grace." Again he clarified the meaning of the Greek text and suggested not so delicately that much exegesis of this passage was fundamentally misguided. The Greek text reads: χαῖρε, κεχαριτωμένη. Erasmus explained this language as a greeting of a specially favored or beloved person. It made little sense, he said, to expound this passage, as many Latin exegetes had done, with reference to medieval categories of grace. The Greek text did not describe Mary as "full of grace." Instead it recorded a salutation appropriate to one who would soon give birth to the author of salvation. Thus Erasmus offered a new translation at Luke 1:28, "Ave gratiosa"—"Greetings, beloved one"—a translation he hoped would draw attention from theological technicalities to the unique event the original author set out to describe.

At other points Erasmus discovered more properly theological implications latent in his revised translation. This was the case, for example, at John 1:1:

GREEK TEXT ᾽Εν ἀϱχῇ ἦν ὁ λόγος.
VULGATE In principio erat verbum.
ERASMUS' TRANSLATION In principio erat sermo.

All three texts might be translated, "In the beginning there was the word." Yet Erasmus fought numerous literary and theological skirmishes in order to justify his choice of words. He pointed out that *verbum* means "a word," where *sermo*, like λόγος, means "word" in the sense of "speech," "discourse," or "oration." The evangelist, Erasmus argued, wanted to convey this sort of rhetorical dimension in Jesus' nature: "Christ is called λόγος for this reason, that whatever the Father speaks, he speaks it through the Son." More than one recent scholar has found in Erasmus' treatment of John 1:1 an important clue to the whole of his humanist theology.[106]

Erasmus' translation and explanation of Rom. 5:12 harbored implications even more fundamental for Christian doctrine. Once again, the texts bear quotation in full:

[106] See especially Boyle, *Erasmus on Language and Method in Theology*, esp. pp. 3-31, where in a strikingly original and sensitive study, Erasmus' treatment of John 1:1 becomes a starting point for the analysis of his rhetorical, humanist theology. See also C.A.L. Jarrott, "Erasmus' *In Principio Erat Sermo*: A Controversial Translation," *Studies in Philology* 61 (1964):35-40.

GREEK TEXT:

διὰ τοῦτο ὥσπερ δἰ ἑνὸς ἀνθρώπου ἡ ἁμαρτία εἰς τὸν κόσμον εἰσῆλθεν καὶ διὰ τῆς ἁμαρτίας ὁ θάνατος, καὶ οὕτως εἰς πάντας ἀνθρώπους ὁ θάνατος διῆλθεν, ἐφ' ᾧ πάντες ἥμαρτον. (Therefore, just as sin entered the world through one man, and through sin death, so also death spread to all men, since all have sinned.)

VULGATE:

Propterea sicut per unum hominem in hunc mundum peccatum intravit, et per peccatum mors, et ita in omnes homines mors pertransiit, in quo omnes peccaverunt. (Therefore, just as sin entered this world through one man, and through sin death, so also death has spread to all men, in whom [referring to "one man," i.e., Adam] all have sinned.)

ERASMUS' TRANSLATION:

Propterea quemadmodum per unum hominem peccatum in mundum introiit, ac per peccatum mors, ita sic in omnes homines mors pervasit, quatenus omnes peccaverunt. (Therefore, just as sin entered the world through one man, and through sin death, so also death has spread to all men, since all have sinned.)

The differences in translation seem minor, but nothing less than the doctrine of original sin stands at issue. Beginning with St. Augustine, Latin theologians had relied on the Vulgate, referred *in quo* ("in whom") to Adam, and taken Rom. 5:12 as providing the clearest scriptural proof for the doctrine of original sin.[107] The Vulgate's translation and this interpretation of it seem strained on the face of things. Erasmus based

[107] See Karl Hermann Schelkle, *Paulus, Lehrer der Väter* (Düsseldorf, 1956), pp. 162-78.

his own translation on the observation that idiomatic Greek uses the prepositional phrase ἐφ' ᾧ not in a relative, but in a causal sense. The translation should therefore read not *in quo* ("in whom"), but *quatenus* ("since"). On this reading, Rom. 5:12 refers only to personal sins and cannot be considered to validate the doctrine of original sin.

Erasmus quickly learned how unpopular this reading could be. In December of 1516 George Spalatin, then court chaplain to Elector Frederick the Wise of Saxony, wrote Erasmus and passed along the opinions of "an Augustinian priest distinguished no less in the holiness of his life than in theological eminence." The Augustinian, unnamed in the letter, highly approved most of Erasmus' works, but advised Erasmus to read Augustine's anti-Pelagian writings in order to grasp better Paul's discussion of original sin in the Epistle to the Romans. Thus did Erasmus first encounter, anonymously, the thought of Martin Luther.[108] Other critics also opened fire on Erasmus' treatment of Rom. 5:12. In the final edition of the *Annotations* Erasmus greatly expanded his note to this passage in order to justify his position. The note grew from a few lines of philological detail to a short treatise on all the problems—grammatical, exegetical, and theological—involved at Rom. 5:12. Erasmus bolstered his grammatical point—that the phrase ἐφ' ᾧ was causal, not relative—by adducing examples of similar usage from other parts of scripture. He strengthened his exegetical point—that Paul referred to personal, not original sin at Rom. 5:12—by reviewing the comments of the Greek Fathers, who largely agreed with Erasmus. Finally, he addressed the theological issues. He denied Pelagianism and affirmed the doctrine of original sin; but he denied absolutely that Rom. 5:12 proved the doctrine and in-

[108] *EE*, no. 501 (2:417-18).

sisted that theologians confront the Pelagians with sound interpretations of the scriptures.

Thus Erasmus' fresh translation emerges as an important element of his New Testament scholarship. There can be no doubt that his version reflected the original Greek text more truly than the Vulgate; indeed, this achievement itself encouraged conservative Roman theologians to reject Erasmus' new translation. Medieval theologians had invested much Catholic doctrine in the precise language of the Vulgate, and any revision of this prized work might undermine important tenets of the Roman faith. Erasmus' entire literary corpus, translation of the New Testament included, found its way onto the first Roman Index of Prohibited Books (1559), and conservative theologians continued all through the sixteenth century to hunt for errors in Erasmus' Latin New Testament.[109]

Exegesis

The last few paragraphs illustrate the close connection between translation and exegesis. Indeed, the success of Erasmus' explanation of the New Testament depended largely on his fresh understanding of the Greek text. In recent years scholars have made significant progress in assessing the work of Erasmus as New Testament exegete.[110] They have analyzed several works where he established general rules of hermeneutics and exegesis—his manual of pious theology, for example, the *Enchiridion militis christiani* (1501); his treatise on the proper method of constructing biblical theology, the *Ratio verae theo-*

[109] Myron P. Gilmore, "Italian Reactions to Erasmian Humanism," in *Itinerarium italicum*, ed. H. A. Oberman and T. A. Brady (Leiden, 1975), pp. 61-115; G. van Calster, "La censure louvaniste du Nouveau Testament et la rédaction de l'index érasmien expurgatoire de 1571," in *Scrinium erasmianum*, ed. J. Coppens (Leiden, 1969), 2:379-436.

[110] See especially the works cited above, notes 9, 83, 84.

logiae (1518); and his handbook for preachers, the *Ecclesiastes, sive concionator evangelicus* (1535). Scholars have devoted attention not only to Erasmus' theoretical treatises, but also to exegetical writings where he put his principles to work. The *Paraphrases*, for example, where Erasmus lightly glossed the entire New Testament, except the Apocalypse, have generated a fair amount of interest. The *Paraphrases* did not lack editorial comment, some of it quite important for understanding Erasmus' thought.[111] But the format of the *Paraphrases* was such that Erasmus could not fully explore even the most important passages. Only in the *Annotations* did he come to grips with the passages that most interested him, examine them in detail, and discuss them from various angles. One must therefore study the *Annotations* in order to understand Erasmus the exegete at work on individual problems and texts.

Erasmus not infrequently illustrated proper exegetical method by negative contrast, i.e., by exposing and correcting the misguided comments of his predecessors. For the most part he appreciated patristic exegetes, and the *Annotations* abound with reports of their explanations. Occasionally, however, even the most sagacious of the Church Fathers erred in Erasmus' view. Origen came into criticism for artificially subtle exegesis at Rom. 1:8 and Rom. 13:1; Jerome for a heavy-handed Platonizing exposition at Eph. 1:17; Ambrosiaster for distorting the literal sense of scripture at Rom. 14:5-6 and Col. 2:18. St. Augustine received a rather larger share of Erasmus' critical attention. Erasmus taxed him at various points for numerical speculation (John 2:18-22), misunderstanding the literal sense (Rom. 14:5), needless allegory (John 11:9-10), forced explanation (Gal. 5:12), and deriving doctrine without sufficient textual warrant (1 Cor. 3:12-15). Yet Erasmus retained a healthy respect for patristic exegesis, and he usually cited the

[111] Roland H. Bainton, "The Paraphrases of Erasmus," *ARG* 57 (1966):67-76.

Fathers, Augustine included, by way of approving, or at least publicizing their exegesis.[112]

The medieval exegetes did not fare so well in the *Annotations*. Erasmus quickly passed off the *Glossa ordinaria* at 2 Tim. 2:15 as "a Rhapsody, which for some unknown reason is called 'ordinary.'" But St. Thomas Aquinas bore the brunt of Erasmus' attack on medieval exegesis. He came under fire for introducing Platonic Ideas into his exegesis (at Col. 1:15), needlessly complicating his explanations (at 2 Cor. 8:19), indulging in useless allegorical speculation (at 1 Tim. 2:15), commenting in ignorance of the Greek text (at Heb. 12:23), distorting the plain sense of scripture to support Church dogma (at 1 Tim. 6:15), proposing trivial numerological explanations (at 1 Cor. 14:19), suggesting inept etymologies (at 1 Cor. 13:4), depending on collections of excerpts instead of original commentaries (at Rom. 2:24), and in general lacking the sort of broad erudition prerequisite to successful exegesis (at 1 Cor. 14:11). Erasmus concentrated his criticism on St. Thomas, but he did not overlook opportunities to score points against other medieval exegetes. He frequently lumped Nicholas of Lyra and Hugh of St. Cher together—e.g., at John 19:13, Acts 28:11, and 1 Tim. 1:18—in denouncing their inept exposition or ignorance of Greek. Erasmus especially scorned Lyra, both inside and outside the *Annotations*. In Erasmus' best-known work, Dame Folly mocked scholastic exegetes in general, and one in particular whom she refused to name, lest he call to mind the Greek proverb about "the ass at the lyre."[113] The whole problem of Erasmus' attitude toward medieval ex-

---

[112] Several recent works point out Erasmus' indebtedness to patristic authorities: Charles Béné, *Érasme et St. Augustin* (Geneva, 1969); Godin, "Fonction d'Origène dans la pratique exégétique d'Érasme"; and Payne, "Erasmus: Interpreter of Romans."

[113] *LB*, 4:491 DE. In his *Adages* Erasmus explained the proverb "asinus ad lyram" as referring to those "who on account of their inexperience have no judgment and unattuned ears." See *LB*, 2:164 B–165 A.

egetes calls for further study. A very impressive recent examination has shown, for example, that Erasmus made much more
use of the *Glossa ordinaria* than his negative evaluations of it
might suggest.[114] Only further analyses can tell to what extent
this pattern holds true for other medieval commentaries.

Few will be surprised to find Erasmus treating medieval
exegetes in such disrespectful fashion, but few will be prepared for the independent attitude he displayed also toward
his humanist predecessors. After all, in the *Apologia* prefaced
to the New Testament, Erasmus openly proclaimed himself a
follower of Lorenzo Valla and Lefèvre d'Étaples.[115] And several times in the *Annotations*, as elsewhere, he favored them
with high praise—Valla, for example, at Acts 22:9 and Lefèvre at Rom. 1:5. Yet when Erasmus cited their specific arguments in the *Annotations*, he usually did so only to set them
aside. The explanation for this lies partly in the fact that Erasmus devoted much more effort to New Testament problems
than his humanist predecessors, so that he sometimes considered their work shallow. Furthermore, Erasmus' own critics
provided him with a motive to put distance between himself
and his predecessors. In a famous letter of 1514, Maarten van
Dorp reported to Erasmus the reservations held by many with
respect to Erasmus' scholarly projects. He suggested to Erasmus, among other things, that in Valla's and Lefèvre's works,
humanist scholarship had exhausted itself; it was not likely to
lead to further discoveries of any interest or importance.[116] In
his reply (1515), Erasmus acknowledged his respect for both
Valla and Lefèvre, but made it clear also that he disagreed

[114] H. J. de Jonge, "Erasmus und die Glossa ordinaria zum Neuen Testament," *Nederlands archief voor kerkgeschiedenis*, n.s. 56 (1975):51-77. This superb analysis ought to serve as a model for future studies of Erasmus' thought
on medieval commentators.
[115] Holborn, pp. 173-74. Cf. *EE*, no. 334 (2:78).
[116] *EE*, no. 304 (2:14-15).

with both at some points.[117] Thus Erasmus looked critically on the works of his humanist predecessors well before his New Testament appeared in print. Nevertheless, with its ominous warning that he represented the views of the theological faculty at the University of Louvain, Dorp's letter probably fortified Erasmus in the resolve to present himself as an independent scholar. Thus already in the first edition of the New Testament, Erasmus reviewed critically the work of Valla and Lefèvre. He charged Valla with caviling at trivial points of grammar and exegesis in notes to Matt. 1:16, Mark 1:4, Mark 7:34, Luke 2:23, Luke 2:38, 1 Cor. 9:5, and Col. 2:18, among others. Finally, as noted above, he found Valla's efforts at the higher criticism somewhat deficient.

Perhaps even more disappointing was the Pauline scholarship of Erasmus' friend, Lefèvre d'Étaples. Lefèvre's *Pauli epistolae* provides a handsome edition of the Pauline epistles in the Vulgate's translation and in Lefèvre's own fresh version, and equips them with an exegetical and philological commentary. From Erasmus' point of view, Lefèvre possessed the right instincts, but lacked the mental toughness required to act properly on them. Lefèvre based his work on a study of the Greek text, but he made erratic and arbitrary textual decisions. More than a few times he allowed tradition, legend, or theological interests to supersede philological considerations. Thus Erasmus found fault with Lefèvre's textual scholarship at 1 Cor. 15:45 and 2 Cor. 10:16; his translations of the Pauline epistles at 1 Cor. 5:4 and 1 Cor. 12:28; and his exegesis at Rom. 1:5 and Col. 2:18. At Heb. 2:7 Erasmus and Lefèvre became involved in a public dispute. Erasmus translated the passage literally from the Greek text: "You have made him [Jesus] a little lower than the angels." Lefèvre considered this translation offensive on Christological grounds, and he pre-

[117] *EE*, no. 337 (2:112).

ferred to bypass the Greek and translate according to the Hebrew text of Ps. 8:6—"You have made him a little lower than
God"—which indeed the author was quoting at Heb. 2:7.
The two men aired their differences in an extended and sometimes bitter polemic on the text, translation, and interpretation of the passage. Only after several attempts at mediation
did Lefèvre tacitly concede defeat.[118] Finally, Erasmus took
Lefèvre to task for his efforts at the higher criticism, which he
considered sadly deficient. Though he did not include them
in the New Testament canon, Lefèvre had published the apocryphal Epistle to the Laodiceans and the spurious Seneca-Paul
correspondence as genuine writings of St. Paul. Erasmus was
immediately struck by the manifest falsity of all these letters,
and in notes to Col. 4:16 and 2 Thess. 2:5 he scornfully dis-
missed them from the Pauline corpus.

Almost all the criticisms of Valla and Lefèvre noted above
occurred in the first edition of Erasmus' New Testament and
Annotations. In later editions of his work Erasmus introduced
a few fresh criticisms, especially of Valla, which suggest another reason for his independent attitude toward his predecessors—this one springing from his own intellectual development. Take as an example Erasmus' note to 1 Cor. 15:10,
where St. Paul credited not himself, but "the grace of God
that is with me" for his successful evangelical labors. In 1516
Erasmus pointed out the Vulgate's slight mistranslation of this
passage and noted that Valla rejected the use of it as scriptural
support for the scholastic category of cooperating grace. In
1519 he added three words, indicating that St. Thomas Aqui-

---

[118] Modern scholarship on this controversy includes Margaret Mann Phillips, *Érasme et les débuts de la Réforme française, 1517-1536* (Paris, 1934), pp.
23-46; Helmut Feld, "Der Humanisten-Streit um Hebräer 2, 7 (Psalm 8,
6)," *ARG* 61 (1970):5-35; and Payne, "Erasmus and Lefèvre d'Étaples as
Interpreters of Paul," which places the quarrel in the context of both men's
Pauline exegesis.

nas accepted the interpretation that Valla rejected. In his fourth edition (1527) he added substantially to the note, saying he found nothing to preclude the scholastic exegesis of the passage. In other words, he sided with St. Thomas against Valla— a highly uncharacteristic course of action for Erasmus. The chronology of the note suggests an explanation. Erasmus' peculiar appreciation of scholastic exegesis appeared only after his bitter controversy with Martin Luther on the freedom of the will (1524-1527), during which Erasmus discovered new virtues in the well-established scholastic theological categories, including that of cooperating grace.[119]

The one contemporary whom Erasmus rarely castigated was his friend, John Colet. Granted, in 1499 Colet and Erasmus debated the nature of Christ's agony in the garden of Gethsemane. But Erasmus respected Colet's thought on the New Testament and encouraged him in 1504 to publish his lectures and commentaries. Colet did not take Erasmus' advice, and his New Testament studies remained unpublished until the late nineteenth century.[120] Colet escaped Erasmus' criticism partly, no doubt, because his works were not widely known. Apart from that, however, I suspect Erasmus found little to upset him in Colet's works. Colet had only a smattering of Greek and was thus unable to address philological issues in an informed manner. He consequently overlooked problems at texts like Rom. 5:12 and 1 Cor. 15:51, where Erasmus presented long discussions. Colet's purpose, however, was not to produce a learned philological analysis of the New Testament, but rather to present an exegetical summary of Pauline doc-

[119] Cf. John B. Payne, *Erasmus: His Theology of the Sacraments* (Richmond, Va., 1970), esp. pp. 19-23, 74-84.

[120] For the debate on Christ's agony, see *EE*, nos. 108-111 (1:245-60). For Erasmus' encouragement to publish, see *EE*, no. 181 (1:404). I have relied on J. H. Lupton's editions of Colet's commentaries: *Enarratio in epistolam S. Pauli ad Romanos* (London, 1873), and *Enarratio in primam S. Pauli epistolam ad Corinthios* (London, 1874).

trine in clear, straightforward fashion, unadorned by scholastic trappings—an enterprise Erasmus could heartily endorse. To the extent that he went beyond a literal explanation, Colet exhibited biases that again appealed to Erasmus. He emphasized the transcendence of God and the heavenly world at Rom. 9:11-13, for example, in providing a mildly Neoplatonic framework for the Pauline epistles. And he frequently developed the moral implications of the text under review, as in long discussions to Rom. 12-14, where he encouraged his readers to exhibit charity, good will, and obedience to authority; and to 1 Cor. 6, where he cautioned against offensive behavior and called for high standards of personal morality.

Thus Erasmus enjoyed a thorough grounding in patristic, scholastic, and humanist exegesis, and he recognized well the limitations, if not always the merits, of his predecessors' efforts. The foundation of Erasmus' own exegesis was a finely tuned sense for words—Greek words and Latin both—and their meanings and functions understood in their whole context. As early as 1501 Erasmus insisted on the necessity of Greek for intelligent exegesis.[121] By the time he published the *Ratio verae theologiae* (1518), however, his thought on proper exegetical method had considerably matured. There he argued in memorable language that the student of scripture must not only master the biblical languages, but also seek to understand biblical literature on its own terms. One must pay attention, that is, "not only to what is said, but also by whom it is said, to whom, with which words, at what time, on what occasion it is said, what precedes and what follows it." One must recognize further the peculiar features of biblical language, which makes liberal use of tropes, allegories, parables, enigmas, idioms, and the like.[122]

---

[121] *EE*, no. 149 (1:352).
[122] Holborn, pp. 181-84, 195-96, 259-78. By far the best study of Eras-

In the *Annotations* Erasmus developed this last observation into a very important insight. At Acts 10:38, commenting on a solecism in the Greek text, he pointedly remarked that "the apostles got their Greek not from Demosthenes' orations, but from vulgar speech." The New Testament was therefore filled with Hebraisms and inelegant expressions. This literary fact did not scandalize Erasmus; indeed, he thought it appropriate that transmission of the gospel was not entrusted to orators, but to simple men who spoke in plain and honest, if sometimes rude fashion. Full understanding of common Greek (*koinē*) became available only in this century, with Adolf Deissmann's studies of the Oxyrhynchus papyri, but Erasmus may be credited with recognizing clearly the colloquial character of New Testament Greek and the demands it placed on the exegete. Deissmann might almost have taken from Erasmus his point that "the historical connecting-points of New Testament Greek are not found in the period of the Epos and the Attic classical literature. Paul did not speak the language of the Homeric poems or of the tragedians and Demosthenes, any more than Luther that of the Nibelungen-Lied."[123]

A striking illustration of Erasmus' close attention to words and their proper usage occurs in his discussion of the terms πίστις and *fides* (both translated usually as "faith") at Rom. 1:17, and right away one begins to perceive the distance between Erasmus and his predecessors in exegesis, both scholastic and humanist. Nicholas of Lyra expounded this text with reference to the categories *fides informis* and *fides charitate formata*, as seen above, and Lorenzo Valla merely changed the

---

mus' hermeneutics is that of John B. Payne, "Toward the Hermeneutics of Erasmus," in *Scrinium erasmianum*, ed. J. Coppens, 2:13-49.

[123] A. Deissmann, *Biblical Studies*, trans. A. Grieve (Edinburgh, 1909), p. 63. See also Deissmann's most important work, *Light from the Ancient East*, 4th ed., trans. L.R.M. Strachan (New York, 1927); and A. T. Robinson, "New Testament Grammar after Thirty Years," in *Festgabe für Adolf Deissmann* (Tübingen, 1927), pp. 82-92.

tense of the verb from present, as in the Vulgate, to future, as in the Greek text. Erasmus, too, presented a new translation that more accurately mirrored the Greek, but he took the occasion, as Valla had not, also to discuss at length the crucial idea of faith. The Latin language possessed no precise equivalent of the Greek word πίστις, he said, though *fides* expressed several of its nuances, which he proceeded to review. A man is said "to have faith in another" (*habere fidem alicui*) when he believes what the other has said. He is said "to give faith" (*dare fidem*) when he solemnly pledges something. He "binds his faith" (*adstringit fidem suam*) who obliges himself to another. He who carries out his promises "redeems his faith" (*liberat fidem suam*). He "lacks faith" (*fide caret*) whom no one believes. He "violates faith" (*fidem violat*) who refuses to honor his commitments. Erasmus continued the discussion at some length and summarized as follows:

> *Fides* therefore is used by the Latins sometimes of the person promising something, sometimes of him who carries out a promise; sometimes of the person believing something, sometimes of him who is believed; sometimes it is an abstract noun, as when we speak of "faith destroyed by the manners of men," meaning that no one fulfills his promises, and no one trusts another.

Then Erasmus turned to the Greek word πίστις. It too is used of someone making or fulfilling a promise, he said, but it can mean other things as well. Sometimes it refers, for example, to a trial (*probatio*) by which we convince someone of something. In that case he is called "faithful" (πίστος) who does not fail another. He "has faith" (πιστεύει) who believes or trusts or commits himself to something. The Vulgate, Erasmus continued, rather mechanically represents πίστις with *fides*, but often the sense would be better served by other Latin words, such as *credulitas* ("belief") or *fiducia* ("trust"). The term *fides* is simply not flexible enough to represent the Greek accurately in all its guises. Sometimes in the Vulgate *fides* stands for an intellectual conviction that even demons can hold, but not infrequently it represents the notion of a trust in God not far removed from "hope" (*spes*). With all this discussion as background, Erasmus addressed the passage at hand, Rom. 1:17. He expounded the two main elements of the text with respect to both *fides Dei* ("faith of God") and *fides hominis* ("faith of man"). The first part of the passage declares that "the justice of God is revealed in [the gospel] from faith into deeper faith." With respect to the *fides Dei*, Erasmus explained that God proved his trustworthiness by fulfilling his promises; with respect to the *fides hominis*, men by degrees increased their knowledge of God and their trust in him. The second part of the passage applies to this teaching the prophecy of Hab. 2:4: "the just man will live by faith." With respect to the *fides Dei*, Erasmus explained that God will not renege on his promises; with respect to the *fides hominis*, the just man places his trust in God.

Most striking in this discussion is Erasmus' profound sensitivity to words and their uses. He ignored the scholastics' categories of *fides informis* and *fides charitate formata*, established in response to the demands of medieval theology, and resorted instead to literary categories, established on the basis of wide reading and close attention to uses made of the words *fides* and πίστις. This explains my earlier generalization that Erasmus founded his exegesis on a finely tuned sense for words, their meanings and functions, understood in their whole context. Students of Erasmus' exegesis these days usually emphasize the moral dimension of his work—his exhortations to pious reform and spiritual renewal—and even in the *Annotations* Erasmus developed moral interpretations of the scriptures.[124]

---

[124] For a representative sampling of recent work see Payne, "Erasmus

But moralism cannot explain all, or even most of Erasmus' commentary on the New Testament. For the larger part of the *Annotations* Erasmus employed his literary and philological insights in an attempt to recover the precise message intended by New Testament authors for their earliest readers. This goal led him primarily to exegesis not of the moral, but of the literal or historical sense of scripture.

For the most part, Erasmus' literal exegesis took the form of a short *explication de texte*: Erasmus illustrated the meanings of words, paraphrased, and discussed the precise sense of various passages. Since he based his exegesis on the Greek text, he was able to slip behind the Vulgate and offer more accurate explanations than earlier exegetes could have provided. At 1 Cor. 13:4, for example, the Vulgate teaches that "charitas patiens est"—"charity is patient." Erasmus explained that behind *patiens est* in Greek there stood the verb μακροθυμεῖ, which suggests that charity is "long-suffering" (*longanimis*), "mild-mannered" (*leni animo*), or "big-minded" (*magnanimis*), or in any case, not inclined toward anger or revenge. At John 14:6 Erasmus again unveiled the sense of the Greek masked by the Vulgate. Jesus announces here that "I am the way and the truth and the life"—ἐγώ εἰμι ἡ ὁδὸς καὶ ἡ ἀλήθεια καὶ ἡ ζωή. In accordance with normal Latin usage, the Vulgate omitted the definite article: "Ego sum via et veritas et vita." Erasmus had pointed out earlier, at John 1:1, that the definite article in Greek often had the force of the Latin demonstrative pronoun *ille* ("this one"). In applying this observation at John 14:6, he offered in a few lines a point that could not be drawn from the Vulgate: "It is to be noted that the article is affixed to each of these nouns, ἡ ὁδὸς, ἡ ἀλήθεια, καὶ ἡ ζωή, so

---

and Lefèvre d'Étaples as Interpreters of Paul," *passim*; Georges Chantraine, "Érasme, lecteur des Psaumes," in *Colloquia erasmiana turonensia*, ed. Jean-Claude Margolin, 2:691-712; and Rabil, *Erasmus and the New Testament*, pp. 100-103.

that we understand by them not just any old way or truth or life, but that true and unique way, truth, and life."

Most of Erasmus' literal exegesis in the *Annotations* resembles this sort of tame explication, but more than a few of his notes touched on sensitive theological issues. Erasmus' goal was to understand and explain what the New Testament meant for its authors and earliest readers. Among other things, this entailed reading out of proper exegesis a great many theological doctrines and concepts popular with medieval commentators. At 1 Cor. 3:12-15, for example, Erasmus denied that the text supported the Church's teaching on purgatory. Commenting on Peter's confession of faith at Matt. 16:18, Erasmus marveled that so many exegetes had distorted the passage and taken it as proof of papal authority in the Church. More controversial were notes where Erasmus addressed Christological issues in such an historical fashion.[125] He was not scandalized by the notion that one could call the Father the "foundation of the deity" or "the only true God," as he openly confessed in notes, respectively, to John 8:25 and John 17:3. Moreover, he removed Rom. 9:5 and Phil. 2:6-7 from the Church's arsenal of anti-Arian ammunition, even though earlier exegetes and theologians accepted these passages as providing good, solid, scriptural proof of orthodox Nicene Christology. Finally, as shown earlier, Erasmus argued several times that scribes had altered original texts in order to remove potentially embarrassing Christological suggestions—e.g., at Matt. 24:36, John 7:1, and 1 Tim. 1:17. Erasmus appended theological disclaimers to many of these notes: he did not side with the Arians and did not seek to aid their cause. In fact he did not hesitate to appropriate texts (e.g., Rom. 1:3-4) for orthodox Christology when he found them clearly attributing both human and divine natures to Jesus. But he insisted that

[125] For an excellent discussion of Erasmus' Christological views see Payne, *Erasmus: His Theology of the Sacraments*, pp. 54-70.

theologians combat Arianism with sound reasoning and honest arguments, not doctored texts and distorted exegesis.

A similar pattern emerges in a series of notes concerning sacramental theology.[126] At 2 Cor. 7:10 Erasmus followed Lorenzo Valla in showing that the Greek word μετάνοια ("repentance") did not precisely match the Latin *poenitentia* ("penitence"), and that it certainly did not imply an elaborate penitential theology built on the elements of contrition, confession, and satisfaction. At Acts 19:18 he argued that the early Church did not know the practice of secret, auricular confession. He denied that matrimony was proved one of the seven sacraments by authority of Eph. 5:32. At none of these points did Erasmus challenge contemporary doctrine: the consensus or authority of the Church persuaded him to accept traditional theology concerning the sacraments. But he refused to allow exegetes or theologians to draw fallacious and anachronistic inferences from the scriptures. These notes (and many others) therefore illustrate well what John Payne has called the "dialectical relationship between the authority of the Church and [Erasmus'] humanistic reason."[127] Proper literal exegesis demands an accurate reconstruction of the texts' original meaning, even if the results prove inconvenient for important doctrines, which then must be justified on grounds other than the scriptures.

The application of humanist reason to New Testament exposition led Erasmus also to problems in the historical background of the New Testament. Thus like Lorenzo Valla, he addressed the question of Dionysius the Areopagite at Acts 17:34. He reviewed Valla's arguments against identifying the Areopagite with the Pseudo-Dionysius: the Areopagites were judges, but the Pseudo-Dionysius was a philosopher; the sup-

---

[126] On this topic see Payne, ibid., who pays close attention to the *Annotations* in an impressive and sensible study.

[127] Ibid., p. 154.

posedly Attic Pseudo-Dionysius mentioned an earthquake reported nowhere outside Judea; and none of the early Fathers referred to the Pseudo-Dionysius. Erasmus also mentioned a work of Valla's, now lost, an epistle written under Dionysius' name that described the earthquake at Jesus' death. Then Erasmus added further considerations that strengthened the case against identifying Dionysius the Areopagite with the Pseudo-Dionysius. In the time of St. Paul and the Areopagite the Church did not employ nearly so many elaborate ceremonies as the Pseudo-Dionysius described in his works. Furthermore, although Eusebius and St. Jerome between them mentioned at least three early Christians named Dionysius, it seemed to Erasmus impossible to identify any of them with the Pseudo-Dionysius, for neither Eusebius nor Jerome attributed to them works resembling those of the Neoplatonic theologian. Thus Erasmus added further detail to Valla's historical and philological arguments against the Pseudo-Dionysius' antiquity and his identity with the Areopagite. Finally, he reported also the experience of William Grocyn, one of England's earliest Greek scholars. Grocyn began to lecture on the Pseudo-Dionysius' *Celestial Hierarchies* with vehement attacks on those who denied the Areopagite's authorship. But before he got halfway through the work, Erasmus said, he began to read more attentively and frankly confessed to his audience that he could no longer believe the work came from the Dionysius converted by St. Paul at Athens.

When Erasmus passed beyond literal and historical explanations, he most often suggested what might be called a moral application of the scriptures: he established New Testament teachings as a standard against which he measured his own times, usually finding them wanting. The *Annotations* are liberally spiced with Erasmus' denunciations of hypocritical mendicants (Mark 6:9), monks and priests who mechanically chant prescribed texts (1 Cor. 14:19), bishops who prey on their

flocks (1 Cor. 9:6), warmongering popes (Acts 5:14), and
venal soldiers (Rom. 6:23). At Matt. 11:30, where Jesus described his yoke as pleasant and his burden as light, Erasmus
lashed out at the "petty human regulations" that weighed down
on sixteenth-century Christians and stifled pious impulses. At
1 Tim. 1:6, where the author discussed aberrant Christians
who devoted themselves to "inane chatter" (ματαιολογία),
Erasmus thought of contemporary theological methods. "As
far as pronunciation goes," he said, "*mataeologia* isn't too far
from *Theologia*." He continued with a many-count indictment
of scholastic theologians who disputed endlessly about the nature of sin but would not teach people to flee it; who wran-
gled over the mystery of the Trinity but never encouraged
adoration of God; who in general posed superfluous and impious questions but failed to inculcate faith, charity, and patience in individual Christians.

Erasmus' attitude toward allegorical exegesis was more
complicated than that toward moral or tropological explanation. In the *Enchiridion militis christiani* (1501) he advised the
reader to study exegetes who passed as far as possible beyond
the literal sense and developed all the subtle implications latent in the scriptures. He suggested Jesus, Paul, Origen, Jerome, Augustine, Ambrose, and even the Pseudo-Dionysius
as examples of such deeply spiritual exegetes.[128] By the time
he published the *Ratio verae theologiae* (1518), however, Erasmus had tempered this view. There he warned against wan-
tonly allegorical explanations that distorted the literal or historical sense. In 1523 he added some passages to the *Ratio*
that singled out Origen, Ambrose, and Hilary for criticism,
charging them with abusing the literal sense and proposing
trivial allegorical explanations.[129] In the *Ecclesiastes, sive concionator evangelicus* (1535), Erasmus censured both stupid lit-

[128] Holborn, pp. 28-38, 67-88.
[129] Holborn, pp. 258-84. For the additions of 1523 see pp. 280-82, 284.

eralism and arbitrary allegory. He allowed allegory when necessity or utility demanded it, but insisted that allegorical explanations conform to piety and the literal sense of the scriptures. Here he especially encouraged development of the tropological or moral sense: all passages of scripture, he said, were relevant to the improvement of morals, but not necessarily to the technical matters of faith and doctrine addressed by proper allegorical exegesis.[130]

Only rarely in the *Annotations* did Erasmus permit allegory that passed clearly beyond the boundaries of the literal sense. He cited with apparent approval, for example, tame allegorical expositions proposed by Jerome at Matt. 3:12 and Cyril at John 7:8. He himself occasionally acknowledged the presence of allegories, typological parallels, and mystical senses in the scriptures, especially in the Pauline epistles, witness notes to Rom. 15:4 and Heb. 1:1. But usually when Erasmus raised the subject of allegory in the *Annotations* it was to reject speculative explanations that violated the literal sense in probing the subtleties and secrets of the scriptures. Thus he disallowed allegorical expositions advanced by Augustine at John 11:9-10, Theophylactus at 1 Cor. 2:13, and both of them along with Jerome and others at Matt. 13:23.

This does not mean, however, that Erasmus lacked interest altogether in spiritual exegesis. In fact, in the later editions of his New Testament—especially in the last edition, which came off the press only sixteen months before his death in July of 1536—Erasmus added a series of reflective passages that suggest a more general spiritual understanding than a mechanical allegorical exposition could provide. Take as an example his comment on 1 Cor. 2:13: "We speak not in the learned language of human wisdom, but in that of the spirit, interpreting spiritual things in a spiritual manner." In the first four editions

---

[130] *LB*, 5:1026-51.

of the *Annotations* Erasmus contented himself with a short philological note, literal exegesis, and critique of Theophylactus' strained allegorical explanation. Inspired by his reading of Chrysostom, he expanded the note in the last edition of his New Testament, emphasizing the gospel's independence of human reason. One does not resort to philosophical arguments to prove the doctrine of Jesus' virgin birth or resurrection, he said, but rather to scriptures or miracles. God created trees without seeds, Adam from mud, Eve from a rib, and earth from nothing. Thus he found it easy to fashion a human body in a virgin's womb and to restore a dead man to life. The later editions of Erasmus' *Annotations* present many such added passages. In 1527, for example, he first published at Rom. 1:17 his long discourse on *fides* discussed earlier. In 1535 he expanded his notes to Rom. 3:21 and Rom. 5:1, emphasizing the role of faith and grace in justification.

Perhaps the most interesting of these late additions to the *Annotations* is that to 1 Cor. 13:13: "Now there remain these three things, faith, hope, and charity, but the greatest of them is charity." In the 1519 edition of the *Annotations* Erasmus presented a few lines of philological comment, which he slightly expanded in 1522. In 1535, however, the note swelled to the size of a small treatise, and it shifted the focus from small points of philology to important matters of doctrine. The bulk of the note consists of a comparison of charity and faith. In view of Erasmus' lifelong campaign to encourage moral and pious reform in Christendom, it will perhaps come as a surprise to learn that here he exalted the importance of faith over charity. Erasmus granted that God found no quality more pleasing than charity, but denied that men could exhibit charity or any other spiritual gift in the absence of faith. Faith he described as "a sort of hand of the mind" by which men grasped and received gifts, including charity, offered by the Holy Spirit. Since faith stands prior to charity, it is therefore the more illustrious quality. Several further arguments tend toward the same end: charity without faith is dead. For faith, Erasmus summarized, is the "root and fount of all spiritual gifts, including even charity itself."

These late additions to the *Annotations* could perhaps be pressed into service by those who argue that Erasmus reflected the influence of Martin Luther's thought in the 1520s and 1530s, or that he attempted in his exegesis of that same period to play a mediatory role between the Lutherans and the Roman Church.[131] It seems to me more likely, however, that they exhibit to us that elder Erasmus whose ethical optimism and faith in active charity had been eroded, not only by the failure of the Roman Church to reform itself so as to meet Erasmus' high standards, but also by the disheartening spectacle of reformers who brought few reforms but many controversies.[132]

Conclusion

Most scholarship on Erasmus' New Testament has placed his work in theological context, and not without reason. Upon publication of the Greek New Testament in 1516, letters rolled in from all parts of Europe praising Erasmus for his services to Christian learning. His exegesis encouraged those who looked for reform in the Church. Luther, Calvin, and Zwingli, to

---

[131] Robert G. Kleinhans, "Luther and Erasmus, Another Perspective," *Church History* 39 (1970):459-69; Tracy, *Erasmus: The Growth of a Mind*, pp. 182, 235; John B. Payne, "The Significance of Lutheranizing Changes in Erasmus' Interpretation of Paul's Letters to the Romans and the Galatians in His *Annotationes* (1527) and *Paraphrases* (1532)," in *Histoire de l'exégèse*," pp. 312-30.

[132] Tracy, *Erasmus: The Growth of a Mind*, esp. pp. 227-36.

name only a few, recognized the opportunities offered by Erasmus' study of the scriptures in their original languages, and all three relied heavily on his Greek New Testament in framing Reformation doctrine and developing a Protestant theology. Meanwhile, Cardinals Cajetan, Contarini, and Sadoleto inaugurated a less well known but equally important tradition of Roman Catholic scholarship on the Greek New Testament.

Without denying the theological significance of Erasmus' work, this chapter I hope makes it clear that his New Testament must be considered also in another context—that of the history of scholarship. It would be an exaggeration to call Erasmus a modern scholar in an unqualified sense of the term. The past four centuries have brought much more data and much better understanding of the New Testament and its problems than Erasmus had at his disposal. Moreover, in the realm of the higher criticism, scholars today approach the New Testament with a fundamentally different attitude from that of Erasmus. Modern students employ advanced techniques, such as form and redaction criticism, designed to dissect the scriptures, analyze each part deeply, and lay bare their differences, so as to illuminate the thought and theology peculiar to the individual human authors of scripture. Erasmus was convinced, however, that the New Testament was basically of a piece. He knew that New Testament authors addressed different problems, that they sometimes disagreed with each other, that Peter and Paul squabbled, and so forth. But for Erasmus the entire Christian canon, with the possible exception of the Apocalypse, exhibited and encouraged those qualities of faith, piety, and charity that he considered necessary to Christendom, but sadly lacking in the sixteenth century. Thus his scholarly writings often do not read like those of contemporary students of the New Testament. He became almost homiletic at points, and he sometimes aimed frankly, not simply to explain and clarify the New Testament, but to employ his research in the cause of moral and religious renewal.

Nonetheless, Erasmus' New Testament studies point well beyond his own age to a new era of scholarship. He demonstrated in a piece of prodigious research that close attention to details of philology, language, and history could lead to important and impressive new understandings of ancient religious documents. In his work, modern New Testament scholarship and scholarly methods took their first great leap forward, and this was perhaps the most enduring of all the legacies Erasmus bequeathed to his cultural heirs.

FIVE

Controversy and the Consolidation of Humanist Scholarship

E RASMUS' New Testament scholarship quickly became the focus of bitter quarrels. Relations between Erasmus and the French humanists, especially Guillaume Budé and Lefèvre d'Étaples, were severely strained by the dispute between Erasmus and Lefèvre on the text, translation, and interpretation of Heb. 2:7. But most of Erasmus' troubles came from another quarter. Conservative scholars and theologians attacked his text, translation, and exegesis, on account of both his methods of scholarship and the specific results he obtained. Though uncoordinated, the conservative reaction was quite a large movement with representatives all over Europe. British critics included Edward Lee, the monk John Batmanson, and Henry Standish, Bishop of St. Asaph; from Louvain the mercurial Maarten van Dorp spoke now for, now against Erasmus, while Jacob Masson (Latomus) and Frans Tittelmans consistently attacked him; in Paris Petrus Sutor, Noel Beda, and the Faculty of Theology denounced him; John Eck questioned his methods from Germany; Stunica and Sancho Carranza led a Spanish defense of tradition against Erasmus' New Testament. Erasmus' liberal religious views and satirical social criticism of course attracted conservative attention to his other works—

194

The Praise of Folly, for example, and the *Colloquies*—and students of Erasmus have recently begun to recognize the ensuing controversial literature as an important source for the reconstruction of his thought.[1] The controversies on the New Testament, though not entirely neglected, have been less thoroughly studied.[2] I make no attempt here to review in detail Erasmus' quarrels with all the figures mentioned above: that would lead to a long, tedious, repetitive account of dubious value, since the different controversies revolved around similar issues and often the same New Testament passages. Instead, this chapter presents a more analytical discussion of the issues themselves in an effort to clarify the early reception of humanist philology.

Controversy

The controversies began even before the publication of Erasmus' Greek New Testament. Prodded by his mentors on

[1] See Franz Bierlaire, *Les colloques d'Érasme* (Liège, 1978), esp. pp. 201-303; and several articles by Myron P. Gilmore: "*De modis disputandi*: The Apologetic Works of Erasmus," in *Florilegium Historiale: Essays Presented to Wallace K. Ferguson*, ed. J. G. Rowe and W. H. Stockdale (Toronto, 1971), pp. 62-88; "Erasmus and Alberto Pio, Prince of Carpi," in *Action and Conviction in Early Modern Europe: Essays in Memory of E. H. Harbison*, ed. T. K. Rabb and J. E. Seigel (Princeton, 1968), pp. 299-318; "Anti-Erasmianism in Italy: The Dialogue of Ortensio Lando on Erasmus' Funeral," *Journal of Medieval and Renaissance Studies* 4 (1974):1-14; and "Italian Reactions to Erasmian Humanism," in *Itinerarium italicum*, ed. H. A. Oberman and T. A. Brady (Leiden, 1975), pp. 61-115.

[2] A. Bludau reviews Erasmus' controversies at some length, emphasizing especially those with Lee and Stunica, *Die beiden ersten Erasmus-Ausgaben des Neuen Testament* (Freiburg-im-Br., 1902), pp. 58-145. Heinz Holeczek discusses the quarrel with Sutor, *Humanistische Bibelphilologie als Reformproblem* (Leiden, 1975), pp. 186-245. For Erasmus' problems with the critics from Louvain see Jerry H. Bentley, "New Testament Scholarship at Louvain in the Early Sixteenth Century," *Studies in Medieval and Renaissance History*, n.s. 2 (1979):51-79.

the Faculty of Theology at Louvain, Maarten van Dorp initiated in September of 1514 a famous series of correspondence
wherein he expressed conservatives' reservations about Erasmus' works, chiefly *The Praise of Folly* and the projected editions of St. Jerome and the Greek New Testament.[3] Dorp
argued in general terms here for the primacy of the Vulgate
in New Testament studies: he disparaged the critical scholarship of Erasmus' humanist predecessors, Valla and Lefèvre; he
argued that the Vulgate offered a text superior to that of the
Greek New Testament, which he thought vitiated by heretical
and schismatic Greeks; he expressed his fear that criticism of
the Vulgate would erode faith in the integrity and validity of
the scriptures. Erasmus replied with common-sense arguments, insisting that serious studies of the New Testament
must be based on the Greek text, though he made no attempt
in correspondence to support his arguments with specific il-
lustrations of his method and the results it produced. Relations between Erasmus and Dorp alternately flamed and fes-
tered over the next few years, and Erasmus' friend Thomas
More himself jumped into the fray before a final reconciliation
was effected in 1520, when Dorp moved openly into the humanists' camp.[4] Meanwhile, without benefit of examining
Erasmus' Greek New Testament, Dorp had anticipated several
of the most common objections to be raised by Erasmus' conservative critics.

Chief among these critics were Edward Lee, Frans Tittelmans, and most formidable of all, Stunica. This discussion will
concentrate on their works, though occasionally those of other

---

[3] The most important letters in this correspondence are *EE*, nos. 304, 337,
347 (2:10-16, 90-114, 126-36).

[4] For a more detailed account of this controversy see Bentley, "New Testament Scholarship at Louvain," esp. pp. 53-60; and Henry de Vocht, *Texts
and Studies about Louvain Humanists in the First Half of the XVIth Century*
(Louvain, 1934), pp. 123-254. For More's intervention see *The Correspondence of Sir Thomas More*, ed. E. F. Rogers (Princeton, 1947), no. 15.

critics will help to illuminate specific issues. Lee's attacks on Erasmus sprang largely from personal pique.[5] Lee and Erasmus met in mid-1517 and enjoyed amicable relations for several months while both lived in Louvain—Erasmus preparing the second edition of his New Testament, and Lee studying Greek at the Trilingual College. A sensitive man and no stranger to pride and ambition, Lee came to believe by mid-1518 that Erasmus had snubbed him by ignoring a set of annotations Lee had prepared, possibly at Erasmus' invitation, on the first edition of the New Testament. The atmosphere around the two men soon darkened with real and imagined insults, and Lee decided to publish against Erasmus. In February of 1520 there appeared in Paris a thick volume containing several of Lee's apologies, epistles, and most importantly, two sets of annotations attacking Erasmus' New Testament.[6]

About the same time Erasmus came also under Stunica's fire.[7] Stunica had long nourished a desire to loose an attack on Erasmus' New Testament. In 1521 Erasmus heard from Juan de Vergara that Stunica had drawn up a set of critical notes upon reviewing the first edition of the New Testament. He made the tactical error, however, of showing his work to Cardinal Ximénez, who forbade its publication unless Stunica submitted his notes to Erasmus and failed to receive a satisfactory response. "Turn out better work if you are able," he told Stunica, "but don't condemn the efforts of others."[8] Stunica

---

[5] The most complete accounts of Erasmus' feud with Lee will be found in Ferguson, pp. 225-34; and Bludau, *Die beiden ersten Erasmus-Ausgaben des Neuen Testaments*, pp. 86-125.

[6] *Annotationes in annotationes novi testamenti Desiderii Erasmi*, and *Annotationes in annotationes posterioris aeditionis novi testamenti Desiderii Erasmi*, printed together with the more general works (Paris, 1520). I shall cite them respectively as the *Annotationes* and *Novae annotationes*, following Lee's own usage.

[7] The only detailed account I know of this controversy is that of Bludau, *Die beiden ersten Erasmus-Ausgaben des Neuen Testaments*, pp. 125-40.

[8] *LB*, 9:284 CE. Cf. also *EE*, nos. 1128, 1216 (4:319, 533). For Vergara's role see *EE*, Appendix XV, no. 1 (4:623-25).

bided his time while the Cardinal lived, but between 1519 and 1524 he published a volume of critical notes on Lefèvre d'Étaple's edition of the Pauline epistles and a series of violent attacks on Erasmus' New Testament scholarship in general.[9]

This feud had hardly ended before Frans Tittelmans began (in 1525) to deliver a series of lectures on the scriptures to his Franciscan brothers in Louvain.[10] He took it upon himself to correct the errors of the humanist New Testament scholars—Valla, Lefèvre, and especially Erasmus—and eventually he published works attacking Erasmus' treatment of the epistle to the Romans and the Apocalypse.[11] As is well known, Erasmus did not take criticism gracefully, and he responded promptly to most of his critics' attacks with apologies reprinted in his collected works.[12]

All these controversies were marred by personal vituperation and criticisms based on an almost willful misunderstanding of Erasmus' *Annotations*. Stunica passed Erasmus off as a simple Dutchman, drenched in beer and butter, who obviously could not possess much understanding of classical and biblical literature. More than once he lectured Erasmus on the greatness of Spain, when he seemed to sense in Erasmus a slur

---

[9] *Annotationes contra Iacobum Fabrum Stapulensem* (Alcalá, 1519); *Annotationes contra Erasmum Roterodamum in defensionem tralationis novi testamenti* (Alcalá, 1520); *Libellus trium illorum voluminum praecursor quibus Erasmicas impietates ac blasphemias redarguit* (Rome, 1522); *Erasmi Roterodami blasphemiae et impietates* (Rome, 1522); *Conclusiones principaliter suspecte et scandolose que reperiuntur in libris Erasmi Roterodami* (Rome, 1523); *Assertio ecclesiasticae translationis novi testamenti a soloecismis quos illi Erasmus Roterodamus impegerat* (Rome, 1524); and *Loca quae ex Stunicae annotationibus, illius suppresso nomine, in tertia editione novi testamenti Erasmus emendavit* (Rome, 1524).

[10] Bentley, "New Testament Scholarship at Louvain," pp. 69-79.

[11] *Collationes quinque super epistolam ad Romanos beati Pauli apostoli* (Antwerp, 1529); *Libri duo de authoritate libri apocalypsis beati Ioannis apostoli* (Antwerp, 1530). See also his more general *Epistola apologetica* (Antwerp, 1530), also directed against Erasmus.

[12] *LB*, 9:123-284 (against Lee); 283-400 (against Stunica); and 967-1016 (against Tittelmans).

on, or at least a lack of appreciation for his native land.[13] Lee and John Eck both became upset with Erasmus' note to Acts 10:38, where he pointed out that the apostles learned their Greek in the streets, not from the study of Demosthenes' orations. Both Lee and Eck proceeded to infer that Erasmus looked condescendingly on apostolic literature and its authority, and both asserted that the Holy Spirit endowed the apostles with their gift of tongues. Lee harangued Erasmus for more than two folios and ended by warning him that "you had best watch what you say"—"Quare cave dicas."[14] Tittelmans saw as the driving force behind humanist scholarship not the desire to improve understanding of biblical writings, but base vanity, impious curiosity, and the urge to criticize and even to ridicule the scriptures.[15] One may reasonably count personal and professional jealousies among the motivations of Erasmus' critics.

For the most part, however, the critics—especially Stunica and Tittlemans—addressed more pertinent and scholarly issues. It will be most convenient here to examine their works under the rubrics employed throughout this study: textual criticism, translation, and exegesis. Erasmus' critics accepted the premise that Latin manuscripts presented a more accurate text of scripture than Greek, whence they proceeded to establish their basic principle of textual criticism: Greek New Testament manuscripts must be corrected against the Vulgate. They did not attempt to revive that peculiar medieval notion discussed above, the idea, based on the misunderstanding of St. Jerome's prologue to the Pentateuch, that Latin manuscripts of the scriptures were better than Greek and Greek better than Hebrew. Both Erasmus and Antonio de Nebrija

---

[13] *Annotationes contra Erasmum*, fol. E iii[v], F iii[r]–F iv[r], G iii[v]–G iv[r].

[14] Lee, *Annotationes*, fol. XLIV[r]–LI[v]. For Eck's objection see *EE*, no. 769 (3:210).

[15] *Collationes quinque*, esp. fol. a 3[v].

had effectively disposed of that piece of lore.[16] The sixteenth-century critics of Erasmus instead simply asserted the superiority of the Vulgate over the Greek text of the New Testament. Dorp rated the Vulgate more accurate than the Greek text in 1514 and 1515, and Latomus, his colleague at Louvain, argued likewise in his dialogue on languages in 1519.[17] All three of Erasmus' chief critics agreed with this assessment, and all three argued openly at one point after another that Greek New Testament manuscripts were inferior to the Vulgate with respect to purity of text.[18]

Of the three, only Stunica was clever enough to counter Erasmus' textual criticism by providing alternative explanations of corruption, explanations that spared the Vulgate responsibility for introducing errors into the text of the New Testament. At 2 Cor. 1:6 he blamed scribes—not the translator—for introducing a variant reading into the Vulgate. At John 7:53–8:11 he argued that John the Evangelist had originally included the story of the adultress in his gospel, but that heretics had erased it from many manuscripts. He suggested no motive that might explain the suppression, but he pointed out on Origen's authority that heretics often tampered with the New Testament. Even more interesting was his treatment of Matt. 21:37, where the owner of the vineyard in the parable sent his son out to the rebellious, murdering servants saying, "Perhaps they will respect my son." Erasmus had ar-

[16] On the origin of the notion see A. Landgraf, "Zur Methode der biblischen Textkritik im 12. Jahrhundret," *Biblica* 10 (1929), esp. pp. 445-56. For Erasmus' and Nebrija's reaction to the medieval belief see *EE*, no. 182 (1:411) and *Tertia quinquagena* (Alcalá, 1516), fol. a ii^v–b ii^r.

[17] See Dorp's letters to Erasmus, *EE*, nos. 304, 347 (2:14-15, 131-32); and Latomus' *De trium linguarum et studii theologici ratione dialogus* in his *Opera*, ed. J. Latomus iunior (the elder's nephew) (Louvain, 1550), fol. 160^{rv}.

[18] See for example Lee's notes to Luke 2:14, 2 Cor. 4:10, and Titus 2:11 in the *Annotationes*; Stunica's notes to Rom. 2:17, 1 Cor. 6:20, 1 Cor. 12:10, and 1 Thess. 2:7 in the *Annotationes contra Erasmum*; and Tittelmans's prologue and note to Rom. 11:6 in the *Collationes quinque* (fol. c 2^r–c 8^v for the prologue).

gued in sophisticated fashion that the word "perhaps" (*forte*) was not geniune. He found it in neither Greek nor old Latin manuscripts, and he explained its presence as an addition by a scrupulous scribe who noticed that the servants in fact did not respect the son, but murdered him instead. Stunica stood Erasmus' explanation on its head: the "perhaps" was indeed genuine, he said, but had been removed from both Greek and Latin manuscripts by those who thought it unseemly for scripture to speak in doubtful terms. There can be no doubt that Erasmus presented the more convincing explanation—no Greek manuscript includes the qualification "perhaps" at Matt. 21:37—but Stunica's note shows that he at least sometimes recognized a responsibility to provide an alternative for views he rejected.

Stunica had worked on the Complutensian editorial team, and he enjoyed a much better knowledge of New Testament manuscripts than either Lee or Tittelmans. These latter almost never cited manuscripts against Erasmus: in rejecting his readings they could only assert stubbornly the accuracy of the Vulgate against Erasmus' Greek text. Stunica, however, often drew on his research in manuscripts in order to refute Erasmus' textual arguments. He placed special value on the Codex Rhodiensis discussed above, a copy of the apostolic epistles that Stunica mentioned by name in rejecting Erasmus' Greek text at five points—2 Cor. 2:3, James 1:22, 2 Pet. 2:2, 1 John 3:16, and 1 John 5:20. Apparently the Codex Rhodiensis presented many readings that supported the Vulgate. It is impossible to know precisely the extent of their agreement, since the manuscript has long been lost. But its close relation to the Vulgate raised Erasmus' suspicions: several times he expressed doubts about its integrity, suggesting that it had been corrected against the Vulgate.[19]

Not even the Rhodiensis supported Erasmus' critics at 1

[19] Besides the note in his *Annotations* to 2 Cor. 2:3, see also his apology to Stunica, *LB*, 9:333 AB, 349 F, 351 C, 351 EF.

John 5:7. Tittelmans did not discuss the problem of the *comma Johannuem*, since he limited his attack to Erasmus' scholarship on the epistle to the Romans and on the Apocalypse, but both Lee and Stunica reacted vigorously to Erasmus' first two editions of the New Testament, which omitted the reference to three heavenly witnesses to Jesus' truth. Stunica evidently knew no Greek manuscript that included the *comma*—in his discussion of the passage he in fact quoted a Greek text that supported Erasmus in omitting the *comma*—so he was forced to argue that *all* Greek codices were corrupted at this point. Lee responded more abusively, predicting that Erasmus' text would encourage the revival of Arianism and would lead to division and discord in the Church. Both Stunica and Lee were motivated by considerations of theology, not philology. But Erasmus buckled under their criticism, and in the third edition of his New Testament he included the *comma*, "lest someone have occasion for slander"—"ne cui sit ansa calumniandi."[20]

Of Erasmus' three chief critics, Stunica and Tittelmans displayed most interest in the issues raised by Erasmus' efforts at the higher criticism. Stunica argued against Erasmus that Matthew's gospel was originally composed in Hebrew and that John the Evangelist wrote the Apocalypse. In both cases he depended on the evidence not of philology, but of traditional authorities: Origen, Chrysostom, Jerome, and Augustine with respect to Matthew; Origen, Chrysostom, and the Pseudo-Dionysius with respect to the Apocalypse.[21] More elaborate was Tittelmans's defense of traditional views on the Apoca-

---

[20] Lee's note occurs in the *Novae annotationes*, fol. CXXVI^r–CXXIX^r. Erasmus' responses to Lee and Stunica occur, respectively, in *LB*, 9:272-284, 353. For the controversy as a whole, see H. J. de Jonge, "Erasmus and the *Comma Johanneum*," *Ephemerides theologicae lovanienses* 56 (1980):381-89; and Bludau, "Der Beginn der Controverse," *Der Katholik*, 3rd ser. 26 (1902), esp. pp. 167-75.

[21] *Annotationes contra Erasmum*, fol. A ii^v–A iii^r, K iii^v–K iv^r.

lypse, presented in a long treatise divided into two books.[22] In the first, Tittelmans culled statements from many Church Fathers in an effort to prove that the Apocalypse was true, authoritative scripture and that John the Evangelist was its author. He cited Origen, Eusebius, Chrysostom, Jerome, and Augustine among his authorities; but he considered as his prime witness the Pseudo-Dionysius, whom Tittelmans of course identified with Dionysius the Areopagite converted at Athens by St. Paul. In the second book of his treatise, Tittelmans addressed more directly the individual points Erasmus made in his note at the end of the Apocalypse. Erasmus expressed doubts, for example, that the same man wrote the gospel of John, the epistles of John, and the Apocalypse of John, because of the striking differences in style exhibited in those works. Tittelmans replied that John the Evangelist wrote all the works, but accommodated his style to his various messages, circumstances, and audiences. In response to Erasmus' deprecating valuation of the Apocalypse's doctrine, Tittelmans relied heavily on the Pseudo-Dionysius to emphasize the book's apostolic gravity. Many people fail to understand the mysteries and enigmas of the Apocalypse, he said, and thus propose distorted and carnal explanations of its teachings. If they would learn to cut through the externals and penetrate to the divine, ineffable truth, they would appreciate the profound and mystical significance of the Apocalypse.

Erasmus' critics therefore depended largely on the authority of the Vulgate and Church Fathers in their criticism, both lower and higher, of the text of the New Testament. Only rarely did they attempt to frame properly philological arguments against those advanced by Erasmus. Yet more than a few times they forced Erasmus to modify his text or reconsider his arguments. The third edition of Erasmus' New Tes-

---

[22] *Libri duo de authoritate libri apocalypsis*. For fuller discussion of this work see Bentley, "New Testament Scholarship at Louvain," esp. pp. 76-78.

tament (1522) reveals especially clearly the influence of his critics' pressure. Most notable was his introduction in that edition of the *comma Johanneum* on the strength of Lee's Codex Monfortianus. But he altered his text at other less sensitive points as well. Stunica went so far as to publish a slim volume (1524) where he claimed to have forced changes in the text or notes at forty-three passages in Erasmus' third edition. Erasmus recognized the validity of his criticism, he said, and modified his work accordingly, but failed to credit Stunica's role in the matter.[23] The charge seems petty, and in any case, most of the alterations involve minor points of exegesis; but there can be no doubt that Erasmus did indeed correct some passages on the basis of Stunica's criticism.[24]

By the late 1520s, Erasmus seemed weary of the controversies his scholarship had engendered, and he made some concessions to his critics. In 1527, for example, he added to his *Apologia* prefaced to the New Testament a passage affirming that the authors of scripture had made no mistakes, that errors crept into scripture only through inattentiveness of copyists and translators. The addition clearly constitutes a sort of recantation of Erasmus' note to Matt. 2:6, where the evangelist had manifestly misused the Hebrew scriptures. Erasmus' note to the passage openly charged the author with introducing human error into the original text of the New Testament. The note proved highly unpopular with conservatives, and

[23] *Loca quae ex Stunicae annotationibus, illius suppresso nomine, in tertia editione novi testamenti Erasmus emendavit.*

[24] See, for example, Erasmus' note to John 12:3. In 1516 and 1519 it read: "Libram unguenti.) λίτραν latinam vocem inflexit in graecam mutata literula B in T." But in 1522 Erasmus offered an entirely new note: "Libram unguenti.) λίτραν. Videri poterat Evangelista Latinam vocem inflexisse in Graecam, nisi λίτραν Iulius Pollux testaretur vocem esse a vetustis scriptoribus Graecis usurpatam, ut probabilius sit Latinos eam vocem a Graecis sumpsisse mutuo." Stunica had made the same point and included a long quotation from Julius Pollux in his *Annotationes contra Erasmum*, fol. D iii[v]–D iv[r]. Cf. also the *Loca*, fol. B ii[rv].

Erasmus had to defend it against the criticism of Lee and John Eck.[25] In this context Erasmus' 1527 addition to the *Apologia* can only be construed as a retraction of the critical views he expressed in his original note to Matt. 2:6. Five years later he gave ground also with respect to the higher criticism, in response to censures voted against him by the Faculty of Theology at the University of Paris, and he agreed to submit his judgment to the authority of the Church. If the Church pronounced St. Paul the author of the epistle to the Hebrews and John the Evangelist the author of the Apocalypse, then Erasmus would drop his criticism and accept the traditional teachings on the authorship of these works.[26]

Erasmus conceded less in the realm of translation than in that of textual criticism, but not for lack of urging. Critics attacked his translation with even greater hostility and intensity than they expended on his text. One of them, Petrus Sutor (Pierre Cousturier), a theologian at the University of Paris, in 1525 devoted a thick treatise to a defense of the Vulgate and attack on Erasmus' new translation. His argument may be briefly summarized: the Vulgate is true, authoritative scripture; St. Jerome translated the entire Vulgate under direct inspiration of the Holy Spirit, and in fact was carried off to the third heaven in preparation for his task; abandoning the Vulgate in favor of new versions, whether Latin or vernacular, constitutes heresy and blasphemy. Erasmus considered Sutor out of his element when it came to philological scholarship. He enjoyed quoting against him the proverb, "ne sutor ultra crepidam"—"let the cobbler keep to his last"—which he explained in his collection of *Adages* with reference to theologians who pass beyond the boundaries of their competence in judging others' works. Erasmus experienced little difficulty exposing the weak philological foundations of Sutor's attack.

[25] *EE*, no. 844 (3:331); *LB*, 9:249 AC.
[26] *LB*, 9:863 D–868 B.

Many Church Fathers, general councils, and orthodox theologians, he showed, had differed among, between, and even with themselves in their readings, and more than a few eminent medieval churchmen had openly challenged the Vulgate's text at many points. Jerome himself had offered in his commentaries numerous, mostly superior translations that differ from the Vulgate's readings. Erasmus agreed that the Holy Spirit was in some way present when Jerome executed his work, but he flatly denied that the Spirit shielded the Vulgate from all errors. He doubted that flaws in the Vulgate obstructed one from attaining faith or salvation, but he argued also the continued need for scholars to point out and improve on the Vulgate's misleading or inaccurate renditions.[27]

Unlike Sutor, Erasmus' other critics descended to the particular: they defended the Vulgate and found fault with Erasmus' revised translations at scores of individual passages. Lee and Tittelmans emerged again as the amateurs, Stunica as the more professional of the critics. Though both had some Greek, Lee and Tittelmans rarely resorted to the Greek text in evaluating Erasmus' translations. Instead they usually relied on the principle of authority: the Vulgate was true scripture; it pleased the Fathers and medieval doctors; it therefore serves as the standard by which Latin translations of the New Testament must be judged. At Acts 26:3 and 28:7 Lee admonished Erasmus to show greater respect for the translator of the Vulgate and to refrain from reckless charges that the translator nodded in his work and allowed monstrous solecisms to creep into the Vulgate. At 2 Cor. 3:14 he defended the traditional translation on the grounds that St. Jerome approved it. Tittelmans

---

[27] Sutor, *De tralatione bibliae et novarum reprobatione interpretationum* (Paris, 1525). Erasmus' reply is printed in *LB*, 9:737-812. For the adage "ne sutor ultra crepidam" see *EE*, no. 1571 (6:68); *LB*, 9:739 A; and *LB*, 2:228 AC. For a good account of this controversy see Holeczek, *Humanistische Bibelphilogie als Reformproblem*, pp. 186-245.

defended the Vulgate against Erasmus' charges on a broad range of issues, including solecism (at Rom. 2:15), improper Latin usage (at Rom. 1:20), unidiomatic Latin style (at Rom. 1:9), inaccurate translation (at Rom. 1:28), and misleading translation (at Rom. 12:1). At Rom. 9:28 he frankly acknowledged that a revised translation would be clearer than the Vulgate's text; yet he defended the traditional version, saying in effect that the translator was not obliged to render the Greek text in the clearest possible way. He had only to take as much care as he could, Tittlemans said, provided he did not positively obscure the sense of the Greek.

More complex was Stunica's response to Erasmus' translation and criticism of the Vulgate. Stunica sometimes exhibited a stubborn conservatism rivaling that of Lee and Tittlemans in his defense of the Vulgate. In his *Annotationes contra Erasmum*, for example, he objected to Erasmus' revision of the traditional formula at Matt. 3:4: "Poenitentiam agite"—"Do penance." "What the old translator put in good and proper Latin," Stunica said, "Erasmus has dared to express in new language hitherto not heard in the Church." He rejected Erasmus' translation and defended the Vulgate on similar grounds at Matt. 6:11 and Eph. 1:21.

Stunica therefore defended tradition against novelty with no less zeal than his fellow critics, but he did so with much more intelligence. He far surpassed both Lee and Tittlemans in his knowledge of Greek and Latin literature, classical, biblical, and patristic. Furthermore, he recognized more clearly than they how philological considerations might be employed in the Vulgate's behalf. Thus he presented a more erudite and, from the scholarly point of view, more persuasive defense of the traditional Latin scriptures. His more scholarly and convincing line of argument appears most clearly in a slim volume, the *Assertio*, where Stunica defended the Vulgate against Erasmus' charges that it contained solecisms and clumsy locution.[28] There he attributed faulty language in many cases not to the Vulgate's translator, but to scribal errors (e.g., at Luke 19:23, Luke 23:29, Acts 5:4, and Rom. 2:15). At other passages he defended the Vulgate's language on the grounds that approved stylists employed similar usage (e.g., at Matt. 22:30, Acts. 17:15, and Heb. 3:3). Yet other peculiar expressions he explained and justified as literal translations of Greek or Hebrew idioms (e.g., at Matt. 7:5, Matt. 8:29, Matt. 20:28, and John 4:9). Stunica's arguments perhaps did not always effectively meet Erasmus' objections: improper Latin made a bad translation, for example, whether or not it literally rendered foreign idioms—or at least it did from Erasmus' point of view. Yet Stunica's works clearly mark him as a more pertinent and diligent researcher than the other critics of Erasmus' translation.

One controversy in particular reveals especially well the unsettling effects Erasmus' translation worked in conservative quarters. I refer to the famous brouhaha concerning Erasmus' revised version of John 1:1: ἐν ἀρχῇ ἦν ὁ λόγος—"In the beginning was the word." In translating λόγος Erasmus replaced the Vulgate's *verbum* with *sermo*—"In principio erat sermo"—and justified his revision with reference to patristic writings and philological considerations. His innovation failed to please some conservatives, however, among them Henry Standish, Bishop of St. Asaph, and an unidentified young Carmelite preacher in Brussels. Standish denounced Erasmus for altering the reading that the Roman Church had seen fit to use for over a thousand years; the Carmelite charged him with condemning and correcting the gospel itself. These concerns apparently sprang from a craving for stability: Standish and the Carmelite spoke for those who distrusted Erasmus'

---

[28] *Assertio ecclesiasticae tralationis novi testamenti a soloecismis quos illi Erasmus Roterodamus impegerat.*

cavalier disruption and revision of the Vulgate's familiar, time-honored formulas. Erasmus' apology for his translation (published in 1520) effectively refuted their charges and demonstrated convincingly that *sermo* expresses much better than *verbum* the sense of the Greek word λόγος.[29] One may doubt, however, whether Erasmus' erudite discussion brought much comfort to those devoted not just intellectually, but emotionally as well, to the traditional phrases and formulas preserved in the Vulgate and revered over the millenium by Latin Christians.

Erasmus' conservative critics objected in similar fashion to his novel explanations and exegeses of many passages. Edward Lee accused him of verging toward Arianism at John 8:26 and Pelagianism at Rom. 5:12; he argued against him that Eph. 5:32 placed marriage among the seven sacraments; and he condemned Erasmus' liberal views on divorce aired in his comment to 1 Cor. 7:39.[30] Stunica trounced Erasmus for criticizing Hugh of St. Cher at 1 Tim. 4:15 and Nicholas of Lyra at 1 Pet. 2:7; at Acts 4:27 he warned Erasmus to avoid the Scylla of Apollinarianism and the Charybdis of Arianism.[31] In one work Stunica catalogued a long list of Erasmus' blasphemous and impious remarks, many of them culled from the *Annotations*. Among other things, he charged Erasmus with insulting popes, monks, mendicants, priests, and doctors; scorning Church ceremonies, sacraments, and doctrines; and arguing against the veneration of relics, the making of pilgrimages, and the waging of war![32] In 1522 Stunica and his

[29] For Erasmus' apology see *LB*, 9:111-122. The best study of the controversy—well worth reading—is that of Marjorie O'Rourke Boyle, *Erasmus on Language and Method in Theology* (Toronto, 1977), pp. 3-31.

[30] *Annotationes*, fol. XL^r–XLI^r, LVII^r–LVIII^v, LXVII^v–LXIX^v; *Novae annotationes*, fol. CXIII^v–CXX^v.

[31] *Annotationes contra Erasmum*, fol. H vi^v–I i^r, K i^r, D vi^v–E i^r.

[32] All these blasphemies Stunica found expressed in the *Annotations: Erasmi Roterodami blasphemiae et impietates*, esp. fol. A iii^r–C iv^v.

close friend, Sancho Carranza, each published a volume attacking Erasmus' notes to three passages: John 1:1, where in the first three editions of the *Annotations* Erasmus said that Christ was openly called God no more than two or three times in the scriptures; Acts 4:27, where he questioned the propriety of referring to Christ as a *servus* ("servant"), or *puer* ("boy" or "servant") as the Vulgate has it; and Eph. 5:32, which he considered no proof that marriage stood among the seven sacraments.[33]

As Reformation controversies heated up in the 1520s, so too did the charges lodged against Erasmus' *Annotations*. Thus Tittelmans not only disapproved Erasmus' note at Rom. 9:5, but warned him also not to abet Christological heretics. Tittelmans devoted the longest discussion of his work to the issue of original sin at Rom. 5:12. He defended the Vulgate's translation of the passage and an Augustinian exegesis of it, basing his argument mostly on the consensus and authority of the Church. But he spiced his comments with suggestions that Erasmus' note would encourage new species of Pelagians, atheists, and heretics—men whom Tittelmans considered increasingly in evidence as he wrote in 1529.[34] Stunica's later writings also ring with accusations of heresy. In a letter to Juan de Vergara of 9 January 1522, Stunica said the intention of his volumes against Erasmus was "to correct this Hollander and compel him to recant," since his writings greatly strength-

[33] Stunica, *Libellus trium illorum voluminum praecursor*; Carranza, *Opusculum in quasdam Erasmi Roterodami annotationes* (Rome, 1522). Erasmus' statement at John 1:1 was suppressed in the editions of 1527 and 1535. It followed the note to the passage "et verbum erat apud Deum" (*LB* 6:337C) and read as follows: "Mos enim hic est divinae scripturae plaerumque dei vocabulum, licet omnibus personis ex aequo commune, patri tribuere, & haud scio an usque legatur dei cognomen aperte tributum Christo, in apostolorum aut evangelistarum literis, praeterquam in duobus aut tribus locis."

[34] *Collationes quinque*, fol. 191ʳ–198ʳ, 113ʳ–135ʳ. See also Bentley, "New Testament Scholarship at Louvain," pp. 69-79.

ened Lutheran heresy.[35] In the preface to his catalog of Erasmus' blasphemies, Stunica promised to prove Erasmus not only
a Lutheran, but the very "standard bearer and prince of the
Lutherans."[36] He renewed the charge a year later, in another
catalog, this one of Erasmus' "suspect conclusions."[37] Stunica
became most abusive, however, in the work mentioned above
where he throttled Erasmus for his exegetical novelities at John
1:1, Acts 4:27, and Eph. 5:32. He took the occasion there
not only to defend the status of marriage as a sacrament, but
also to assess the damage done to orthodoxy by Erasmus'
comments at Eph. 5:32. He saw Erasmus and the German
Hebraist Johann Reuchlin as Luther's chief forerunners; he
considered Erasmus' note to Eph. 5:32 directly related to Luther's denial that marriage stood among the sacraments. He
promised a volume on "the parallel views of Erasmus and Luther," though he never published such a work. Finally, he
asserted that Erasmus and Luther held positions so close that,
in his famous quip, "either Erasmus lutherizes or Luther
erasmusizes—"ἤ ἔρασμος λουτερίζει, ἤ λουτέριος ἐρα-
σμίζει, idest aut Erasmus luterizat aut Luterius erasmizat."[38]

The Reformation in fact worked an ambiguous influence
on New Testament studies. On the one hand, as is well known,
the Protestant reformers rallied round the principle *sola scrip-
tura*. They preached on scripture, translated it into vernacular
languages, commented on it, and pressed it into the service of
their own theological and ecclesiastical programs. Reading and
study of the Bible—particularly the New Testament—reached
new heights of popularity in the sixteenth century. The Reformation thus proved a great boon for New Testament studies in that it stimulated new interest in the scriptures.

---

[35] *EE*, Appendix XV, no. 2 (4:625-28, esp. 626).
[36] *Erasmi Roterodami blasphemiae ac impietates*, fol. A ii[rv].
[37] *Conclusiones principaliter suspecte et scandolose*, fol. A ii[r], A iv[r].
[38] *Libellus trium illorum voluminum praecursor*, esp. fol. G iv[v]–G v[v].

On the other hand, the controversies that attended the Reformation all but poisoned the free intellectual atmosphere required to sustain the humanists' brand of independent, critical scholarship on the New Testament. I do not mean to say that humanist scholarship altogether vanished: even during the darkest days of theological wrangling, the best scholars continued to recognize the necessity of basing biblical studies on firm philological foundations. Most prominent of these perhaps were John Calvin among the Protestant reformers and Cardinal Cajetan among the Catholics.[39] Yet beginning about the 1530s, one might reasonably argue, the initiative in New Testament scholarship passed from the hands of the philologists into those of theologians and polemical exegetes. Problems of doctrine and discipline, not philology or criticism, engaged the attention of most students of the New Testament, whether Protestant or Catholic, in the middle and later years of the sixteenth century.[40] Meanwhile, sixteenth-century scholars broke little new philological ground after Erasmus. Editions of the Greek New Testament, for example, most often reprinted the text of Erasmus or the Complutensian circle, with a few emendations drawn from a handful of other edi-

---

[39] For excellent studies of these men's work see T.H.L. Parker, *Calvin's New Testament Commentaries* (London, 1971); A. F. von Gunten, "La contribution des 'Hebreux' a l'oeuvre exégètique de Cajétan," in *Histoire de l'exégèse*, pp. 46-83; and Denis Janz, "Cajetan: A Thomist Reformer?" *Renaissance and Reformation* 18 (1982):94-102.

[40] Four articles in the volume *Histoire de l'exégèse* illustrate particularly well the fact that theology and exegesis dominated philology and criticism during the later sixteenth century: Hans Hermann Holfelder, "Schriftauslegung und Theologie bei Johannes Bugenhagen (1485-1558). Zur theologische Vorgeschichte seiner Kirchenordnung," pp. 265-85; Philippe Denis, "Le recours à l'écriture dans les églises de la Réforme au XVIe siècle: exégèse de Mt 18, 15-17 et pratique de la discipline," pp. 286-98; Bernard Roussel, "La découverte de sens nouveax de l'épitre aux Romains par quelques exégètes français du milieu du XVIe siècle," pp. 331-41; and Ernst Koch, "Paulusexegese und Bundestheologie. Bullingers Auslegung von Gal. 3, 17-26," pp. 342-50. See also Bentley, "New Testament Scholarship at Louvain."

tions or manuscripts.[41] This state of affairs contrasted sharply with that in the realm of classical scholarship, where throughout the sixteenth century advances were registered on every front by scholars in the Erasmian tradition, including Beatus Rhenanus, Zasius, Budé, Dorat, the Étiennes, Scaliger, Casaubon, and Lipsius, to name only the most important figures.[42]

Consolidation

Humanist scholarship therefore did not come quickly to dominate New Testament studies, largely because of religious passions inflamed by the Reformation. Liberal humanist scholarship has always been a fragile creature, and only a little reflection will bring to mind cases where it fell victim to political or ideological causes. But once developed, humanist scholarship cannot be entirely ignored, for it places at the scholar's disposal those methods and principles that have proven to be his most useful and reliable tools. Even in the sixteenth century humanist scholarship commanded attention, though it failed to dominate New Testament studies. No serious scholar could afford to overlook the work of Erasmus, for example: whether he accepted or rejected Erasmus' arguments, he had to come to grips with them. Thus Erasmus' most formidable critic, Stunica, recognized the obligation, when rejecting Erasmus' arguments, to provide alternative explanations and re-

[41] Bruce M. Metzger, *The Text of the New Testament*, 2nd ed. (New York, 1968), pp. 95-106.

[42] Rudolf Pfeiffer, *History of Classical Scholarship from 1300 to 1850* (Oxford, 1976), pp. 71-123. Cf. esp. pp. 82 and 93, where Pfeiffer emphasizes that "it was on the Erasmian model . . . that true [read: philological] scholarship prospered, not on that of the biblical exegesis of the reformers and the new Protestant Scholasticism, still less in the narrow traditionalism of the Catholic counter-reformation" (p. 82).

213

port the results of his own independent research. Similarly, Cardinal Guglielmo Sirleto (1514-1585) later in the century defended the Vulgate against the criticisms of Valla and Erasmus, but did so on the basis of exhaustive research in patristic works and manuscripts of the Greek New Testament.[43]

Sooner or later, humanist scholarship was bound to find spokesmen who would consolidate the methods and discoveries of the early humanist scholars and establish them as normative for serious students of the New Testament. This is precisely what happened in the seventeenth and eighteenth centuries.[44] John Mill began to accumulate variant readings—he eventually collected some 30,000—from Greek manuscripts, early translations, and the works of the Church Fathers. Johann Bengel began to formulate reliable canons and principles of textual criticism. Perhaps most important among the seventeenth- and eighteenth-century scholars, however, was Johann Jakob Wettstein, editor of a still impressive edition of the Greek New Testament.[45] The "Prolegomena" to this work makes it clear that Wettstein was well acquainted with Erasmus' New Testament and *Annotations*. There he taxed Erasmus at times for working in haste, exaggerating the age of his manuscripts, and improper emendations, among other things.[46] But elsewhere his debt to Erasmus' work is more plain. As an appendix to his edition he published a short work of "Animadversiones," where he developed nineteen canons of textual criticism. Two of them he illustrated with points made by Erasmus in the *Annotations*: no. VII, which argues that a smoother Greek reading is less likely authentic than a coarser

[43] Hildebrand Höpfl, *Kardinal Wilhelm Sirlets Annotationen zum Neuen Testament* (Freiburg-im-Br., 1908).

[44] Metzger, *The Text of the New Testament*, pp. 106-18.

[45] C. L. Hulbert-Powell, *John James Wettstein, 1693-1754* (London, 1938).

[46] See Wettstein's *Novum Testamentum graecum*, 2 vols. (Amsterdam, 1751-1752), 1:44-45, 120-27.

variant; and no. XII, which argues that a more orthodox reading is not necessarily preferable to a less orthodox or apparently heretical variant.[47] He might easily have cited Erasmus' *Annotations* to illustrate others of these nineteen critical principles as well: no. X, for example, which cautions scholars against variant readings that agree with other passages of scripture; no. XIV, which attributes high value to readings preserved in works of the Church Fathers; or no. XV, which warns editors against readings that are not witnessed by the Fathers, but settle a point that was controversial in patristic times.[48]

Only a thorough study of New Testament scholarship between Erasmus and Wettstein would enable one to determine precisely to what extent the humanists directly influenced the development of philological scholarship on the New Testament. In the lack of such a study, I should like to suggest three general ways that the Renaissance humanists contributed to the development of modern New Testament scholarship.

In the first place, the humanists began to assemble and make available the basic data that New Testament scholars depend upon. They examined manuscripts and other sources of textual information; they reported the various readings encountered in those sources; and they published the first standard editions of the Greek New Testament. Neither Erasmus' New Testament nor the Complutensian approaches the quality of modern critical editions, but both served scholarship by providing a starting point for future research. This is particularly true of Erasmus' editions, equipped as they were with the *Annotations* and their straightforward discussions of textual problems. In any case, only with the appearance of published

---

[47] Wettstein, ed., *Novum Testamentum graecum*, 2:851-74, esp. 859-62, 864-67.

[48] Wettstein, ed., *Novum Testamentum graecum*, 2:863, 867-68.

editions of the Greek New Testament did it become possible to assess meaningfully the value of new textual discoveries. Without a standard to measure them against, a large body of variant readings will lead the critic to confusion or insanity, not comprehension. The editions of both Erasmus and the Complutensian circle may appear faulty when compared with modern texts of the Greek New Testament, but in the lack of such works, it would have been almost impossible for later scholars to advance the discipline of New Testament textual criticism.

In the second place, the humanists developed several specific methods and principles important for accurate scholarly work on the New Testament. Erasmus' formulation of the principle of the harder reading illustrates this creative impulse in its most sophisticated form. But Valla and the Complutensian editors also learned to think about textual problems from the point of view of the scribe, and thus to attempt their solution on properly philological grounds. Scholars today no doubt use techniques more refined than those developed by their Renaissance counterparts, but the humanists must be credited with imparting to modern New Testamant scholarship its thoroughly philological character.

Finally, the humanists displayed a fresh historical attitude that made possible a more accurate understanding of the world of biblical antiquity. Valla expelled the Pseudo-Dionysius and the concept of cooperating grace from the New Testament. Erasmus accepted and bolstered his arguments, then extended the insights to matters of basic Christian doctrine. Thus he recognized that the Christology of New Testament authors was far removed from that of the patristic and medieval Church, that New Testament authors simply did not think Jesus was divine in the same sense as did the Fathers at Nicaea. One might even describe this historical approach as an early attempt at demythologization of the New Testament: I do not mean that the humanists anticipated Rudolf Bultmann's efforts to peer behind the mythological language of the New Testament itself, but they did endeavor to strip the New Testament of the many legends and misunderstandings accreted onto it during the Middle Ages. They understood the New Testament writings as the literary product of an antique past whose problems, interests, aspirations, and manner of expression differed from those of the present. More than any previous scholar, they rendered the New Testament an object of detached literary, historical, and philological analysis, as well as a source of theological doctrine.

In all of this, Erasmus contributed most significantly to the development of modern New Testament scholarship. Valla set out primarily to look behind the Latin mask of the Vulgate and penetrate to a more pure understanding of New Testament writings. In the process he found some (though rare) occasion to comment on variant readings, suggest emendations, and draw the religious or theological implications of his philological discoveries. The Complutensian team set out primarily to provide a standard edition, without annotation, of the scriptures in their original languages and most important versions. One or more anonymous members of the circle prepared, but did not publish a set of notes correcting the Vulgate in light of their Greek New Testament; Nebrija applied philological criteria to New Testament problems in a manner not too dissimilar from that of Valla; Stunica placed his talents entirely in the service of conservative orthodoxy and the Vulgate. Only in Erasmus' work does one find philological criteria applied thoroughly to all aspects of New Testament scholarship: in several thousand notes he evaluated a vast body of Greek and Latin textual data, considered from all angles the best Latin representation of the Greek text, and offered explanations of the Greek text sensitive to literary, historical, and philological realities.

Thus already in Erasmus the revolution in scholarship, initiated by Valla, reached a point of impressive maturity and independence. The humanists set aside the tradition of New Testament study developed by medieval scholars, who from about the eleventh century, like medieval thinkers in general, had increasingly allowed logic and dialectic to dictate the questions they asked and the methods they used to answer them.[49] But the humanists exhibited discontinuity also with the Reformation tradition of New Testament study. They played a prominent role in promoting the Reformation in its early stages, as many studies have shown.[50] But unlike the reformers, major and minor alike, the humanists declined the opportunity to produce long commentaries expounding the scriptures in the light of new theological principles and systems; they limited themselves instead to the production of accurate texts, translations, and historical explanations of the New Testament.

Breaking with the medieval tradition, failing to anticipate the Reformation style, the humanists exhibited continuity instead with the modern world with respect to New Testament scholarship. Humanist philology came to dominate New Testament study and created a new brand of scholarship that has worked a profound influence on modern culture. Humanist philology not only made possible a more accurate understanding of the New Testament, but also led to a new vision of Christian antiquity itself. With the humanists' works, the New Testament world began to retreat into history, and the Chris-

[49] Cf. two articles by Richard McKeon: "Renaissance and Method in Philosophy," *Studies in the History of Ideas* 3 (1935):37-114; and "The Transformation of the Liberal Arts in the Renaissance," in *Developments in the Early Renaissance*, ed. B. S. Levy (Albany, 1972), esp. pp. 161-69.

[50] To cite only two important and recent works: Lewis W. Spitz, *The Religious Renaissance of the German Humanists* (Cambridge, Mass., 1963); and Bernd Moeller, *Imperial Cities and the Reformation*, trans. H.C.E. Midelfort and M. U. Edwards (Philadelphia, 1972), esp. pp. 19-38, 54.

tian scriptures would figure in later centuries less as the arbiter of doctrine, more as the object of professional philological and historical analysis. By no means do I wish by this interpretation to try to restore currency to the old, discredited notion that the Renaissance humanists posed a secular or anti-religious alternative to a supposedly spiritual, Christian worldview developed in the Middle Ages. The fundamentally Christian character of the humanists' thought is now well established. Far from weakening the Christian tradition, the humanists took philological studies as a new way to express their devotion to that tradition. One can only take at face value the refrain Erasmus often repeated in his prefatory and apologetic works, that he undertook his scholarly labors not in order to harm religion, but rather to provide purer texts and an improved understanding of the New Testament.

Yet one must also recognize in the humanists' works the first attempts to apply philological criteria in establishing accurate texts, producing sensitive translations, and providing sound, historical explanations of the New Testament. That is to say, in their efforts one finds the first attempts at modern New Testament scholarship.

Bibliography

MANUSCRIPTS CONSULTED

Basle. Öffentliche Bibliothek der Universität Basel. A. III. 15; A. N. III. 11; A. N. III. 12; A. N. IV. 1; A. N. IV. 2; A. N. IV. 4; A. N. IV. 5; O. II. 23; O. II. 27.

Brussels. Archives generaux du Royaume. Manuscrits divers, 5234.

Cambridge. University Library. Dd. VII. 3.

Hasselt (Belgium). Rijksarchief. MS. 6681 b.

Hatfield (Hertfordshire). Hatfield House. Cecil Papers, MS. 324.

Leicester. Country Record Office. Codex Leicesterensis.

London. British Library. Reg. 1. E. V. 1; Reg. 1. E. V. 2.

Madrid. Archivo Histórico Nacional. Universidades y colegios, libro 1091 F; Universidades y colegios, libro 1092 F.

Madrid. Archivo Histórico Universitario, Universidad Complutense de Madrid. 105-Z; 106-Z-22; 117-Z-1; 117-Z-45; 118-Z-28; 118-Z-29; 118-Z-30; 119-3.

Oxford. Corpus Christi College. E. 4. 9; E. 4. 10.

Paris. Bibliothèque Nationale. MS. grec 59; MS. grec 108; MS. grec 109; MS. grec 110; MS. grec 111.

Seville. Biblioteca Colombina. 7-1-10.

Vatican City. Biblioteca Apostolica Vaticana. Pal. lat. 45; Urb. lat. 5; Urb. lat. 6.

PUBLISHED PRIMARY SOURCES

Aland, Kurt; Black, Matthew; Martini, Carlo; Metzger, Bruce; and Wikgren, Allen, eds. *The Greek New Testament*. 2nd ed. (New York, 1968).

Aquinas, Thomas. *Opera omnia*. 25 vols. (Parma, 1852-1873).

Beatus Rhenanus. *Briefwechsel des Beatus Rhenanus*. Edited by A. Horowitz and K. Hartfelder (Leipzig, 1886).

221

Bede. *Expositio actuum apostolorum et retractio.* Edited by M.L.W. Laistner (Cambridge, Mass., 1939).

Biblia complutense. 6 vols. (Alcalá, 1514-1517).

Budé, Guillaume. *Omnia opera.* 4 vols. (Basle, 1557).

Carranza de Miranda, Sancho. *Opusculum in quasdam Erasmi Roterodami annotationes* (Rome, 1522).

Colet, John. *Opera.* Edited by J. H. Lupton. 5 vols. (London, 1867-1876).

Dorp, Maarten van. *Oratio in praelectionem epistolarum divi Pauli* (Antwerp, 1519).

Epistolae aliquot eruditorum . . . quo magis liqueat, quanta sit insignis cuiusdam sycophantae virulentia (Antwerp, 1520).

Epistolae aliquot eruditorum, ex quibus perspicuum quanta sit Eduardi Lei virulentia (Basle, 1520).

Erasmus. *Opera omnia Des. Erasmi Roterodami.* Edited by J. LeClerc. 10 vols. (Lugdunum Batavorum, 1703-1706).

―――. *Opera omnia Desiderii Erasmi Roterodami* (Amsterdam, 1969-).

―――. *Opus epistularum Des. Erasmi Roterodami.* Edited by P. S. Allen, H. M. Allen, and H. W. Garrod. 12 vols. (Oxford, 1906-1958).

―――. *Erasmi opuscula.* Edited by W. K. Ferguson (The Hague, 1933).

―――. *Ausgewählte Werke,* Edited by H. and A. Holborn (Munich, 1933).

―――, ed. *Novum Instrumentum omne, diligenter ab Erasmo Roterodamo recognitum & emendatum* (Basle, 1516).

―――, ed. *Novum Testamentum omne, multo quam antehac diligentius ab Erasmo Roterodamo recognitum, emendatum ac translatum* (Basle, 1519).

―――, ed. *Novum Testamentum omne, tertio iam ac diligentius ab Erasmo Roterodamo recognitum* (Basle, 1522).

―――, ed. *Novum Testamentum ex Erasmi Roterodami recognitione, iam quartum* (Basle, 1527).

―――, ed. *Novum Testamentum iam quintum accuratissima cura recognitum a Des. Erasmo Roter.* (Basle, 1535).

―――. *Collected Works of Erasmus* (Toronto, 1974-).

―――. *Erasmus and Cambridge: The Cambridge Letters of Erasmus.* Edited by H. C. Porter. Translated by D.F.S. Thompson (Toronto, 1963).

Ficino, Marsiglio. *Opera omnia.* 4 vols. (Basle, 1576).

Gómez de Castro, Alvar. *De rebus gestis a Francisco Ximenio Cisnerio, archiepiscopo toletano, libri octo* (Alcalá, 1569).

In Edouardum Leum quorundam e sodalitate literaria Erphurdiensis Erasmici nominis studiossorum epigrammatae (Mainz, 1520).

Lake, Kirsopp, ed. *Codex 1 of the Gospels and Its Allies* (Cambridge, 1902).

Latomus, Jacobus. *Opera.* Edited by J. Latomus iunior (Louvain, 1550).

LeClerc, Jean. *Ars critica.* 2 vols. (Amsterdam, 1697).

Lee, Edward. *Annotationes in annotationes novi testamenti Desiderii Erasmi* (Paris, 1520).

―――. *Annotationes in annotationes posterioris aeditionis novi testamenti Desiderii Erasmi* (Paris, 1520).

―――. *Apologia ad diluendas quorundam calumnias* (Paris, 1520).

―――. *Epistola apologetica qua respondent duabus Desiderii Erasmi epistolis* (Paris, 1520).

Lefèvre d'Étaples, Jacques, ed. *Pauli epistolae* (Paris, 1512).

―――, ed. *Quincuplex Psalterium* (Paris, 1513).

Migne, J.-P., ed. *Patrologiae cursus completus. Series graeca.* 161 vols. (Paris, 1857-1904).

―――, ed. *Patrologiae cursus completus. Series latina.* 221 vols. (Paris, 1844-1890).

Mill, John, ed. *Novum Testamentum* (Oxford, 1707).

More, Thomas. *Correspondence of Sir Thomas More.* Edited by E. F. Rogers (Princeton, 1947).

Nebrija, Antonio de. *Apologia cum quibusdam sacrae scripturae locis non vulgariter expositis* (Alcalá, 1516).

―――. *Apologia earum rerum quae illi obiiciuntur* (Granada, 1535).

―――. "Epistola del maestro de Lebrija al Cardenal." *RABM*, 3rd ser. 8 (1903):493-96.

―――. *Gramática castellana.* Edited by P. Galindo Romeo and L. Ortiz Muñoz (Madrid, 1946).

―――. *Hymnorum recognitio cum aurea illorum expositione* (Granada, 1535).

―――. *Introductiones latinae, cum commento* (Salamanca, 1495).

―――. *De litteris graecis* (Barcelona, 1523).

―――. *De litteris hebraicis cum quibusdam annotationibus in scripturam sacram* (Alcalá, 1515).

223

Nebrija, Antonio de. *Nebrissensis biblica.* Edited by P. Galindo Romeo and L. Ortiz Muñoz (Madrid, 1950).

——. *Segmenta ex epistolis Pauli, Petri, Iacobi & Ioannis, necnon ex prophetis quae in re divina leguntur per anni circulum tam in diebus dominicis quam in sanctorum festis & profestis* (Alcalá, 1516).

——. *Tertia quinquagena* (Alcalá, 1516).

——. *Tertia quinquagena* (Granada, 1535).

——. *De vi ac potestate litterarum* (Barcelona, 1523).

Nestle, E., and Aland, Kurt, eds. *Novum Testamentum graece et latine.* 25th ed. (Stuttgart, 1969).

Nicholas of Lyra. *Biblia sacra cum glossa interlineari, ordinaria, et Nicolai Lyrani postilla, eiusdemque moralitatibus, Burgensis additionibus, & Thoringi replicis.* 6 vols. (Venice, 1588).

Poggio Bracciolini. *Opera omnia.* Edited by R. Fubini. 4 vols. (Turin, 1963-1969).

Stromer, Heinrich. *Duae epistolae* (Leipzig, 1520).

Stunica (Diego López Zúñiga). *Annotationes contra Erasmum Roterodamum in defensionem tralationis novi testamenti* (Alcalá, 1520).

——. *Annotationes contra Iacobum Fabrum Stapulensem* (Alcalá, 1519).

——. *Assertio ecclesiasticae translationis novi testamenti a soloecismis quos illi Erasmus Roterodamus impegerat* (Rome, 1524).

——. *Conclusiones principaliter suspecte et scandolose que reperiuntur in libris Erasmi Roterodami* (Rome, 1523).

——. *Erasmi Roterodami blasphemiae et impietates* (Rome, 1522).

——. *Libellus trium illorum voluminum praecursor quibus Erasmicas impietates ac blasphemias redarguit* (Rome, 1522).

——. *Loca quae ex Stunicae annotationibus, illius suppresso nomine, in tertia editione novi testamenti Erasmus emendavit* (Rome, 1524).

Sutor, Petrus. *De tralatione bibliae et novarum reprobatione interpretationum* (Paris, 1525).

Tittelmans, Frans. *Collationes quinque super epistolam ad Romanos beati Pauli apostoli* (Antwerp, 1529).

——. *Elucidatio in omnes epistolas apostolicas* (Lyons, 1546).

——. *Epistola apologetica* (Antwerp, 1530).

——. *Libri duo de authoritate libri apocalypsis beati Ioannis apostoli* (Antwerp, 1530).

Valla, Lorenzo. *Opera omnia.* Edited by E. Garin. 2 vols. (Turin, 1962).

————. *Collatio novi testamenti.* Edited by A. Perosa (Florence, 1970).

————. *De falso credita et ementita Constantini donatione.* Edited by W. Setz (Weimar, 1976).

————. *De libero arbitrio.* Edited by M. Anfossi (Florence, 1934).

————. *De vero falsoque bono.* Edited by M. de P. Lorch (Bari, 1970).

Vallejo, Juan de. *Memorial de la vida de fray Francisco Jiménez de Cisneros.* Edited by A. de la Torre y del Cerro (Madrid, 1913).

Vio, Thomas de (Cardinal Cajetan). *Epistolae Pauli et aliorum apostolorum* (Paris, 1532).

————. *Evangelia cum commentariis* (Venice, 1530).

Wettstein, Johann Jakob, ed. *Novum Testamentum graecum.* 2 vols. (Amsterdam, 1751-1752).

Wordsworth, John, and White, Henry J., eds. *Novum Testamentum domini nostri Iesu Christi latine.* 3 vols. (Oxford, 1889-1954).

————, eds. *Novum Testamentum latine. Editio minor* (Oxford, 1911).

Ziegler, Jakob. *Libellus adversus Iacobi Stunicae maledicentiam, pro Germania* (Basle, 1523).

SECONDARY WORKS

Alberti, G. B. "Erodoto nella traduzione latina di Lorenzo Valla." *Bollettino del comitato per la preparazione dell'edizione nazionale dei classici greci e latini,* n.s. 7 (1959):65-84.

————. "Tucidide nella traduzione latina di Lorenzo Valla." *Studi italiani de filologia classica* (1957):224-49.

Aldridge, John W. *The Hermeneutic of Erasmus* (Richmond, Va., 1966).

Anderson, Marvin W. *The Battle for the Gospel: The Bible and the Reformation, 1444-1589* (Grand Rapids, 1978).

Augustijn, C. *Erasmus en de Reformatie* (Amsterdam, 1962).

Bailey, J. W. "Erasmus and the Textus Receptus." *Crozer Quarterly* 17 (1940):271-79.

Bainton, Roland H. *Erasmus of Christendom* (New York, 1969).

————. "The Paraphrases of Erasmus." *ARG* 57 (1966):67-76.

Barozzi, L., and Sabbadini Remigio. *Studi sul Panormita e sul Valla* (Florence, 1891).

Baruzi, Jean. "Introduction d'un cours sur les diverses interprétations de Saint Paul au seizième siècle et les résultats de l'exégèse contemporaine." *Revue de théologie et de philosophie,* n.s. 17 (1929):81-102.

Bataillon, Marcel. *Erasmo y España.* Translated by A. Alatorre. 2nd ed. (Mexico City, 1966).

Beck, Hans-Georg. *Kirche und theologische Literatur im byzantinischen Reich* (Munich, 1959).

Bedouelle, Guy. *Lefèvre d'Étaples et l'intelligence des écritures* (Geneva, 1976).

——. *Le "Quincuplex Psalterium" de Lefèvre d'Étaples* (Geneva, 1979).

Béné, Charles. *Érasme et St. Augustin* (Geneva, 1969).

Bentley, Jerry H. "Biblical Philology and Christian Humanism: Lorenzo Valla and Erasmus as Scholars of the Gospels." *SCJ* 8, no. 2 (1977), pp. 9-28.

——. "Erasmus, Jean Le Clerc, and the Principle of the Harder Reading." *RQ* 31 (1978):309-21.

——. "Erasmus' *Annotationes in Novum Testamentum* and the Textual Criticism of the Gospels." *ARG* 67 (1976):33-53.

——. "Gerard Morinck's Orations on the New Testament." *Humanistica lovaniensia* 29 (1980):194-236.

——. "New Light on the Editing of the Complutensian New Testament." *Bibliothèque d'humanisme et Renaissance* 42 (1980):145-56.

——. "New Testament Scholarship at Louvain in the Early Sixteenth Century." *Studies in Medieval and Renaissance History*, n.s. 2 (1979):51-79.

Berger, Samuel. *La Bible au XVIe siècle* (Nancy, 1879).

Bierlaire, Franz. *Les colloques d'Érasme* (Liège, 1978).

Bietenholz, Peter G. *History and Biography in the Work of Erasmus of Rotterdam* (Geneva, 1966).

Billanovich, G. "Petrarch and the Textual Tradition of Livy." *JWCI* 14 (1951):137-208.

Bischoff, Bernhard. *Mittelalterliche Studien*. 2 vols. (Stuttgart, 1967).

Bludau, A. "Der Beginn der Controverse über die Aechtheit des *Comma Johanneum* (1 Joh. 5, 7. 8.) im 16. Jahrhundert." *Der Katholik*, 3rd ser. 26 (1902):25-51, 151-75.

——. *Die beiden ersten Erasmus-Ausgaben des Neuen Testaments und ihre Gegner* (Freiburg-im-Br., 1902).

Bolgar, R. R. *The Classical Heritage and Its Beneficiaries* (Cambridge, 1954).

——, ed. *Classical Influences on European Culture, A.D. 500-1500* (Cambridge, 1971).

——, ed. *Classical Influences on European Culture, A.D.1500-1700* (Cambridge, 1976).

Bouwsma, William J. "The Renaissance and the Drama of Western History." *AHR* 84 (1979):1-15.

Boyle, Marjorie O'Rourke. *Erasmus on Language and Method in Theology* (Toronto, 1977).

Branca, Vittore. "Ermolao Barbaro and Late Quattrocento Venetian Humanism." In *Renaissance Venice*, edited by J. R. Hale, pp. 218-43 (Totowa, N.J., 1973).

Bywater, Ingram. *The Erasmian Pronunciation of Greek, and Its Precursors* (London, 1903).

Calster, G. van. "La censure louvaniste du Nouveau Testament et la rédaction de l'index érasmien expurgatoire de 1571." In *Scrinium erasmianum*, edited by J. Coppens, 2:379-436, (Leiden, 1969).

Cambridge History of the Bible. 3 vols. (Cambridge, 1963-1970).

Camporeale, Salvatore. *Lorenzo Valla. Umanesimo e teologia* (Florence, 1972).

Cantimori, Delio. *Eretici italiani del Cinquecento* (Florence, 1939).

Cavallera, F. "St. Jérôme et la Vulgate des Actes, des Épitres et de l'Apocalypse." *Bulletin de littérature ecclésiastique* 21 (1920):269-92.

———. *Saint Jérôme*. 2 vols. (Louvain, 1922).

Cessi, Roberto. "Paolinismo preluterano." *Rendiconti dell'Accademia nazionale dei lincei* (Classe di scienze morali, storiche e filologiche) 8th ser. 12 (1957):3-30.

Chantraine, Georges. "Érasme, lecteur des Psaumes." In *Colloquia erasmiana turonensia*, edited by J.-C. Margolin, 2:671-712 (Toronto, 1972).

———. "Le mustèrion paulinien selon les Annotations d'Érasme." *Recherches de science religieuse* 58 (1970):351-82.

———. *"Mystère" et "philosophie du Christ" selon Érasme* (Namur, 1971).

Chomarat, Jacques. "Les *Annotations* de Valla, celles d'Érasme et la grammaire." *Histoire de l'exégèse*, pp. 202-28.

———. "Érasme lecteur des Elegantiae de Valla." In *Acta conventus neo-latinis Amstelodamensis*, edited by P. Tuynman et al., pp. 206-43 (Munich, 1979).

———. "Grammar and Rhetoric in the Paraphrases of the Gospels by Erasmus." *Erasmus of Rotterdam Society Yearbook* 1 (1981):30-68.

Clark, K. W. "Observations on the Erasmian Notes in Codex 2." *Texte und Untersuchungen zur Geschichte altchristlichen Literatur* 73 (1959):749-56.

Colloquium erasmianum (Mons, 1968).

Coppens, J. "Érasme exégète et theologien." *Ephemerides theologiae lovanienses* 44 (1968):191-204.

————, ed. *Scrinium erasmianum.* 2 vols. (Leiden, 1969).

Coppola, Goffredo. *La critica neotestamentaria di Erasmo da Rotterdam* (Bologna, 1943).

Courants religieux et humanisme (Paris, 1959).

Delitzsch, Franz. *Handschriftliche Funde.* 2 vols. (Leipzig, 1861-1862).

————. *Studien zur Entstehungsgeschichte der Polyglottenbibel des Cardinals Ximenes* (Leipzig, 1871).

————. *Complutensische Varianten zum alttestamentlichen Texte* (Leipzig, 1878).

————. *Fortgesetzte Studien zur Entstehungsgeschichte der complutensischen Polyglotte* (Leipzig, 1886).

DeMolen, Richard, ed. *Essays on the Works of Erasmus* (New Haven, 1978).

Denifle, Heinrich. *Die abendländischen Schriftausleger bis Luther über Justitia Dei (Rom. 1,17) und Justificatio* (Mainz, 1905).

————. "Die Handschriften der Bibel-Correctorien des 13. Jahrhunderts." *Archiv für Literatur- und Kirchengeschichte des Mittelalters* 4 (1888):262-311, 471-601.

Dolores de Asis, Maria. *Hernán Núñez en la historia de los estudios clásicos* (Madrid, 1977).

Dorey, T. A., ed. *Erasmus* (London, 1970).

Dress, Walter. *Die Mystik des Marsilio Ficino* (Berlin, 1929).

Duhamel, P. Albert. "The Oxford Lectures of John Colet." *Journal of the History of Ideas* 14 (1953):493-510.

Eisenstein, Elizabeth L. *The Printing Press as an Agent of Change.* 2 vols. (Cambridge, 1979).

Étienne, Jacques. *Spiritualisme érasmien et theologiens louvanistes* (Louvain, 1956).

Farrar, F. W. *History of Interpretation* (London, 1886).

Fatio, O., and Fraenkel, P., eds. *Histoire de l'exégèse au XVIe siècle* (Geneva, 1978).

Feld, Helmut. *Die Anfänge der modernen biblischen Hermeneutik in der spätmittelalterlichen Theologie* (Wiesbaden, 1977).

————. "Der Humanisten-Streit um Hebräer 2, 7 (Psalm 8, 6)." *ARG* 61 (1970):5-35.

Fois, Mario. *Il pensiero cristiano di Lorenzo Valla nel quadro storico-culturale del suo ambiente* (Rome, 1969).

Fox, Adam. *John Mill and Richard Bentley: A Study of the Textual Criticism of the New Testament, 1675-1729* (Oxford, 1954).

Friedman, Jerome. "Servetus and the Psalms: The Exegesis of Heresy." In *Histoire de l'exégèse*, pp. 164-78.

————. "Sixteenth-Century Christian-Hebraica: Scripture and the Renaissance Myth of the Past," *SCJ* 11, no. 4 (1980) pp. 67-85.

Gaeta, Franco. *Lorenzo Valla. Filologia e storia nell'umanesimo italiano* (Naples, 1955).

Garofalo, Salvatore. "Gli umanisti italiani del secolo XV e la Bibbia." *Biblica* 27 (1946):338-75.

Gasquet, Francis A., Cardinal. "Roger Bacon and the Latin Vulgate." In *Roger Bacon Essays*, edited by A. G. Little, pp. 89-99 (Oxford, 1914).

Geanakoplos, Deno J. *Greek Scholars in Venice* (Cambridge, Mass., 1962).

————. *Interaction of the "Sibling" Byzantine and Western Cultures in the Middle Ages and Italian Renaissance (330-1600)* (New Haven, 1976).

Gerl, Hanna-Barbara. *Rhetorik als Philosophie. Lorenzo Valla* (Munich, 1974).

Gilmore, Myron P. "Anti-Erasmianism in Italy: The Dialogue of Ortensio Lando on Erasmus' Funeral." *Journal of Medieval and Renaissance Studies* 4 (1974):1-14.

————. "Erasmus and Alberto Pio, Prince of Carpi." In *Action and Conviction in Early Modern Europe: Essays in Memory of E. H. Harbison*, edited by T. K. Rabb and J. E. Seigel, pp. 299-318 (Princeton, 1968).

————. "*De modis disputandi*: The Apologetic Works of Erasmus." In *Florilegium Historiale: Essays Presented to Wallace K. Ferguson*, edited by J. G. Rowe and W. H. Stockdale, pp. 62-88 (Toronto, 1971).

————. "Italian Reactions to Erasmian Humanism." In *Itinerarium italicum*, edited by H. A. Oberman and T. A. Brady, pp. 61-115 (Leiden, 1975).

Godin, André. "Fonction d'Origène dans la pratique exégétique d'Érasme: les Annotations sur l'épitre aux Romains." In *Histoire de l'exégèse*, pp. 17-44.

Grafton, Anthony. "Joseph Scaliger's Edition of Catullus (1577) and the Traditions of Textual Criticism in the Renaissance." *JWCI* 38 (1975):155-81.

Grafton, Anthony. "On the Scholarship of Politian and Its Context." *JWCI* 40 (1977):150-88.

———. "The Origins of Scholarship." *American Scholar* (Spring, 1979):236-61.

Gray, Hanna H. "Valla's *Encomium of St. Thomas Aquinas* and the Humanist Conception of Christian Antiquity." In *Essays in History and Literature Presented by the Fellows of the Newberry Library to Stanley Pargellis*, edited by H. Bluhm, pp. 37-51 (Chicago, 1965).

Gregory, C. R. *Das Freer-Logion* (Leipzig, 1908).

———. *Textkritik des Neuen Testaments*. 3 vols. (Leipzig, 1900-1909).

Greitemann, N. "Erasmus als exegeet." *Studia catholica* 12 (1936):294-305, 365-87.

Grimm, Harold J. "Lorenzo Valla's Christianity." *Church History* 18 (1949):75-88.

Gunten, A. F. von. "La contribution des 'Hebreux' à l'oeuvre exégètique de Cajétan." In *Histoire de l'exégèse*, pp. 46-83.

Hadot, Jean. "La critique textuelle dans l'édition du Nouveau Testament d'Érasme." In *Colloquia erasmiana turonensia*, edited by J.-C. Margolin, 2:749-60 (Toronto, 1972).

Hagen, Kenneth. *A Theology of Testament in the Young Luther: The Lectures on Hebrews* (Leiden, 1974).

———. *Hebrews Commenting From Erasmus to Bèze, 1516-1598* (Tübingen, 1981).

Hailperin, Herman. *Rashi and the Christian Scholars* (Pittsburgh, 1963).

Hall, Basil. "The Trilingual College of San Ildefonso and the Making of the Complutensian Polyglot Bible." In *Studies in Church History*, vol. 5, edited by G. J. Cuming, pp. 114-46 (Leiden, 1969).

Harris, J. Rendel. *The Origin of the Leicester Codex of the New Testament* (Cambridge, 1887).

Harth, Dietrich. *Philologie und praktische Philosphie. Untersuchungen zum Sprach- und Traditionsverständnis des Erasmus von Rotterdam* (Munich, 1970).

Höpfl, Hildebrand. *Kardinal Wilhelm Sirlets Annotationen zum Neuen Testament* (Freiburg-im-Br., 1908).

Holeczek, Heinz. *Humanistiche Bibelphilologie als Reformproblem bei Erasmus von Rotterdam, Thomas More und William Tyndale* (Leiden, 1975).

Hufstader, Anselm. "Lefèvre d'Étaples and the Magdalen." *Studies in the Renaissance* 16 (1969):31-60.

230

Hulbert-Powell, C. L. *John James Wettstein, 1693-1754* (London, 1938).

Hulley, K. K. "Principles of Textual Criticism Known to St. Jerome." *Harvard Studies in Classical Philology* 55 (1944):87-109.

Hussey, J. M. *Church and Learning in the Byzantine Empire, 867-1185* (New York, 1963).

Janz, Denis. "Cajetan: A Thomist Reformer?" *Renaissance and Reformation* 18 (1982):94-102.

Jarrot, C.A.L. "Erasmus's Annotations and Colet's Commentaries on Paul: A Comparison of Some Theological Themes." In *Essays on the Works of Erasmus*, edited by R. L. DeMolen, pp. 125-44 (New Haven, 1978).

———. "Erasmus' Biblical Humanism." *Studies in the Renaissance* 17 (1970):119-52.

———. "Erasmus' *In Principio Erat Sermo*: A Controversial Translation." *Studies in Philology* 61 (1964):35-40.

———. "John Colet on Justification." *SCJ* 7 (1976):59-72.

Jayne, Sears. *John Colet and Marsilio Ficino* (Oxford, 1963).

Jonge, H. J. de. "Erasmus und die Glossa ordinaria zum Neuen Testament." *Nederlands archief voor kerkgeschiedenis*, n.s. 56 (1975):51-77.

———. "Erasmus and the *Comma Johanneum*." *Ephemerides theologicae lovanienses* 56 (1980):381-89.

———. "Novum testamentum a nobis versum. De essentie van Erasmus' uitgave van het Nieuwe Testament." *Lampas* 15 (1982):231-48.

Kelley, Donald R. *Foundations of Modern Historical Scholarship* (New York, 1970).

Kelly, J.N.D. *Jerome* (New York, 1975).

Kenney, E. J. *The Classical Text* (Berkeley, 1974).

Kleinhans, Robert G. "Luther and Erasmus, Another Perspective." *Church History* 39 (1970):459-69.

Kohls, Ernst-Wilhelm. *Die Theologie des Erasmus*. 2 vols. (Basle, 1966).

Kristeller, Paul O. *Renaissance Thought: The Classic, Scholastic, and Humanist Strains* (New York, 1961).

Krumbacher, Karl. *Geschichte der byzantinischen Literatur*. 2nd ed. (Munich, 1897).

Kümmel, Werner G. *The New Testament: The History of the Investigation of Its Problems*. Translated by S. M. Gilmour and H. C. Kee (Nashville, 1972).

Lake, Kirsopp, and Lake, Silva, *Family 13 (The Ferrar Group)* (London, 1941).

Landgraf, A. "Zur Methode der biblischen Textkritik im 12. Jahrhundert." *Biblica* 10 (1929):445-74.

Langlois, Charles-Victor. "Nicolas de Lyre, frère mineur." *Histoire littéraire de la France* 36 (1927):355-400.

Lemus y Rubio, Pedro. "El maestro Elio Antonio de Lebrixa." *Revue hispanique* 22 (1910):459-508; 29 (1913):13-120.

Lindeboom, J. *Het bijbelsch humanisme in Nederland* (Leiden, 1913).

Logan, George M. "Substance and Form in Renaissance Humanism." *Journal of Medieval and Renaissance Studies* 7 (1977):1-34.

Lowry, Martin. *The World of Aldus Manutius* (Ithaca, 1979).

Lubac, Henri de. *Exégèse médiévale.* 4 vols. (Paris, 1959-1964).

Lyell, James P. R. *Cardinal Ximénes* (London, 1917).

Maas, Paul. *Textual Criticism.* Translated by B. Flower (Oxford, 1958).

Mancini, Girolamo. *Vita di Lorenzo Valla* (Florence, 1891).

Mara, M. G. "L'esegesi erasmiana di alcuni passi della *Lettera ai Romani.*" *Studi storico religiosi* 1 (1977):165-82.

————. "La II Epistola di Pietro: testo e annotazioni erasmiane." *Archeologia classica* 25-26 (1973-1974):376-94.

Margolin, Jean-Claude, ed. *Colloquia erasmiana turonensia.* 2 vols. (Toronto, 1972).

Massaut, Jean-Pierre. *Critique et tradition à la veille de la Réforme en France* (Paris, 1974).

Mattingly, Garrett. *Renaissance Diplomacy* (Baltimore, 1964).

McKeon, Richard. "Renaissance and Method in Philosophy." *Studies in the History of Ideas* 3 (1935):37-114.

————. "The Transformation of the Liberal Arts in the Renaissance." In *Developments in the Early Renaissance*, edited by B. S. Levy, pp. 158-223 (Albany, 1972).

McNeil, David O. *Guillaume Budé and Humanism in the Reign of Francis I* (Geneva, 1975).

Mestwerdt, Paul. *Die Anfänge des Erasmus* (Leipzig, 1917).

Metzger, Bruce M. *The Early Versions of the New Testament* (Oxford, 1977).

————. "Explicit References in the Works of Origen to Variant Readings in New Testament Manuscripts." In his *Historical and Literary Studies*, pp. 88-103 (Leiden, 1968).

————. "Patristic Evidence and the Textual Criticism of the New Testament." *New Testament Studies* 18 (1971-1972):379-400.

————. "The Practice of Textual Criticism among the Church Fathers." *Texte und Untersuchungen* 115 (1975):340-49.

————. "The Punctuation of Rom. 9:5." In *Christ and Spirit in the New Testament*, edited by B. Lindars and S. S. Smalley, pp. 95-112 (Cambridge, 1973).

————. *New Testament Studies: Philological, Versional, and Patristic* (Leiden, 1980).

————. "St. Jerome's Explicit References to Variant Readings in Manuscripts of the New Testament." In *Text and Interpretation*, edited by E. Best and R. Wilson, pp. 179-90 (Cambridge, 1979).

————. *The Text of the New Testament*. 2nd ed. (New York, 1968).

————. *A Textual Commentary on the Greek New Testament*. 3rd ed. (New York, 1971).

Morisi, Anna. "A proposito di due redazioni della *Collatio Novi Testamenti* di Lorenzo Valla." *Bollettino dell'istituto storico italiano per il Medio Evo e archivo muratoriano* 78 (1967):345-81.

————. "La filologia neotestamentaria di Lorenzo Valla." *Nuova rivista storica* 48 (1964):35-49.

Mühlenberg, Ekkehard. "Laurentius Valla als Renaissancetheolog." *Zeitschrift für Theologie und Kirche* 66 (1969):466-80.

Napoli, Giovanni di. *Lorenzo Valla. Filosofia e religione nell'umanesimo italiano* (Rome, 1971).

Nader, Helen. " 'The Greek Commander' Hernán Núñez de Toledo, Spanish Humanist and Civic Leader." *RQ* 31 (1978):463-85.

————. *The Mendoza Family in the Spanish Renaissance, 1350-1550* (New Brunswick, N.J., 1979).

Nauert, Charles G. "The Clash of Humanists and Scholastics: An Approach to Pre-Reformation Controversies." *SCJ* 4 (1973):1-18.

————. "Humanists, Scientists, and Pliny: Changing Approaches to a Classical Author." *AHR* 84 (1979):72-85.

Norton, F. J. *Printing in Spain, 1501-1520* (Cambridge, 1966).

Odriozola, Antonio. "La caracola del bibliofilo nebrisense. Extracto seco de bibliografia de Nebrija en los siglos XV y XVI." *Revista de bibliografía nacional* 7 (1946):3-114.

Oelrich, Karl Heinz. *Der späte Erasmus und die Reformation* (Münster, 1961).

Olmedo, Felix G. *Nebrija (1441-1522)* (Madrid, 1942).

O'Malley, John W. "Some Renaissance Panegyrics on Aquinas." *RQ* 27 (1974):174-92.

Panofsky, Erwin. *Renaissance and Renascences in Western Art* (New York, 1969).

Parker, T.H.L. *Calvin's New Testament Commentaries* (London, 1971).

———. "The Sources of the Text of Calvin's New Testament." *Zeitschrift für Kirchengeschichte* 73 (1962):272-98.

Pasquali, Giorgio. *Storia della tradizione e critica del testo*. 2nd ed. (Florence, 1952).

Payne, John B. *Erasmus: His Theology of the Sacraments* (Richmond, Va., 1970).

———. "Erasmus and Lefèvre d'Étaples as Interpreters of Paul." *ARG* 65 (1974):54-82.

———. "Erasmus: Interpreter of Romans." *Sixteenth Century Essays and Studies* 2 (1971):1-35.

———. "The Significance of Lutheranizing Changes in Erasmus' Interpretations of Paul's Letters to the Romans and the Galatians in His *Annotationes* (1527) and *Paraphrases* (1532)." In *Histoire de l'exégèse*, pp. 312-30.

———. "Toward the Hermeneutics of Erasmus." In *Scrinium erasmianum*, edited by J. Coppens, 2:13-49 (Leiden, 1969).

Petris, Alfonso de. "Le teorie umanistiche del tradurre e l' *Apologeticus* di Giannozzo Manetti." *Bibliothèque d'humanisme et Renaissance* 37 (1975):15-32.

Pfeiffer, Rudolf. *Ausgewählte Schriften* (Munich, 1960).

———. *Humanitas erasmiana* (Leipzig, 1931).

———. *History of Classical Scholarship from the Beginnings to the End of the Hellenistic Age* (Oxford, 1968).

———. *History of Classical Scholarship from 1300 to 1850* (Oxford, 1976).

Phillips, Margaret Mann. *Érasme et les débuts de la Réforme française, 1517-1536* (Paris, 1934).

Prete, Sesto. "Leistungen der Humanisten auf dem Gebiete der lateinischen Philologie." *Philologus* 109 (1965):259-69.

———. *Observations on the History of Textual Criticism in the Medieval and Renaissance Periods* (Collegeville, Minn., 1970).

Preus, James Samuel. *From Shadow to Promise: Old Testament Interpretation from Augustine to the Young Luther* (Cambridge, Mass., 1969).

Proctor, Robert. *The Printing of Greek in the 15th Century* (Oxford, 1900).

Rabil, Albert. *Erasmus and the New Testament: The Mind of a Christian Humanist* (San Antonio, 1972).

Radetti, Giorgio. "La religione di Lorenzo Valla." In *Medioevo e Rinascimento. Studi in onore di Bruno Nardi*, 2:595-620 (Florence, 1955).

Reicke, Bo. "Erasmus und die neutestamentliche Textgeschichte." *Theologische Zeitschrift* (1966):254-65.

Revilla Rico, Mariano. *La Políglota de Alcalá* (Madrid, 1917).

Reynolds, L. D., and Wilson, N. G. *Scribes and Scholars*. 2nd ed. (Oxford, 1974).

Rice, Eugene F. "John Colet and the Annihilation of the Natural." *Harvard Theological Review* 45 (1952):141-63.

Riggenbach, Eduard. *Die ältesten lateinischen Kommentare zum Hebräerbrief* (Leipzig, 1907).

Rizzo, Silvia. *Il lessico filologico degli umanisti* (Rome, 1973).

Roussel, B. "Histoire de l'église et histoire de l'exégèse au XVIe siècle." *Bibliothèque d'humanisme et Renaissance* 37 (1975):181-92.

Russell, A. T. *Life of Bishop Andrewes* (London, 1863).

Sabbadini, Remigio. *Il metodo degli umanisti* (Florence, 1920).

———. *Le scoperte dei codici latini e greci ne' secoli XIV e XV*. 2 vols. (Florence, 1967).

Salembier, Louis. "Une page inédite de l'histoire de la Vulgate." *Revue des sciences ecclésiastiques* 56-62 (1887-1890).

Sandys, J. E. *History of Classical Scholarship*. 3 vols. (Cambridge, 1903-1920).

Schelkle, Karl Hermann. *Paulus, Lehrer der Väter* (Düsseldorf, 1956).

Schlingensiepen, Hermann. "Erasmus als Exeget auf Grund seiner Schriften zu Matthäus." *Zeitschrift für Kirchengeschichte* 48 (1929):16-57.

Scholderer, Victor. *Greek Printing Types, 1465-1927* (London, 1927).

Schwarz, W. "The History of Principles of Bible Translation in the Western World." *Babel* 9 (1963):5-22.

———. "The Meaning of *Fidus Interpres* in Medieval Translation." *Journal of Theological Studies* 45 (1944):73-78.

———. *Principles and Problems of Biblical Translation* (Cambridge, 1955).

———. "Studies in Luther's Attitude towards Humanism." *Journal of Theological Studies* 56 (1955):66-76.

———. "The Theory of Translation in Sixteenth-Century Germany." *Modern Language Review* 40 (1945):189-99.

Scrivener, Frederick Henry. *A Plain Introduction to the Criticism of the New Testament* (Cambridge, 1861).

Simon, Richard. *Histoire critique des principaux commentateurs du Nouveau Testament* (Rotterdam, 1693).

———. *Histoire critique des versions du Nouveau Testament* (Rotterdam, 1690).

———. *Histoire critique du texte du Nouveau Testament* (Rotterdam, 1689).

Smalley, Beryl. *The Study of the Bible in the Middle Ages*. 2nd ed. (Oxford, 1952).

Spicq, C. *Ésquisse d'une histoire de l'exégèse latine au Moyen Age* (Paris, 1944).

Spitz, Lewis W. *The Religious Renaissance of the German Humanists* (Cambridge, Mass., 1963).

Streeter, B. H. *The Four Gospels* (New York, 1925).

Struever, Nancy S. *The Language of History in the Renaissance* (Princeton, 1970).

Tarelli, C. C. "Erasmus's Manuscripts of the Gospels." *Journal of Theological Studies* 44 (1943):155-62; 48 (1947):207-208.

Tasker, R.V.G. "The Complutensian Polyglot." *Church Quarterly Review* (April 1953), pp. 197-210.

Telle, Emile V. *Érasme de Rotterdam et le septième sacrament* (Geneva, 1954).

Thompson, C. R. *The Translations of Lucian by Erasmus and St. Thomas More* (Ithaca, 1940).

Timpanaro, Sebastiano. *La genesi del metodo del Lachmann* (Florence, 1963).

Torre y del Cerro, Antonio de la. "La Universidad de Alcalá. Datos para su historia." *RABM*, 3rd ser. 20 (1909):412-23; 21 (1909):48-71, 261-85, 405-33.

Tracy, James D. "Erasmus Becomes a German," *RQ* 21 (1968):281-88.

———. *Erasmus: The Growth of a Mind* (Geneva, 1972).

———. *The Politics of Erasmus* (Toronto, 1978).

———. "Erasmus and the Arians: Remarks on the *Consensus Ecclesiae*." *Catholic Historical Review* 67 (1981):1-10.

Trapp, J. B. "Notes on Manuscripts Written by Peter Meghen." *The Book Collector* 24 (1975):80-96.

Tregelles, Samuel P. *An Account of the Printed Text of the Greek New Testament* (London, 1854).

Trillitzsch, Winfried. "Erasmus und Seneca." *Philologus* 109 (1965):270-93.

Trinkaus, Charles. *In Our Image and Likeness.* 2 vols. (Chicago, 1970).

———, and Heiko Oberman, eds. *The Pursuit of Holiness in Late Medieval and Renaissance Religion* (Leiden, 1974).

Turner, Cuthbert H. *The Early Printed Editions of the Greek Testament* (Oxford, 1924).

Vernet, André. "Les manuscrits grecs de Jean de Raguse (d. 1443)." *Basler Zeitschrift für Geschichte und Altertumskunde* 61 (1961):75-108.

Villa Amil y Castro, José. *Catálogo de los manuscritos existentes en la biblioteca del noviciado de la Universidad central* (Madrid, 1878).

Vocht, Henry de. *History of the Foundation and the Rise of the Collegium Trilingue Lovaniense, 1517-1550.* 4 vols. (Louvain, 1951-1955).

———. *Texts and Studies about Louvain Humanists in the First Half of the XVIth Century* (Louvain, 1934).

Waszink, J. H. "Einige Betrachtungen über die Euripidesübersetzung des Erasmus und ihre historische Situation." *Antike und Abendland* 17 (1971):70-90.

West, Martin L. *Textual Criticism and Editorial Technique* (Stuttgart, 1973).

Westgate, R.I.W. "The Text of Valla's Translation of Thucydides." *Transactions and Proceedings of the American Philological Association* 67 (1936):240-51.

Wiles, Maurice F. *The Divine Apostle: the Interpretation of St. Paul's Epistles in the Early Church* (Cambridge, 1967).

Winkler, Gerhard B. *Erasmus von Rotterdam und die Einleitungsschriften zum Neuen Testament* (Münster, 1974).

Zippel, G. "L'autodifesa di Lorenzo Valla per il processo dell'inquisizione napoletana (1444)." *Italia medioevale e umanistica* 13 (1970):59-94.

———. "La 'Defensio quaestionum in philosophia' di Lorenzo Valla, e un noto processo dell'inquisizione napoletana." *Bollettino dell'istituto storico italiano per il Medio Evo e archivio muratoriano* 69 (1957):319-47.

———. "Lorenzo Valla e le origini della storiografia umanistica a Venezia." *Rinascimento* 7 (1956):93-133.

Zuntz, G. *The Text of the Epistles: A Disquisition upon the Corpus Paulinum* (London, 1953).

Index

239

Library of Congress Cataloging in Publication Data

Bentley, Jerry H., 1949–
Humanists and Holy Writ.

Bibliography: p.
Includes index.
1. Bible. N.T.—Criticism, interpretation, etc.—History—
Middle Ages, 600-1500. 2. Bible. N.T.—Criticism,
interpretation, etc.—History—16th century. 3. Humanists—
Europe. 4. New Testament scholars—Europe. I. Title.
BS2350.B46 1983   225.6'09'024   83-42547

ISBN: 978-0-691-15560-9

Jerry H. Bentley is Associate Professor of History at the
University of Hawaii. This is his first book.

CPSIA information can be obtained at www.ICGtesting.com
Printed in the USA
BVOW041314260612

293656BV00002B/1/P